THE THERAPIST'S NOTEBOOK

THE THERAPIST'S NOTEBOOK

Volume 3

More Homework, Handouts, and Activities for Use in Psychotherapy

CATHERINE FORD SORI
LORNA L. HECKER
AND ASSOCIATES

Routledge
Taylor & Francis Group
New York London

Routledge
Taylor & Francis Group
711 Third Avenue
New York, NY 10017

Routledge
Taylor & Francis Group
2 Park Square
Milton Park, Abingdon
Oxon OX14 4RN

Routledge is an imprint of Taylor & Francis Group, an Informa business

International Standard Book Number-13: 978-0-7890-3522-6 (Softcover)

Library of Congress Cataloging-in-Publication Data

The therapist's notebook 3 : more homework, handouts, and activities for use in psychotherapy / [edited by] Catherine Ford Sori, Lorna L. Hecker, and associates.
p. ; cm.
Includes bibliographical references and index.
ISBN-13: 978-0-7890-3522-6 (soft : alk. paper)
1. Psychotherapy--Problems, exercises, etc. I. Sori, Catherine Ford. II. Hecker, Lorna L. III. Title: More homework, handouts, and activities for use in psychotherapy.
[DNLM: 1. Psychotherapy--methods. 2. Adolescent. 3. Child. WM 420 T39849 2008]

RC480.5.H3483 2008
616.89'14--dc22 2007051969

Visit the Taylor & Francis Web site at
http://www.taylorandfrancis.com

and the Routledge Web site at
http://www.routledge.com

This book is dedicated in memory of Alfredo R. Sori (1939–2007), whose life exemplified love and commitment to family and friends,

and to

our loves, Horacio John Sori and Jonathan Lee,

our children, Marisa, Marlene, Al, Ann, Paul, Jessica, and Heather

(and all their children),

and Aaron and Noah,

and our parents and family members, whose love, support, and encouragement provided the foundation for our lives from which we work.

Contents

Preface

Since the original *Therapist's Notebook* was published in 1998 (Hecker & Deacon), the *Therapist's Notebook* series has provided a myriad of field-tested activities, homework, and handouts for therapists to use in their daily practice. People seemed to really *use* the therapist's notebooks, and we are delighted in the success of the series. It seems that we have accomplished our goal: to produce a book that did not gather dust! We are back again with *The Therapist's Notebook III: More Homework, Handouts & Activities for Use in Psychotherapy* with yet more creative ideas for therapists from innovative clinicians in the field. Authors have field tested their interventions and they are ready to share them with the reader. The authors have uniquely blended theory, science, and creativity into interventions, handouts, homework, and activities.

Therapists spend long hours with clients and can sometimes lose their imagination or inspiration. Yet, it is important that therapy feel generative for clients as well as therapists. You will find in these pages the boost you have been looking for. The creativity at your fingertips can revive sessions and bring therapy to life for clients and therapists alike. You will also find not only that the creativity extolled in this volume will inspire you to use the chapter at hand, but also that creativity begets creativity, and you will take, mold, and shape ideas in ways we never would have imagined.

Likewise, you can expand your theoretical repertoire or adapt the activities to your own preferred approach. In this book, authors share the theoretical basis for their chapters. Theories reflected in the chapters include narrative, solution focused, choice theory, reality therapy, experiential, Bowenian, structural, social learning theory, art and play therapies, and couples approaches including Gottman and emotionally focused therapy. Client populations covered in this volume are children and adolescents, adults, couples, families, and groups.

Highlights of this book include renowned play therapist Risë VanFleet sharing how she carefully and creatively integrates dogs in working with children, Dan Wiener sharing a dynamic experiential technique he uses with couples, and Israela Meyerstein providing a fun and easy way to measure progress in couples therapy with her "Are We There Yet?" chapter. Therapists share uncommon ways for livening up therapy while accomplishing therapeutic goals. Some of these include integrating dance in therapy, utilizing rap and hip-hop with children, turning therapy sessions into quiz shows, creatively using ropes with couples, utilizing blog pages online, making the therapy room floor into a game board for families, unique ways to address sexual issues, and much more.

Organization of the Book

In the table of contents, we have grouped chapters according to their primary topic, but there is much overlap. Many chapters could easily have been listed under several categories. The sections are "Children and Adolescents," "Adults," "Couples," and "Families and Groups." The chapters follow the same format as those in previous *The Therapist's Notebook* books. First is the title of the chapter and name of the author or authors, followed by the *type of contribution* contained in the chapter. This is an activity that can be used by clinicians in session, a homework assignment that can be given to clients (or a combination of both), a handout that can be used in therapy or sent home with the client, or a combination of all three.

What follows next is an *objective* section that contains a summary of the purpose of the chapter. The *rationale for use* section explains more thoroughly when the activity, homework, or handout is appropriate and how it can be utilized. In the *instructions* section that follows, authors give a clear description of how to execute the activity, handout, or homework. In the *brief clinical vignette* section, the authors provide intimate case examples (all client names and identifying information have been changed to protect client confidentiality) that offer readers insight in how to apply the activity, homework, or handout. *Suggestions for follow-up* is the next section; here, advice is provided on how to expand on the material provided in the near or distant future. A *contraindications for use* section is offered to alert the reader to times that the intervention might be inappropriate or harmful. Finally, this book expands upon the references typically found in the literature: Three different types of reference sections are provided. After the *reference* section is the *professional readings and resources* section, which offers therapists an ample list of additional resources for further study on the topic or issues discussed in the chapter. The next section is *bibliotherapy sources for the client*, which clinicians can use to recommend resources to their clients. These sources may include books, Websites, compact discs, or videos.

Many chapters contain reproducible handouts at the end, with Haworth's blessing to reproduce them for private use. They are designed to use with clients in implementing the activity, as an informational handout for the client, or as a resource for the clinician. They are also designed to make the life of the therapist a little easier because they are ready-made and available at his or her fingertips.

We hope you enjoy *The Therapist's Notebook III: More Homework, Handouts & Activities*, and that the ideas shared in this book are practical, lend fun and creativity to your work, and, most importantly, aid your clients in leading better lives.

Reference

Hecker, L., Deacon, S., et al. (1998). *The therapist's notebook: Homework, handouts, and activities for use in psychotherapy.* Binghamton, NY: The Haworth Press.

Acknowledgments

We would like to acknowledge our many contributors without whom this book would not be possible. The knowledge, creativity, intuition, and insight that they share are stellar. We also want to thank all of the wonderful people at Taylor & Francis who guided this process through to fruition. Thanks also go out to Kathy Schultz, Julie Ramisch, Marvin Ford, and John Sori for their toiling behind the scenes. We also appreciate the patience of our families and friends, who always put us out "on loan" to the writing and editing process.

Thanks to John and Jonathan for their steadfast support and love.

Cheers to the joy of enduring friendship.

Editors

Catherine Ford Sori, PhD, is an associate professor of marriage and family counseling at Governors State University in University Park, Illinois, and associate faculty at the Chicago Center for Family Health. Her special interests include training issues related to children in family therapy, family play therapy, children and families facing illness and bereavement, divorce and stepfamily issues, and integrating spirituality in therapy. Dr. Sori was the director of Children and Family Services at the Cancer Support Center in Homewood, Illinois. She is frequently invited to present on topics pertaining to children, families, illness, bereavement, and family play therapy. She received her PhD in marriage and family therapy from Purdue University, and practiced for several years at Samaritan Counseling Center in Munster, Indiana.

Dr. Sori's publications include journal articles in the *Journal of Marital and Family Therapy,* the *Family Journal;* the *Journal of Clinical Activities, Assignments & Handouts in Psychotherapy Practice;* the *Journal of Couple & Relationship Therapy;* the *American Journal of Family Therapy;* and the *Journal of Family Psychotherapy.* She coauthored (with Lorna L. Hecker, PhD, and associates) *The Therapist's Notebook II: More Homework, Handouts & Activities for Use in Psychotherapy* (Haworth Press, 2007) and *The Therapist's Notebook for Children and Adolescents: Homework, Handouts and Activities for Use in Psychotherapy* (2003). Her other books include *The Therapist's Notebook for Integrating Spirituality in Counseling,* volumes I and II (with Karen Helmeke, PhD) (2006) and *Engaging Children in Family Therapy: Creative Approaches to Integrating Theory and Research in Clinical Practice* (2006). She has also developed the training program for Kids Support, a national training program for the treatment of cancer in the family.

Dr. Sori is on the editorial boards for the *Journal of Couple and Relationship Therapy* and the *Journal of the Illinois Counseling Association.* She is a clinical member of the American Association for Marriage and Family Therapy (AAMFT), a licensed marriage and family therapist, and an AAMFT-approved supervisor. She is also a member of the American Counseling Association and the Association for Play Therapy. She is a classical pianist and lives in Highland, Indiana, with her husband, John. They have seven children and are awaiting their 20th grandchild.

Lorna L. Hecker, PhD, LMFT, is a professor of marriage and family therapy at Purdue University Calumet in Hammond, Indiana, where she is on the faculty in the marriage and family therapy master's program in the Department of Behavioral Sciences. She teaches graduate courses in ethics and professional issues and couples therapy. She is also the director of the Purdue University Calumet Couple and Family Therapy Center. She is a clinical member of the American Association of Marriage and Family Therapy (AAMFT) and an AAMFT-approved supervisor. Her clinical interests include couples therapy, divorce, and trauma recovery.

Dr. Hecker and Catherine Ford Sori coedited *The Therapist's Notebook II: More Homework, Handouts & Activities for Use in Psychotherapy* (Haworth Press, 2007). She coauthored (with Catherine Ford Sori, PhD, and associates) *The Therapist's Notebook for Children and Adolescents: Homework, Handouts and Activities for Use in Psychotherapy* (Haworth, 2003), and coauthored (with Sharon Deacon and associates) *The Therapist's Notebook: Homework, Handouts and*

Activities for Use in Psychotherapy (Haworth, 1998). She also coedited (with Joseph Wetchler) *An Introduction to Marriage and Family Therapy* (Haworth, 2003). She has an upcoming book, *Ethics and Professional Issues in Couple and Family Therapy,* with Haworth Press. Dr. Hecker is the founding editor of the *Journal of Clinical Activities, Assignments & Handouts in Psychotherapy Practice*. She has also published articles in the *Journal of Marital and Family Therapy, Journal of Contemporary Family Therapy,* the *American Journal of Family Therapy,* and the *Journal of Family Psychotherapy.* She lives in Munster, Indiana, with her two sons, Aaron and Noah.

Contributors

Mark S. Carich, PhD, coordinates the Sexually Dangerous Persons Assessment and Treatment Program for the Illinois Department of Corrections at Big Muddy River Correctional Center. He has been working with the program since 1989 and with sex offenders since 1984. He conducts training on an international basis on topics related to sex offender assessment and treatment. Dr. Carich has published extensively on the topic, coauthoring several books, including the *Adult Sexual Offender Assessment Report* (Safer Press, 2003), *The Handbook for Sexual Abuser Assessment & Treatment* (Safer Press, 2001), and *Contemporary Treatment of Adult Male Sex Offenders* (Russell House, 2003), among others.

F. Scott Christopher, PhD, is a professor of family studies in the School of Social and Family Dynamics at Arizona State University. Dr. Christopher teaches courses in advanced human sexuality as well as family relationships that are a part of the Marriage and Family Therapy Program. He has served as an associate editor for the *Journal of Sex Research* and has published in the areas of premarital sexuality, sexual aggression, and intimate partner abuse.

Shannon B. Dermer, PhD, is currently an associate professor at Governors State University in University Park, Illinois. She has a PhD in marriage and family therapy from Kansas State University and a master's degree in psychology from Illinois State University. Dr. Dermer's interests include postmodern models, qualitative research, couples counseling, sex therapy, and creativity in counseling and therapy.

Megan L. Dolbin-MacNab, PhD, is an assistant professor in the Marriage and Family Therapy Program at Virginia Polytechnic Institute and State University. She has published in *The Therapist's Notebook for Children and Adolescents,* the *Journal of Marital and Family Therapy, Family Relations,* and *Research in Human Development.* Her research is focused on predicting risk and resilience in grandparent-headed families. Clinically, she is interested in grandparent-headed families and also specializes in working with couples facing infertility.

Kimanne Foraker-Koons, MA, is a graduate of the Marriage and Family Counseling Program at Governors State University in University Park, Illinois. She worked with a local psychologist to design and create "Ident Dolls," which are used to help sexually and physically abused children. With a background in law enforcement, she assisted in creating Lock Out Child Crime (L.O.C.K.), an organization responsible for changing, improving, and strengthening state and federal laws pertaining to child molesters and the victims of child molestation. She works with families to strategize their way through difficult life events using play therapy, art therapy, and family mediation.

Adam S. Froerer, M Ed, is a PhD student in marriage and family therapy at Texas Tech University. He received his master's degree in marriage and family therapy from the University of Oregon. His research interests include solution-focused brief therapy and medical family therapy.

Miriam Claire Godwin, MS, LMFT, is a student in the medical family therapy PhD program at East Carolina University. She is a teaching instructor for the Department of Child Development and Family Relations at East Carolina University and maintains a small private practice as a licensed marriage and family therapist in Greenville, North Carolina. She earned an MS in marriage and family therapy at East Carolina University. Her research and clinical interests include working with at-risk adolescents and their families (in the home and collaboratively with their schools) and with families who have a member with an autism spectrum disorder, and incorporating the use of art into family therapy interventions.

Dreena E. Greenwood, BA, is currently finishing her master's degree in counseling at Governors State University in University Park, Illinois. She has been employed with the Department of Children and Family Services for 24 years and volunteers with the youth in the community.

April Michele Hames, MM Ed, is a doctoral student in the Medical Family Therapy Program at East Carolina University. She maintains a small private music therapy practice where she incorporates a biopsychosocial–spiritual approach. She holds an internship position at the Brody School of Medicine in the Department of Internal Medicine. Currently, she is facilitating a fibromyalgia support group at the East Carolina University Family Therapy Clinic. She received her MM Ed in music education and music therapy from East Carolina University. Her research and clinical interests include perceived locus of control in chronic illness, relationship trajectories in chronic illness, and the role of hope in therapeutic outcomes.

Dianne E. Jeffries, MSW, has a master's degree in clinical social work. She is currently working at the YWCA Domestic Violence Prevention and Intervention Program in Lafayette, Indiana. She has been facilitating reflection groups for women who are survivors of domestic violence. Her interests include group therapy, domestic violence, coping mechanisms, and self-esteem for domestic violence survivors.

Gunnur Karakurt, MS, has a master's degree in social psychology from Middle East Technical University in Turkey. She is currently working toward her PhD in marriage and family therapy at Purdue University. Her interests include emotionally focused family therapy, affect regulation in families, aggression and violence, sexual abuse, and feminism and multiculturalism. She is currently completing a clinical internship at the YWCA Domestic Violence Prevention and Intervention Program in Lafayette, Indiana.

Tiffani S. Kisler, PhD, is an assistant professor of marriage and family therapy in the Department of Human Development and Family Studies at the University of Rhode Island. Dr. Kisler teaches courses in theories of marriage and family therapy, human sexuality, sex therapy, and marriage and family relationships for the masters program in marriage and family therapy. Her clinical specialties include female sexual functioning, sexual aggression, and relational and sexual satisfaction. She has published on topics such as marital sexuality and sexual aggression.

Margaret R. Kohut, MSW, earned her master's degree in social work from the University of Oklahoma, going on to specialize in criminal justice, addiction therapy, and behavioral forensics. She served as an Air Force officer for 17 years as a clinical social worker and psychotherapist. Now retired from active duty due to a service-related medical condition, Kohut uses her proficiency in the helping professions through her full-time business, Rocky Mountain Way Freelance Writing. She has a lengthy publication history in both academic and commercial writing. Kohut is a keen advocate of helping others through her 11 miniature dachshunds in animal-assisted therapy. She and her husband, Dr. Tristan Kohut, live in Anaconda, Montana.

Kimberly Laninga, BA, is currently working on her master's degree in marriage and family counseling and for a certificate in stress management from Governors State University. She is passionate about working with adults who have survived severe childhood abuse and those trying to extricate themselves from addictions. In addition, she seeks to empower individuals to develop healthy boundaries in all areas of life. She is married with one daughter and resides with her family in Lockport, Illinois.

Michelle T. Mannino, BA, is currently pursuing her master's degree in child and family studies with an emphasis in marriage and family therapy at Purdue University Calumet in Hammond,

Indiana. Her clinical interests include medical family therapy and bereavement, eating disorders, and sex therapy.

William F. Martin, LCSW, is a psychotherapist in private practice with couples, adults, and adolescents, specializing in the use of guided imagery and psychodrama to heal trauma. He leads intensive psychodrama weekends for the Victories of the Heart Program and has extensive experience leading short- and long-term groups for men living with HIV/AIDS. He is on the faculty of the Chicago Center for Family Health and a former lecturer at the University of Chicago School of Social Services Administration.

Jill Matson, MA, completed her master's degree in marriage and family counseling at Governors State University in University Park, Illinois. With Shannon B. Dermer and Shannon D. Smith, she has been published in the Illinois Counseling Association's journal with a work entitled "Systems Theory and Narrative Therapy: Enhancing Multicultural Sensitivity of Career Theory and Counseling." She enjoys working with couples and families and looks forward to pursuing a doctorate in counselor education.

Melissa L. McVicker, BA, is currently pursuing her master's degree in marriage and family therapy at Purdue University Calumet, Hammond, Indiana. She is an intern therapist at the Purdue Couple and Family Therapy Center and intends to specialize in child therapy.

Israela Meyerstein, LCSW-C, LMFT, a family and couples therapist with 30 years experience, is in private practice in the Baltimore community. An approved supervisor with the American Association for Marriage and Family Therapy, Meyerstein has taught and supervised mental health professionals of all disciplines in both academic and clinical settings. She also has numerous published articles and book chapters on family treatment, medical issues, and spirituality.

Susan N. Perkins, MA, is a PhD candidate in the Marriage and Family Therapy Program at Virginia Polytechnic Institute and State University. She is currently working as a child and family clinician at New River Valley Community Services in Blacksburg, Virginia. She has published on gerontology and on students' metaphors for learning research. Her research interests include common factors, theory development, therapy process, and the use of technology for therapy, research, and training.

Patricia A. Robey, MA, LPC, NCC, RTC, is a senior faculty member of the William Glasser Institute. She has taught the concepts of choice theory and reality therapy in the United States, Canada, Europe, and Asia, addressing the application of these ideas in the fields of counseling, corrections, education, business, and health care as well as to individuals interested in personal growth and development. Robey is a lecturer at Governors State University, where she teaches master's level students in counseling. As a counselor at Oak Lawn Family Services in Illinois, she works with individuals, groups, families, couples, and children. She is currently pursuing her doctorate in counselor education at Northern Illinois University.

Errol Rodriguez, PhD, CRC, is a psychologist at Jacobi Medical Center's Family and Youth Addiction Program. He is also adjunct professor at the State University of New York at Westchester Community College and a consultant for Inter-Care, an outpatient chemical dependency program in New York City. In addition, he is a certified rehabilitation counselor with a private practice in New York City. Dr. Rodriguez's clinical interests include treatment of addictive disorders, substance abuse and the family system, child and adolescent psychotherapy, and psychological testing.

Rita L. Sanders, MA, received her master's degree in school counseling at Governors State University in University Park, Illinois. She is divorced and mother of one daughter, Emily. Her professional interests are in the areas of prevention and treatment of child abuse, family therapy, and advocacy for children and adolescents.

Sara A. Smock, PhD, is an assistant professor at Texas Tech University in the Marriage and Family Therapy Program. She is the book review editor for the *Journal of Couple and Relationship Therapy.* Dr. Smock's primary interest is testing the solution-focused brief therapy model, including process and outcome research.

Risë VanFleet, PhD, RPT-S, is a licensed psychologist and registered play therapist-supervisor with 35 years of clinical and leadership experience in a variety of settings. She is the president of the Family Enhancement & Play Therapy Center, Inc. in Boiling Springs, Pennsylvania, and clinical consultant for its affiliated Beech Street Program. Her specialties include filial therapy, play therapy, disaster mental health, chronic medical illness in families, assisting families with trauma and attachment-related problems, and animal-assisted play therapy. Dr. VanFleet is the founder of the International Collaborative on Play Therapy and a past president/board chair of the Association for Play Therapy. She is the author of *Filial Therapy: Strengthening Parent–Child Relationships Through Play, A Parent's Handbook of Filial Play Therapy;* coeditor with Dr. Louise Guerney of the *Casebook of Filial Therapy;* and author and photographer of *The Faces of Play: A Photographic Exploration of the Importance and Joys of Playfulness.* Her latest book is *Play Therapy for Kids and Canines: Benefits for Children's Developmental and Psychosocial Health* (in press). Dr. VanFleet has received two prestigious national awards for her work. She is an approved evaluator with the American Kennel Club's Canine Good Citizen® Program and is involved with the Association of Pet Dog Trainers, the International Society for Anthrozoology, and the International Association of Animal Behavior Consultants. She is responsible for the Playful Pooch Program and offers training programs in canine-assisted play therapy.

Charles A. Waehler, PhD, is an associate professor and training director in the Collaborative Program in Counseling Psychology at the University of Akron. He has authored the book *Bachelors: The Psychology of Men Who Haven't Married* (Praeger, 1996). He is a practicing psychologist with Cornerstone Comprehensive Psychological Services in Medina, Ohio. His research interests include personality assessment and the counseling process.

Elsa K. Weber, PhD, is an associate professor of early childhood in the Department of Behavioral Sciences at Purdue University Calumet in Hammond, Indiana. She taught preschool and kindergarten for 12 years. Her current research interests are in children's social development—specifically, the development of children's conception of autonomy and the personal.

Daniel J. Wiener, PhD, ABPP, RDT-BCT, CGP, is a professor in the Department of Counseling and Family Therapy at Central Connecticut State University. A licensed psychologist and marriage and family therapist, he is the founder of Rehearsals for Growth, a drama therapy of relationships that uses improvisational theater exercises. In addition to numerous professional articles and book chapters, he is the author of *Rehearsals for Growth* and has edited three books on the uses of action methods in psychotherapy.

Teresa L. Young, BA, is a graduate student at Purdue University Calumet working toward her master's degree in child and family studies with an emphasis in marriage and family therapy. Her clinical interests include sex therapy, eating disorders, and couples therapy.

SECTION I: CHILDREN AND ADOLESCENTS

– 1 –

Playful Pooches

Using Canine Interactions to Enhance Therapeutic Outcomes for Children and Adolescents

Risë VanFleet

Type of Contribution: Activity

Objective

This chapter offers some general guidelines and specific therapeutic methods for incorporating properly trained and handled canines into therapy with children and adolescents. Interactions between children and dogs, especially playful ones, can assist with a wide range of therapeutic objectives, including the building of skills, competence, and confidence; facilitating healthy attachment relationships; and strengthening emotional and behavioral regulation.

Rationale for Use

The benefits of the human–animal bond have been clearly demonstrated for children and adults. Studies have shown that human interactions with animals have beneficial (1) health effects, such as lowered blood pressure, improved recovery from serious illnesses, and stress reduction; (2) social effects, such as companionship, support, a sense of belonging, security, and social lubricant effects; and (3) developmental effects, such as improved learning, language development, understanding of the natural world, physical development, and social and emotional development (Beck & Katcher, 2003; Becker & Morton, 2002; Goodall & Bekoff, 2002; Hart, 1995; Jalongo, 2004; Knapp, 1998; Melson, 2001; Podberscek, Paul, & Serpell, 2000; Schoen, 2001; Serpell, 1995, 1996). Barker and Barker's (1988) review of a survey of 13,000 readers of *Psychology Today* showed that pet owners firmly believed that pets improved the quality of family relationships by reducing tensions and increasing fun, conversation, exercise, time spent together, and compassion.

Interest in the field of animal-assisted therapy (AAT) has been growing rapidly due to its clinical success and a developing research base (Chandler, 2005; Fine, 2000, 2006; Mallon & Levinson, 1997). A wide range of animals has been used to

- Assist with occupational therapy (Velde, Cipriani, & Fisher, 2005)
- Elevate mood and improve quality of life in nursing facilities (Colombo, Buono, Smania, Raviola, & De Leo, 2006; Lutwack-Bloom, Wijewickrama, & Smith, 2005)
- Promote positive educational experiences for children (Jalongo, 2004; Jalongo, Astorino, & Bomboy, 2004
- Reduce depression (Antonioli & Reveley, 2005)
- Help children with autism (Sams, Fortney, & Willenbring, 2006)
- Reduce anxiety and improve quality of life for psychiatric clients (Barker & Dawson, 1998; Nathans-Barel, Feldman, Berger, Modai, & Silver, 2005)

Facilitate youth adjustment and overcome family conflict (Strand, 2004)
Assist with post-traumatic stress disorder and chronic medical illness (Altschuler, 1999; Gorczyca et al., 2006)
Improve adolescent anger management (Hanselman, 2001)

Many other applications have also been used. Animals have been used in mental health programs (Carpenter, 2005; Fine, 2006; Hayden, 2005; Kruger & Serpell, 2006; Woolley, 2005), school and residential settings (Jalongo; Sullivan, 2006; www.greenchimneys.org; www.gressmountainranch.com), prisons and youth detention centers (Bondarenko, 2007), and at a variety of disaster and recovery sites (Greenbaum, 2006; Kohr, 2006; Shane, 2006).

More frequent and better designed research studies are emerging, adding to a substantial body of empirical data. Chandler (2005) has reviewed studies showing the positive impact of AAT in such areas as anxiety, depression, self-esteem, child development, motivation, and child and adolescent social and emotional problems. Kaminski, Pellino, and Wish (2002) found improvements in children's heart rates, mood, and happiness as a result of a pet therapy group. Fine (2000, 2006) has described research methodology, relevant measures, and the current empirical support for AAT.

Animal-assisted therapy has used visits, petting and grooming, and a wide variety of other interactions between human and nonhuman animals to promote positive therapeutic outcomes. More recently, the value of cross-species play has been explored more fully as a means of enhancing therapy with children (Thompson, 2007; VanFleet, in press). Many animals, including humans, actively play during their early years and, to a lesser extent, throughout their lives. People and other animals are usually able to read the play signals and communications of other species (Bekoff, 2007) and can engage in play activities together. The importance and power of play for healthy child development is well established (Elkind, 2007; Sutton-Smith, 1997), and the rapidly growing field of play therapy is a developmentally attuned, empirically based way to engage children effectively in therapy (Bratton, Ray, Rhine, & Jones, 2005; Kaduson & Schaefer, 2000, 2006; Kottman, 1995; Landreth, 2002; O'Connor & Schaefer, 1994; Reddy, Files-Hall, & Schaefer, 2005; Terr, 1990; VanFleet, 2005, 2006a, 2006b; Wilson & Ryan, 2005). The use of cross-species play in conjunction with play therapy seems a natural combination.

The blending of animal-assisted therapy and play therapy shows promise as a multimodal approach to many child problems. VanFleet (2007a) has defined animal-assisted play therapy, or pet play therapy, as the use of animals in the context of play therapy, in which appropriately trained therapists and animals engage with children and families primarily through systematic play interventions, with the goal of improving children's developmental and psychosocial health as well as the animal's well-being. Play and playfulness are essential ingredients of the interactions and the relationship (p. 17).

An exploratory survey revealed that many play therapists incorporate animals into their work (VanFleet, 2007b), and Thompson (2007) is conducting an investigation of the impact of canines in nondirective play therapy on child progress.

Although many different types of animals can be used in playful and therapeutic ways with children and adolescents, this chapter focuses on the use of canines. Dogs are uniquely suited to this type of play therapy work:

They play readily with children.
Children are drawn to them.
They are accepting and nonjudgmental.
They show empathy and a remarkable ability to read human cues and behaviors.
They can learn a large array of behaviors, tricks, sports, and interactions.
They often enjoy touch and action.

They have some of the same social and behavior problems as children and adolescents.
They focus on the here and now.
They seek out human attachment.

All of these characteristics can be employed in the service of therapy. The remainder of this chapter outlines several ways that dogs can be incorporated into play therapy interventions.

Instructions

A number of considerations are important before using dogs in child and adolescent therapy. Proper selection and training of the dog and its therapist or handler is essential. A thorough understanding of animal-assisted therapy and play therapy or other forms of child psychotherapy must precede the incorporation of canines with clients. The therapist must carefully consider the capabilities and interests of the dog and use them in a manner that helps children meet therapeutic goals while protecting the welfare and motivation of the dog. Canine-assisted play therapy needs to be applied systematically in the service of therapy while demonstrating a caring awareness of the needs of the dog.

Training

All canines used for therapy must be obedient and under the control of the handler (usually the therapist). Credentials such as the American Kennel Club's Canine Good Citizen® Award (www.akc.org/events/cgc.program.cfm) and certifications by the Delta Society (www.deltasociety.org) or Therapy Dogs International (www.tdi-dog.org) are excellent ways to prepare a canine-handler team for therapy work. Chandler's (2005) book is an excellent resource for more information on this topic. Further preparation for play therapy work entails encouraging play behaviors that come naturally to each particular dog. For example, retrievers are likely to excel at games such as ball playing and Frisbee; scent hounds might be enticed to play "search" and "find it" games. Many dogs have quirky, funny behaviors that can be honed for use in play sessions with children and adolescents.

Child Preparation

Therapists should prepare children in advance for meeting and working with the dog. This part of the process is important, not only for showing children how to interact with the therapy dog, but also for teaching them skills for meeting any unfamiliar dog. Children often approach dogs too straightforwardly, and these behaviors can be interpreted by some canines as aggression. Many children suffer dog bites because they grasp the dog's face, put their hands over the dog's head and neck to pet it, or approach the dog directly from the front using unpredictable movements. Although therapy dogs are trained to accept these behaviors, many dogs feel threatened by them and protect themselves with their mouths. Therapists who show children how to draw in their arms and permit the dog to sniff them first (e.g., Pelar's [2005] "Be a Tree" technique), drop training treats on the floor, approach the dog from an angle, and stroke the dog's chest rather than its head are teaching children skills that generalize to interactions with other dogs as well (VanFleet, in press). An informative book on canine calming signals (Rugaas, 2006) and DVDs produced by Kalnajs (2006a, 2006b) show therapists and other dog handlers how to read the body language of the whole dog, and this information can easily be taught to children as well. Books by Dunbar (1996) and Donaldson (2005) provide exceptionally useful explanations and procedures for understanding and working with dogs in a positive manner.

It is useful for children to learn some basic canine obedience commands, such as "look" (to get the dog to look at one's eyes prior to other commands), "come," "sit," "down," "stay," "off," "heel," and "good." Because children learn best through play, this can be accomplished by playing "dog" with younger child clients. The therapist explains the commands, asking children to pretend they are dogs and follow the commands as the therapist gives them. The therapist does this in a lighthearted, playful manner, laughing and praising the child (as dog) for following the commands. Then the therapist reverses roles and allows the child to practice the commands. The therapist takes the role of dog and follows the child's commands, periodically reinforcing the child's efforts and making suggestions as needed. This simple game quickly prepares even very young children to meet the therapy dog. Adolescents are likely to remember the commands after the therapist explains them, but a playful practice session with a stuffed toy dog or canine puppet can add levity to the training and strengthen the client's memory of the commands. In keeping with basic play therapy principles, the therapist uses playfulness and humor to create and maintain an emotionally safe climate.

Interventions

There are many ways to use canines in the context of child and adolescent therapy. VanFleet (in press) has described numerous canine-assisted play activities that can be used to help children reach a wide range of therapeutic goals. To stay within the scope of this chapter, three general goals and approaches are described here. Each description includes the therapeutic goal of the intervention and how to conduct it. In all cases, these approaches should not be used without proper training—obedience and therapy training for the canine and dog handling and play therapy training for the therapist.

Building skills, competence, and confidence. Many children lack confidence and suffer from anxiety, shyness, trauma, poor peer or family relationships, and low self-esteem. Canine-assisted therapy can build children's knowledge and skills about dogs and strengthen their self-esteem and confidence as their dog-handling competence develops. Brief training sessions with the dog can accomplish these goals. The therapist explains the use of any equipment (such as a Martingale collar, Gentle Leader head halter, and/or leash), demonstrates its use, and then watches as the child tries. As the child implements the commands, the therapist avoids interfering with the process unless safety issues require it, praises the child's efforts, and makes simple suggestions to ensure the child's success. The process of therapist demonstration, child practice, and therapist feedback is continued with just one or two commands at a time until the child masters them.

Children often need help with voice intonation. Their voices must convey excitement when calling the dog to them, genuine pleasure when praising the dog, and firm control when correcting the dog. Children tend to use high-pitched voices when giving all commands, and they need help using a deep voice when saying "No!" to the dog. At other times, they may become punitive toward the dog, and the therapist shows them alternative ways of managing the situation. Again, therapist modeling followed by child practice helps skill mastery. When giving suggestions, the therapist makes suggestions for alternative behaviors rather than focusing on what the child is doing wrong. The therapist should keep the overall tone of the session pleasant, patient, positive, and playful to help the child and the canine feel relaxed.

Children learn remarkably well from the therapist's demonstrations, so it is important to be consistent and clear when showing them how a particular command is given, executed, corrected, or praised. The therapist emphasizes how the frequent use of praise, consistency, and gentle correction helps build a respectful relationship with the dog. This relationship can serve as a metaphor for human-to-human relationships as well.

Once children master some of the dog training skills, the therapist can suggest putting on an "obedience show" for the parents or caregivers. This often builds the child's confidence as a training "expert" while teaching the parents training commands and methods that they may not know. It is not unusual for families to take the child's lead and begin using the same commands and training methods with their own pet dogs. This builds children's confidence as well.

Similarly, if the therapist has trained agility dogs, he or she can involve the children or adolescents in agility work (www.usdaa.com; www.nadac.com; www.akc.org; www.ukcdogs.com). This also builds children's skills, fosters a healthy child–canine relationship, and provides physical release of anxiety or energy. An innovative program, On Course for Kids (Crevling, personal communication, 2006; www.dogsofcourse.com), uses trained volunteer human–canine agility teams to work with child cancer patients. The child actually joins the agility team and participates while dogs run the course as part of a fundraising event that benefits a local childlife cancer program.

Facilitating healthy attachment relationships. Many children and adolescents, especially those with histories of maltreatment, find it difficult to trust people. They have been neglected or injured by those most responsible for caring for them, and it is not uncommon for those in placement to have been moved from home to home. One symptom of their distress is that they sometimes injure animals. Several canine-related activities can help reverse these trends and help these children learn about healthy relationships.

First, the mere presence of a dog in a therapeutic setting can reduce resistance. Gonski (1985) found that children in a child welfare setting responded immediately and positively to therapy dogs, and their resistance was eliminated almost immediately. When children find it difficult to trust people, the presence of dogs communicates to them that therapy is not going to be a serious, "talking" place, but an experience with many avenues of expression and relationship.

Second, if the therapist uses a rescued dog as a canine therapist, children are often interested in hearing the dog's story. They can relate to a canine that was unwanted and living in a shelter or rescue facility—much as they have lived in foster or kinship care. The canine's story should be based on the truth, but the therapist tells it in a manner that helps the child see the parallels. The therapist emphasizes the hopeful ending, such as:

> Spottie waited and waited for someone to adopt him, and sometimes he worried that no one would come. But then one day, our family saw him and fell in love with him. And even though he's had some problems because of his rough start in life, we would never give him up! Don't you think Spottie is lovable? His first owners must have been very foolish to give him up. Spottie is very happy now, though, and so are we.

Third, the therapist can teach children how to groom, pet, or massage the dog, showing them the special places where the dog likes to be touched. This helps children learn caregiving, appropriate touch and pressure, and how to prevent injury to the dog or themselves. The therapist demonstrates various grooming or touching techniques, invites the child to try, and then provides reinforcement and suggestions to keep the child on track. "Tellington Touch" (Tellington-Jones, 1993) is a massage technique that has a calming effect on animals and is useful for teaching children to touch with the right amount of pressure. During grooming or petting activities, the therapist can also encourage the child to watch the dog's reactions and to adjust accordingly. For example, if the dog keeps moving away, this may signal that it has had enough or that the pressure is too intense. Children readily learn to watch and adjust—perhaps one way to facilitate the development of empathy.

Fourth, engaging in a variety of play activities with the therapy dog builds a relationship. It is quite common for children to show interest in the dog, its feelings, and its welfare after just a session or two of play.

Fifth, well-trained canines can be used in the room during nondirective play therapy. Because dogs seem to be accepting and eager to please, children feel close to them. A play therapist can provide empathic listening responses via the dog and help the dog engage in imaginary play as directed by the child, such as "Look, Spottie, Sara is making a special meal for us. She's giving you your supper." (The therapist makes slurping noises as the dog sniffs the bowl Sara has placed on the floor.) "Mmm, mmm. Spottie, you sure like that supper." Then, when seeing the big smile on Sara's face, the therapist says, "You're proud of the supper you made. You're happy that Spottie liked it so much!"

Strengthening behavioral and emotional regulation. There are many ways that canines can play with children in play therapy. The specific type of play depends on the dog's natural inclinations to play (i.e., what it naturally enjoys doing), the child's needs and wishes, and the therapeutic goals. After a brief period of obedience training, the therapist can suggest one or two play activities with the dog. These can include canine-assisted nondirective play therapy, as described in the previous section, or directed games such as fetch, tugging on a rope toy, running together, jumping over obstacles, modified agility activities, find it! (a canine version of hide-and-seek), or a variety of tricks. The therapist gives the child the instruction, "You can play and have fun with Spottie. There are just a couple of rules. First, whatever you do must be fun for *both* of you and, second, your job is to keep yourself safe and keep Spottie safe."

During all directive interventions, the therapist monitors the play interactions, praising the child for things done well such as playing safely, praising the dog, letting the dog "win" some of the time, watching and responding to the dog's signals, and helping the dog calm down if play becomes too rambunctious or potentially dangerous. The therapist also gives suggestions of ways to maintain safety or to calm the play if needed. For example, if the dog jumps up on the child and the child has difficulty managing it, the therapist reminds the child to say "off!" with a deep voice and/or to stand up or turn away and ignore the dog until it gets down. The therapist gives just a few suggestions during each interaction so that the child can absorb the learning without feeling overwhelmed or criticized. Praise for the child's efforts and behaviors should far outweigh corrective suggestions.

Clinical Vignette

Randy was a 14-year-old foster child who had lived in nine different homes since he was 10. Two prior adoptive placements had failed. He had a traumatic abuse history, including severe physical abuse and neglect. In his placements, he often was withdrawn and sullen with intermittent angry outbursts. He could not bear being corrected, fearing that even the slightest criticism revealed his inadequacy. Whenever he began feeling close to his caregivers, he pushed them away with his tantrums, during which he often destroyed property. He had caused mild injury to cats and dogs in some of his placements by pulling their tails, locking them in closets, and holding their front paws so that the animal balanced on its hind legs for long periods of time.

Randy was involved in a multimodal treatment approach, including individual nondirective play therapy, cognitive behavioral play therapy, filial therapy with his foster mother, behavior management, and canine-assisted play therapy. Play therapy was used with Randy because he disliked talking about his situation and because he played readily and imaginatively. The therapist introduced him to Kirrie, her play therapy dog, after four sessions, one of which included preparation to meet the dog. When Kirrie, a border collie mix, first met him, she immediately licked his hands and face. He laughed aloud—the first time the therapist had heard him do so. Randy told the therapist he would love to work with Kirrie regularly, and the dog participated in his treatment for approximately 15 minutes at the end of each session.

During the early canine-assisted play sessions, Randy helped the therapist train Kirrie. He learned the commands quickly and accepted the therapist's suggestions to use his "deep, strong voice" when correcting Kirrie. He never did anything that could hurt the dog. When Kirrie complied with his commands, he often turned around and looked at the therapist with a grin on his face. The therapist was able to praise many aspects of his interactions with the dog, and his growing confidence showed in his demeanor. After a 5-minute obedience training segment, Kirrie and Randy played together, usually using a long rope toy. Randy learned to pull on the rope toy with sufficient strength to give

Kirrie some resistance, yet allowed her to "win" some of the interactions by letting go of the rope. Kirrie immediately brought the rope toy back to him, nudging him to play more. At times, their play became a bit rough, and the therapist suggested that Randy help Kirrie calm down by playing more slowly or taking a brief break. Within two sessions, Randy learned to watch for this level of intensity and to make the needed adjustments without needing reminders. He was able to calm himself and the dog successfully, and the therapist told him, "That's great. You're finding ways to calm down a bit. Great control! You're keeping both of you safe. That's just the way to do it."

The therapist incorporated new child–canine play activities into later play sessions. Randy and Kirrie typically engaged in brief obedience training to start and then participated in other play activities to help Randy meet some of his therapeutic goals. As his self-regulation improved, Randy played ball with Kirrie and learned to incorporate new commands to govern the way she ran for the ball (e.g., telling her to "stay" before running out for the ball, which direction to run, and so on). These complex sequences required Randy to have patience and manage his own impulses, watch the dog's responses, praise or correct the dog, and decide when Kirrie was tired and needed to stop. Randy also helped train Kirrie in several new tricks.

Finally, Randy occasionally asked to have Kirrie join his nondirective play sessions. He often placed a camouflage bandanna around her neck, telling her she was an Army search-and-rescue dog. He played themes related to his trauma and attachment. He usually cast himself in the role of a soldier who was fighting in a war. Sometimes he pretended to be shot, and Kirrie had to find him. He told the therapist that she was the medic who had to help him once Kirrie found him. He often giggled when Kirrie searched the room and found him hiding behind the puppet theater or in the corner beneath a pile of stuffed animals.

In addition to filial therapy and parent consultation, Randy's foster mother occasionally joined some of the canine-assisted play sessions. Randy demonstrated for her the obedience training, grooming, and tricks that he had mastered with Kirrie. His foster mother told the therapist that his behavior at home with her golden retriever improved markedly after Randy's first session with Kirrie, and he behaved appropriately with her dog for the remainder of his placement with her. He now knew how to create a relationship with a dog, how to keep himself and the dog safe, and how to enjoy the relationship. He also communicated more openly with his foster mother, sharing observations and stories about dogs. These benefits also seemed to transfer when Randy was adopted 1 year later. The adoptive family reported that Randy showed them all of the canine commands and then applied them with their three family dogs. Randy is now 16 years old and has been reading a great deal about animals. He has expressed interest in becoming a veterinary assistant someday.

Randy's involvement with Kirrie helped him relax during therapy sessions, and he quickly learned to create healthy relationships with dogs. He transferred this knowledge to other canines in his life, as well as to people, becoming more communicative—initially about dog topics and later about other matters of importance to him. He was able to work more fully on his trauma issues, especially when he could pet or lie down with Kirrie at the end of the session. He viewed Kirrie as an important support. Involvement with Kirrie and the other canines in his life also improved Randy's motivation for some of his school work. He began to select and read library books about dogs and dog training, and he took pictures of himself training the foster mother's dog to school to show his homeroom teacher and classmates.

Suggestions for Follow-Up

When using canines in play therapy or other work with children and adolescents, follow-up is particularly important if the child lives with dogs or other animals at home. If so, helping the family incorporate some of the new skills with family pets is important for generalizing what the child has learned. Helping families recognize, encourage, and support the child's new skills at home can continue to build the child's sense of competence and confidence, healthy attachments, and self-regulation.

Contraindications for Use

Using dogs or other animals in therapy with children and adolescents is not always wise. Pet dander and animal-transmitted diseases can cause allergic reactions or endanger some (but not all) children with compromised immune systems. Parents have their own unique reactions to animals, and their consent to use therapy dogs should always be acquired first. Improperly or inadequately socialized and trained animals should not be used. They increase the chances of injury to children, the therapist, or themselves. The therapist should always monitor for stress and stop interactions if either the child or the dog appears tired, anxious, or stressed. Finally, the therapist must *always* be present with the child and dog. Disastrous injuries can happen very quickly, so if the therapist must leave the room, the dog and/or child should go too.

References

Altschuler, E. L. (1999). Pet-facilitated therapy for posttraumatic stress disorder. *Annals of Clinical Psychiatry, 11*(1), 29–30.

Antonioli, C., & Reveley, M. A. (2005). Randomized controlled trial of animal facilitated therapy with dolphins in the treatment of depression. *British Medical Journal, 331,* 7527.

Barker, S. B., & Barker, R. T. (1988). The human–canine bond: Closer than family ties? *Journal of Mental Health Counseling, 10*(1), 46–56.

Barker, S. B., & Dawson, K. S. (1998). The effects of animal-assisted therapy on anxiety ratings of hospitalized psychiatric patients. *Psychiatric Services, 49*(6), 797–801.

Beck, A. M., & Katcher, A. H. (2003). Future directions in human–animal bond research. *American Behavioral Scientist, 47*(1), 79–93.

Becker, M., & Morton, D. (2002). *The healing power of pets: Harnessing the amazing ability of pets to make and keep people happy and healthy.* New York: Hyperion.

Bekoff, M. (2007). *The emotional lives of animals.* Novato, CA: New World Library.

Bondarenko, N. (2007). *BBC and Canine Partners: Helping at-risk children.* Unpublished document.

Bratton, S. C., Ray, D., Rhine, T., & Jones, L. (2005). The efficacy of play therapy with children: A meta-analytic review of treatment outcomes. *Professional Psychology: Research & Practice, 36*(4), 376–390.

Carpenter, M. L. (2005). Trying to bridge the gap: The traditional mental health professional and animal assisted therapy. *Equine Facilitated Mental Health Association Newsletter*, Spring, 6–7.

Chandler, C. K. (2005). *Animal assisted therapy in counseling.* New York: Routledge.

Colombo, G., Buono, M. D., Smania, K., Raviola, R., & De Leo, D. (2006). Pet therapy and institutionalized elderly: A study on 144 cognitively unimpaired subjects. *Archives of Gerontology and Geriatrics, 42*(2), 207–216.

Donaldson, J. (2005). *The culture clash: A revolutionary new way of understanding the relationship between humans and dogs* (2nd ed.). Berkeley, CA: James & Kenneth.

Dunbar, I. (1996). *How to teach a new dog old tricks: Sirius puppy training* (2nd ed.). Berkeley, CA: James & Kenneth.

Elkind, D. (2007). *The power of play: How imaginative, spontaneous activities lead to healthier and happier children.* New York: Perseus.

Fine, A. H. (Ed.). (2000). *Handbook on animal-assisted therapy: Theoretical foundations and guidelines for practice.* San Diego: Academic Press.

Fine, A. H. (Ed.). (2006). *Handbook on animal-assisted therapy: Theoretical foundations and guidelines for practice* (2nd ed.). San Diego: Academic Press.

Gonski, Y. A. (1985). The therapeutic utilization of canines in a child welfare setting. *Child and Adolescent Social Work Journal, 2,* 93–105.

Goodall, J., & Bekoff, M. (2002). *The ten trusts: What we must do to care for the animals we love.* New York: Harper Collins (Harper San Francisco).

Gorczyca, K., Fine, A. H., Spain, C. V., Callaghan, D., Nelson, L., Popejoy, L., et al. (2006). History, development, and theory of human–animal support services for people with AIDS/HIV and other disabling chronic conditions. In A. H. Fine (Ed.), *Handbook on animal-assisted therapy: Theoretical foundations and guidelines for practice* (2nd ed.). San Diego: Academic Press.

Greenbaum, S. D. (2006). Introduction to working with animal-assisted crisis response animal handler teams. *International Journal of Emergency Mental Health, 8*(1), 49–63.

Hanselman, J. L. (2001). Coping skills interventions with adolescents in anger management using animals in therapy. *Journal of Child & Adolescent Group Therapy, 11*(4), 159–195.

Hart, L. A. (1995). Dogs as human companions: A review of the relationship. In J. Serpell (Ed.), *The domestic dog: Its evolution, behavior and interactions with people* (pp. 161–178). New York: Cambridge University Press.

Hayden, A. J. (2005). An exploration of the experiences of adolescents who participated in equine-facilitated psychotherapy: A resiliency perspective. *Dissertation Abstracts International, Section B: The Sciences and Engineering, 65*(12-B), 6653.

Jalongo, M. R. (Ed.). (2004). *The world's children and their companion animals: Developmental and educational significance of the child/pet bond.* Olney, MD: Association for Childhood Education International.

Jalongo, M. R., Astorino, T., & Bomboy, N. (2004). Canine visitors: The influence of therapy dogs on young children's learning and well-being in classrooms and hospitals. *Early Childhood Education Journal,* 32(1), 9–16.

Kaduson, H. G., & Schaefer, C. E. (Eds.). (2000). *Short-term play therapy for children.* New York: The Guilford Press.

Kaduson, H. G., & Schaefer, C. E. (Eds.). (2006). *Short-term play therapy for children* (vol. 2). New York: Guilford.

Kalnajs, S. (2006a). *The language of dogs: Understanding canine body language and other communication signals* (DVD set). Madison, WI: Blue Dog Training & Behavior.

Kalnajs, S. (2006b). *Am I safe? The art and science of canine behavior assessments.* Madison, WI: Blue Dog Training & Behavior.

Kaminski, M., Pellino, T., & Wish, J. (2002). Play and pets: The physical and emotional impact of child-life and pet therapy on hospitalized children. *Children's Health Care, 31*(4), 321–335.

Knapp, C. (1998). *Pack of two: The intricate bond between people and dogs.* New York: Delta.

Kohr, G. C. (2006). *K-9 and critical stress management.* Unpublished document.

Kottman, T. (1995). *Partners in play: An Adlerian approach to play therapy.* Alexandria, VA: American Counseling Association.

Kruger, K. A., & Serpell, J. A. (2006). Animal-assisted interventions in mental health: Definitions and theoretical foundations. In A. H. Fine (Ed.), *Handbook on animal-assisted therapy: Theoretical foundations and guidelines for practice* (2nd ed.). San Diego: Academic Press.

Landreth, G. L. (2002). *Play therapy: The art of the relationship* (2nd ed.). Philadelphia: Brunner–Routledge.

Lutwack-Bloom, P., Wijewickrama, R., & Smith, B. (2005). Effects of pets versus people visits with nursing home residents. *Journal of Gerontological Social Work, 44*(3–4), 137–159.

Mallon, G. P., & Levinson, B. M. (1997). *Pet-oriented child psychotherapy* (rev. ed.). Springfield, IL: Charles C Thomas.

Melson, G. F. (2001). *Why the wild things are: Animals in the lives of children.* Cambridge, MA: Harvard University Press.

Nathans-Barel, I., Feldman, P., Berger, B., Modai, I., & Silver, H. (2005). Animal-assisted therapy ameliorates anhedonia in schizophrenia patients. *Psychotherapy and Psychosomatics, 74*(1), 31–35.

O'Connor, K. J., & Schaefer, C. E. (Eds.). (1994). *Handbook of play therapy: Advances and innovations* (vol. 2). New York: Wiley.

Pelar, C. (2005). *Living with kids and dogs...without losing your mind: A parent's guide to controlling the chaos.* Woodbridge, VA: C&R Publishing.

Podberscek, A. L., Paul, E. S., & Serpell, J. A. (2000). *Companion animals and us: Exploring the relationships between people and pets.* New York: Cambridge University Press.

Reddy, L., Files-Hall, T., & Schaefer, C. E. (Eds.). (2005). *Empirically based play interventions for children.* Washington, DC: American Psychological Association.

Rugaas, T. (2006). *On talking terms with dogs: Calming signals* (2nd ed.). Wenatchee, WA: Dogwise Publishing.

Sams, M. J., Fortney, E. V., & Willenbring, S. (2006). Occupational therapy incorporating animals for children with autism: A pilot investigation. *American Journal of Occupational Therapy, 60*(3), 268–274.

Schoen, A. M. (2001). *Kindred spirits: How the remarkable bond between humans and animals can change the way we live.* New York: Broadway Books.

Serpell, J. (Ed.). (1995). *The domestic dog: Its evolution, behavior and interactions with people.* New York: Cambridge University Press.

Serpell, J. A. (1996). *In the company of animals* (2nd ed.). New York: Cambridge University Press.

Shane, F. T. (2006). *Canines in crisis: Mitigating traumatic stress through canine crisis intervention.* Upper Montclair, NJ: K-9 Disaster Relief Foundation.

Strand, E. B. (2004). Interparental conflict and youth maladjustment: The buffering effects of pets. *Stress, Trauma and Crisis: An International Journal, 7*(3), 151–168.

Sullivan, P. (2006). The healing power of animals. *Healing Magazine, 11*(1), 10–11.

Sutton-Smith, B. (1997). *The ambiguity of play.* Cambridge, MA: Harvard University Press.

Tellington-Jones, L. (1993). *The Tellington touch.* Newark, NJ: Penguin.

Terr, L. (1990). *Too scared to cry: How trauma affects children...and ultimately us all.* New York: Basic Books.

Thompson, M. J. (2007). *Effects of a trained therapy dog in child-centered play therapy on children with anxiety disorders.* Unpublished doctoral dissertation proposal.

VanFleet, R. (2005). *Filial therapy: Strengthening parent–child relationships through play* (2nd ed.). Sarasota, FL: Professional Resource Press.

VanFleet, R. (2006a). *Child-centered play therapy* (DVD workshop). Boiling Springs, PA: Play Therapy Press.

VanFleet, R. (2006b). *Introduction to filial therapy* (DVD workshop). Boiling Springs, PA: Play Therapy Press.

VanFleet, R. (2007a). *Pet play therapy: A workshop manual.* Boiling Springs, PA: Play Therapy Press.

VanFleet, R. (2007b). *Preliminary results from the ongoing pet play therapy study.* Boiling Springs, PA: Play Therapy Press; www.play-therapy.com/pets_study.html.

VanFleet, R. (2008). *Play therapy with kids and canines: Benefits for children's developmental and psychosocial health.* Sarasota, FL: Professional Resource Press.
Velde, B. P., Cipriani, J., & Fisher, G. (2005). Resident and therapist views of animal-assisted therapy: Implications for occupational therapy practice. *Australian Occupational Therapy Journal, 52*(1), 43–50.
Wilson, K., & Ryan, V. (2005). *Play therapy: A nondirective approach for children and adolescents* (2nd ed.). Philadelphia: Elsevier.
Woolley, C. C. (2005). Changes in child symptomatology associated with animal-assisted therapy. *Dissertation Abstracts International; Section B: The Sciences and Engineering, 65*(12-B), 6681.
www.akc.org
www.akc.org/events/cgc.program.cfm
www.deltasociety.org
www.dogsofcourse.com
www.greenchimneys.org
www.gressmountainranch.com
www.nadac.com
www.tdi-dog.org
www.usdaa.com
www.ukcdogs.com

Professional Readings and Resources

Beck, A., & Katcher, A. (1996). *Between pets and people: The importance of animal companionship* (rev. ed.). West Lafayette, IN: Purdue University Press.
Delta Society. (2004). *Team training course manual: A Delta Society® program for animal-assisted activities and therapy.* Bellevue, WA: Delta Society.
Masson, J. M. (1997). *Dogs never lie about love: Reflections on the emotional life of dogs.* New York: Three Rivers Press.
McConnell, P. B. (2005). *For the love of a dog: Understanding emotion in you and your best friend.* New York: Ballantine Books.

Bibliotherapy Sources for the Client

Elkind, D. (2007). *The power of play: How imaginative, spontaneous activities lead to healthier and happier children.* New York: Perseus.
Herriot, J. (1986). *James Herriot's dog stories.* New York: St. Martin's Paperbacks.
Pelar, C. (2005). *Living with kids and dogs...without losing your mind: A parent's guide to controlling the chaos.* Woodbridge, VA: C&R Publishing.
VanFleet, R. (2006). *The faces of play: A photographic exploration of the importance and joys of playfulness.* Boiling Springs, PA: Play Therapy Press.

KidsRap
Using Hip-Hop to Promote and Punctuate Change

Catherine Ford Sori

Over the last thirty to forty years, youth culture has shifted; where once there were moldable young people you could just tell what to do, there are now young people telling folk what they ain't gonna do!

Smith and Jackson
2005, p. 65

So *when* you're *stuck* and don't know *what* to do
With that *"resistant,"* mute *kid,* who's just a *lookin'* at you,
Ya can't *just* sit back! Ya gotta *meet* him where he's *at!*
So get *up* on your feet, start a *movin'* to the *beat!*
Clinician's *Rap...Uh!...*Kid's *Rap...Uh!*

Type of Contribution: Activity, Homework, Handouts

Objective

The purpose of this activity is to utilize hip-hop with children, adolescents, and families to emphasize how youth can overcome problems and maintain the therapeutic gains they have achieved. Because this activity is culturally relevant to most youths it has great appeal. It is also an excellent method to engage and empower young clients to overcome problems in a playful and familiar modality that incorporates music and movement. This strength-based activity can be adapted for use with individual children or adolescents, with families, and with children's groups. It can be used to accomplish three goals: (1) to promote joining between the therapist and clients; (2) as a means for youth to express themselves in ways that are meaningful and relevant to their culture; and (3) to promote and punctuate change and progress toward therapeutic goals.

Rationale for Use

To be "hip" you must understand the hip-hop culture. While not all of us are knowledgeable about the hip-hop culture, it is now part of the fabric of contemporary, mainstream American society (Gadsden, 2007). If you work with youth, whether they are African American, Caucasian, Latino, Asian, or multicultural; whether they are from rural areas, affluent suburbs, or inner cities; and regardless of whether they love hip-hop or not, they are all being influenced by it (Smith & Jackson, 2005). To understand the youth culture of today, "you have to understand urban America" because "what affects the hood every day and becomes commonplace there becomes all the rave in the suburbs among middle- and upper-class white, black and Latino kids" (Smith & Jackson, p. 64). In fact,

Smith and Jackson claim that "if you truly want to understand the culture that youth live in today, it's important to understand hip-hop—as a culture, not just a music form" (p. 62).

While hip-hop originated in the South Bronx in the early 1970s in the African-American community as a reaction to the "poverty, tension over economic injustices, social injustice and social change" (Smith & Jackson, 2005, p. 67), it is now a Wall Street economy. Hip-hop is big business, with major corporations like McDonald's using it in their advertising. In discussing the influence of hip-hop on current culture, Nelson George (1998) wrote in *Hip Hop America*:

> Now we know that rap music, and hip hop style as a whole, has utterly broken through from its ghetto roots to assert a lasting influence on American clothing, magazine publishing, television, language, sexuality, and social policy as well as its obvious presence in records and movies.... Advertisers, magazines, MTV, fashion companies, beer and soft drink manufacturers, and multimedia conglomerates like Time-Warner have embraced hip-hop as a way to reach not just black young people, but all young people. (p IX)

History of Hip-Hop

Hip-hop was born in the years between 1965 and 1984, and originated in the streets of the Bronx. During that time when youths in the Bronx experienced great political tension and poverty, hip-hop started with "deejayin'" at parties and emceeing in parks. In 1979 the SugarHill Gang burst onto the national music scene with their album "Rapper's Delight," which sold two million copies. It became the voice of a disenfranchised people who had historically been ignored by mainstream America (Williams-Alleyne, 1996). But soon the popularity of hip-hop swept beyond the hood and it was suddenly a mainstream phenomenon, embraced by many youths regardless of race or ethnicity (Williams-Alleyne). In fact, 70% of the records were purchased by Caucasian American teenagers (Smith & Jackson, 2005).

While many people may think that the terms rap and hip-hop are synonymous, they are not (Gadsden, 2007). Hip-hop is a subculture, and rap is only one component (although the most recognized) of many other elements that come together to produce that subculture (Smith & Jackson, 2005). Hip-hop uses rap to provide commentary on the everyday experiences of living in the hood, with "rappers functioning as inner-city journalists who through their rap, dance and graffiti report on what's going on in the city and the world at large" (Smith & Jackson, 2005, p. 62). While many in the hood had learned a mindset of hopelessness that allowed for few dreams or aspirations, rap gave an empowering voice to a powerless group of young people crying out to be heard. Its message was one of common experiences and futility counterbalanced with resiliency. According to Smith and Jackson:

> Hip-hop brings the hope back. Even if it offers no change, it at least gives confirmation that your situation is recognized and identified. The hip-hop culture being birthed out of this anxiety has created a new voice of resistance for a disenfranchised group of people. Young people needed a way to begin understanding the struggles of urban life, and the hip-hop subculture, using rap as its medium, was the vehicle that would speak into this culture and be its voice to the world. (p. 68)

Elements of Hip-Hop

While Smith and Jackson (2005) identify at least 10 elements of hip-hop (deejayin', emceeing, breaking, graffiti art, street language, street entrepreneurship, beat box, street knowledge, street fashion, and hip-hop spirituality), only five are relevant for this chapter. Those are emceeing (rapping), breaking, graffiti art, beat box, and spirituality. Each is discussed briefly next.

Emceeing (rapping). Using a microphone, rappers chant verses that may or may not rhyme or use alliteration, but that follow the rhythmic beat of the music. Often there is little or no melody; the focus is on the rhythm and on the lyrics, which ideally "tell a story, teach morals or history, give a report on street life, or celebrate life" (Smith & Jackson, 2005, p. 76). Emcees are lyricists who have a message for the heart, soul, or mind, and who share ideas on how to live in today's world. These skilled artists are stewards of the heritage of hip-hop culture; however, in recent years many rappers spin a different message, often about materialism and sex. This unfortunate transformation has occurred since the record labels began to dictate the lyrics (Smith & Jackson).

Breaking. Breaking is a dance style that incorporates combinations of stylized movements from gymnastics, spinning, and capoeira (from Africans enslaved in Brazil), all in sync with the break beats of the songs (Smith & Jackson, 2005). Rival gangs had "battles," which today have evolved into competitions that are quite elaborate and give hope, purpose, and identity to many young people living in the hood. This is forcefully portrayed in the 2005 film *Rize* (LaChapelle).

Graffiti art. While illegal, graffiti art utilized spray paint on abandoned buildings, walls, or subways. Many graffiti artists are quite creative, and record promoters and big businesses have hired graffiti artists and use these techniques in their advertisements (Smith & Jackson, 2005).

Beat box. Rhythm is an essential element of rap, and street rappers used whatever was handy to create a beat—even their mouths (the "box" in the term beat box) (Smith & Jackson, 2005). This beat forms the foundation upon which the lyrics are rapped.

Spirituality. Hip-hop has spiritual elements, first, because it utilizes music, and music is often linked to spirituality. In fact, the call-and-response tradition found in the Black church can be found in rap (Williams-Alleyne, 1996). Second, Afrika Bambaataa, who started the Zulu Nation, recognized a spiritual link between the music of hip-hop and the subculture that resulted, and he sought to bring peace to the hood by using hip-hop music and dance (Smith & Jackson, 2005). Many current artists promote a sense of spirituality in their lyrics, and others are even utilizing rap in hip-hop Christian churches (e.g., Gadsden, 2007; *The Hip-Hop Church*, see Smith & Jackson). However, it is important to note that much mainstream hip-hop has moved from its spiritual roots toward expressions of materialism and sex.

Use in Therapy

Rap is a useful intervention because it reaches kids through a culturally relevant modality, and it can be utilized in therapy in several ways. First, clients can create their own rap. This can be used as a family intervention, where family members come together to create music and dance to promote change, or to punctuate progress that has already occurred. As an alternative, young clients could create their own raps individually or as sibling subsystems, perhaps to perform for family members. Finally, clinicians can create a rap for clients and perform it as a pseudo "reflection" on the changes and strengths the clinician sees in the clients.

KidsRap as discussed in this chapter can be viewed through the lenses of three theories: family play therapy, structural family therapy, or narrative therapy. These will be briefly introduced next.

Family Play Therapy: A Metamodel

Family play therapy has been described as a metamodel that "fits" with many schools of family therapy, including structural, experiential, solution focus, and narrative (Dermer, Olund, & Sori, 2006). When families play together the therapist is able to observe how they organize around a task, how they interact, whose ideas are privileged and utilized in the activity (and whose are discarded), and their level of enjoyment (Gil & Sobol, 2000). In addition, the content of the session—what the child or family produces (i.e., artwork, a sandtray, a puppet interview, storytelling) offers therapists a symbolic window into the problem as it is metaphorically represented. As a family play therapy intervention, *KidsRap* could be utilized within many theoretical frameworks. This chapter explains how to integrate it within a structural family therapy or narrative theoretical perspective.

Structural Family Therapy

Structural family therapy, founded by Salvador Minuchin in the early 1970s (e.g., Minuchin, 1974), emphasizes the importance of parental hierarchy and clear boundaries that define the roles and rules of the family. According to Minuchin, problems emerge in families during transitions in the life cycle, when one or more family members encounter stress from outside the family, or when idiosyncratic problems occur. The therapist's role is to alter the family structure to create new possibilities for families to solve their problems. This often occurs when the boundaries around individuals or the family are altered and the parent's role in the hierarchy is strengthened. Key structural interventions include an emphasis on the therapist joining with each family member, and asking family members to talk directly to one another. These conversations, known as enactments, allow the therapist to assess the patterns of communication, to hypothesize about the boundaries and structure in the family, and to intervene by suggesting new ways for families to communicate with one another that alters the boundaries and structure of the family.

When used in a structural family therapy framework, *KidsRap* allows the clinician to observe the family in an enactment as they create their hip-hop. Parents may be put in charge of directing the activity, overseeing the creation of the rap, assigning roles, and structuring the rehearsal and performance. The rap itself and how it is performed often reveal how the family is organized, including any coalitions and patterns of complementarity, and it also offers therapists an opportunity to intervene to alter the family structure.

Narrative Therapy

Narrative therapy rests on the assumption that people create stories to make sense of their lives and their experiences. These stories (or narratives) are greatly influenced by society. Clients believe and internalize these stories as absolute "truths," which narrative therapists call clients' dominant stories. One goal of therapy is to uncover subjugated stories that are different from dominant stories, and offer an alternative "truth" about the client and his or her relationship with the problem. Narrative therapists often seek to uncover the subjugated story by externalizing the problem. When the problem is externalized it does not lie within clients, but is outside them and therefore more accessible and amenable to change. One popular saying in narrative therapy is that "the person is not the problem; the problem is the problem." For example, Mary is not labeled "depressed," but "sadness" may be the problem that Mary says is influencing her. To externalize a problem, the therapist asks clients what name they would give to their problem, or what they might call their problem. Examples of what some younger clients might name the problem could be "Distraction Monster," "Mr. Anger," or "Bickering Bill." Once the problem is externalized, the child and parents can explore ways to defeat the influence of the problem. Narrative therapy, which emphasizes the importance of language, helps clients discover "unique outcomes" (times when they are not influenced by the problem, or when they have overcome it in the past), and to explore additional ways to defeat the externalized problem (see Freedman & Combs, 1996; Freeman, Epston, & Lobovits, 1997; Shilts & Duncan, 2003; Sholtes, 2003; Simons & Freedman, 2000; White & Epston, 1990).

From a narrative perspective, *KidsRap* can be used after clients have externalized the problem, and rap can be written to (a) identify unique outcomes, (b) clarify steps each client has taken toward reaching his or her goal or goals, (c) punctuate how far clients have come in diminishing the influence of the externalized problem or problems on their lives, and (d) describe how the their world will be when the externalized problem no longer oppresses them.

Materials Needed

- Play microphones—one for each family member (these do a nice job of echoing the voice and can be purchased for under $4.00)—or a toy karaoke machine
- A simple drum, box, or a book that can be used as a percussion "instrument" (optional: include small rhythm instruments)
- Paper, pencils, and erasers, or a large blackboard
- A video camera or digital camera
- Tape recorder

Instructions

This activity generally works best if used in the middle to late stages of therapy with families who have children and/or adolescents. However, it can also be used in the early stages of therapy to both join with resistant young clients in a culturally relevant manner, and to assess the family's structure or to uncover unique outcomes to the problem. The first step to prepare clients for this activity is to review progress clients have made toward a goal and specific things they have done that have improved their situation. The following additional steps are suggested for implementing this activity.

Clients Create Their Own Rap

The instructions for clients creating their own rap are similar to those for doing a family puppet interview (Gil, 1994; Irwin & Malloy, 1994). While the following steps outline how to utilize this activity with a family, they can easily be adapted for use with an individual young client:

1. Explain that you have an idea for a fun activity to help them as a family to document all the hard work they have done, the strengths they have as individuals and as a family, and the progress they have made in reaching their goals. If the family has externalized the problem, discuss how they have defeated the influence of the problem. Take notes so that the family can use them in writing their rap.
2. Explore clients' knowledge about the roots of hip-hop and rap, how it has changed over the years (with more emphasis today on materialism and sex), and how many are trying to "take back" the positive aspects originally found in hip-hop (Gadsden, 2007) and use it to help kids and strengthen families.
3. Explain that even if they do not feel they have musical talent or have little interest in hip-hop, the activity you are proposing should be a fun way for them to come together to create something together or to celebrate the victories they are having over their problems. Tell them this has helped other families and invite them to experiment with you. (Note: If a parent does not want to actually do the rap, he or she could tap out the rhythm on a small drum, box, or book, make background rhythmic vocal noises, or simply help coach the children in writing the lyrics.)
4. Tell them that this activity has three steps: (1) After you leave the room they will write a rap together that has a beginning, a middle, and an end and expresses what they have all done to reach their goal or goals and/or to defeat their externalized problem. (2) They will decide how to perform the rap and practice it a few times. They can decide if they want to include simple or elaborate dance movements, what tempo the rap should be, who will sing the rap, and if

they want a "musical accompaniment" (e.g., someone drumming rhythms, snapping fingers, or making background vocal noises). Encourage all family members to be involved. (3) The family will perform the hip-hop for the counselor. Handout 2.1 provides questions and information to help guide clients through this process. The parents may be put in charge of the activity if the therapist wants to observe how the executive subsystem functions. Other times it may be useful to just observe who assumes leadership in directing the activity or to suggest that a child be in charge.

5. The clinician can leave the room while the family creates their hip-hop. Another alternative is for the therapist to sit quietly and unobtrusively in a corner of the room to observe the family members' interactions and relationships as they write the rap, assign roles, and rehearse their performance. Usually 20 minutes is ample time for them to write and rehearse it.
6. The clinician returns when the clients are ready and serves as the audience while the family performs the hip-hop.
7. Follow-up discussions should focus on two general areas: content (the actual work the family produced) and process (how the family interacted while creating the hip-hop) (see Gil & Sobol, 2000; Sori, 2006b).
8. To process the *content,* clinicians can go over the rap line by line and discuss what each phrase means to each family member. Content questions might include:
   - What emotions were triggered in each person in different phrases?
   - Which lines had the strongest impact?
   - (If they have externalized their problems) What effect does hearing this have on their externalized problem? How do you think the problem felt in hearing this? Did this increase or decrease the size or influence of the problem? If it decreased the size of the problem, how much was the decrease (using scaling questions: see Shilts & Duncan, 2003; Sori, 2006a)? How might this activity be useful in the future as part of their arsenal in defeating the problem?
   - What effect does hearing this have on each family member and his/her relationship to the problem?
   - What does this rap say about their individual and family strengths?
   - What message does this rap send to others?
   - What is the "moral of the story?"
   - What title would each one give to his or her rap?
9. Next, clinicians should explore what the *process* was like for them to cocreate this hip-hop that tells their story. Process questions might include:
   - What was it like for each of you to do this activity?
   - How did you decide what to write? Whose ideas to use?
   - How did you decide what roles you would play in performing it?
   - How did your thinking and emotions change throughout this activity?
   - What was the hardest part in doing this together? The best part?
   - What did you learn from this?
10. The session might end with the clinician asking the family to practice this at home three times that week, just in case the problem thinks they have forgotten how much power the family has to defeat its influence, or to encourage children to comply with a parent's request.
11. If possible, a video and audio tape should be made of the clients' performance, which clients can take home to review. Another option is to pose the family and take digital photos for the family to keep. These visual and auditory reproductions serve as reminders and positive reinforcement, and help clients to internalize and visualize the message, as well as to remember their playful experience in cocreating the hip-hop.

"Hip-Hop Reflecting Teams"—Clinicians Rap for Clients to Punctuate Progress

While at first it may seem daunting for clinicians to use hip-hop in therapy, it is really not so hard to do. All of us remember childhood chants and jingles, such as jump rope or hand-clapping songs, nursery rhymes, and advertisement jingles. With a bit of imagination and courage, anyone can do it—and it not only helps clients, but also can help therapists feel more alive in the session!

Using hip-hop works well if the clinician has a cotherapist or team members behind a one-way mirror. However, courageous and playful clinicians can perform this as a solo for clients, which is an excellent way to liven a family with deadpan or resistant youth! In fact, you can perform the hip-hop from a one-down position, apologizing afterward for your lack of expertise and asking for the assistance of the "experts"—the youth in the family!

Whether done with a team or as a solo, the clinician should prepare in advance (unless he or she has exceptional improvisational rhyming skills!). When used within a narrative framework, the first step prior to the session is to list the externalized problems or goals the clients have identified. Next, write down the clients' strengths and the steps they have taken to defeat their externalized problem or to reach their goals. Then write a rap that has some of the elements discussed earlier (e.g., rhyme, alliteration, rhythm, etc.) and tells a "thick" story of exactly what the clients have done to make progress. If possible include specific examples that reflect how each family member has found ways to "conquer" the enemy. It is often helpful to include a brief "chorus" of a few repeated words (e.g., "uh-huh, uh-huh" or "they cool, they cool") between every two stanzas to make the performance easier. While this is easier than it may sound, if you need help with rhyming, the *Hip-Hop Rhyming Dictionary* by Mitchell (2003) is a very useful and inexpensive resource.

Then decide what movements will be incorporated into the rap, and what words might be emphasized. Finally, rehearse, rehearse, and rehearse! Practice in front of a mirror, record yourself, and if you are really brave, try it out for your colleagues or supervisor!

Brief Clinical Vignette One: Family-Created Hip-Hop: "Good Touch–Bad Touch"

Mrs. Wilson, an African-American professional single parent, initiated therapy for herself and her 9-year-old twin daughters, Sarena and Sabrina, and 5-year-old son, James. They came in because someone had attempted to sexually abuse James. Mrs. Wilson had sent her children to a neighborhood store for some bread, and when her daughters came out of the back door of the store into the alley they saw an 8-year-old boy from their neighborhood pull down their brother's pants and start to touch his genitals. Sarena started yelling while Sabrina ran over to stop the assault, and the boy ran away. The girls helped their brother; then they all ran home to tell their mother, who talked to the mother of the child and then called the school. Mrs. Wilson told the school counselor what had happened and it was reported to child protective services. The school counselor recommended family therapy and referred them for services.

The first few sessions of family therapy were spent assessing the degree of trauma to the children and felt quite heavy, with Mrs. Wilson being very distressed over how this had happened to her children. Mrs. Wilson felt somehow responsible, and that if she were a better mother she could have somehow protected her children. She was naturally concerned about her children's safety, so much time was spent discussing ways to keep them safe. To empower Mrs. Wilson and strengthen her role as protector, the therapist coached her on how to explain the difference between good touch (who could touch them and where) and bad touch (inappropriate touch). She was encouraged to discuss appropriate boundaries with her children and what they should do if anyone attempted to touch them in an improper way.

To strengthen her role, to make this lesson more kid friendly, and to help ensure that the children internalized Mrs. Wilson's lesson, the therapist asked Mrs. Wilson to be in charge of a play activity: The family was invited to make up a hip-hop together. After giving the instructions discussed previously, the therapist left the room. Mom, with the assistance of the three children, wrote the following rap:

Good Touch...Bad Touch...

Good touch and bad touch ain't the same thing!
Bad touch is bad, if you know what I mean.
I get to pick who gets to touch me,
People got to respect my boundaries!
My body is mine, and the parts covered up
By my bathing suit, nobody can touch!
If somebody comes and tries to touch me,
I'll run and scream and kick 'em in the knee!
I'll tell my Mom, or a teacher or a cop
And they'll be in trouble—not a little, but a lot!
So you gotta know just what to do
If someone's bad touch comes a lookin' for you.
Good touch, bad touch, I know what they mean!
Bad touch is banned, not allowed on the scene!
Uh-huh (echoed Uh-huh),
Uh-huh (echoed Uh-huh).

They practiced their rap a few times, standing in front of the one-way mirror, which reflected their images. The children danced and snapped their fingers to the beat and pretended that they were on stage performing. Mom kept them on task when one would deviate from the script with too much improvising. When Mom signaled they were ready, the therapist came back in the room and gave them each a toy microphone that amplified and reverberated their voices. With Mom as the director, they performed their hip-hop for the therapist with great energy and excitement, and the therapist audiotaped the performance so that the family could take a copy home. After a few "encores" Mom asked the kids to sit down, and the therapist discussed their process in creating the rap, and what the words meant. While Mrs. Wilson had made up most of the words, the kids had given their input, and they had decided what movements and rhythmic sounds they wanted to use. The children were able to explain in their own words what the rap lyrics meant, and the family was encouraged to practice the hip-hop along with the tape three times in the next week.

In the following weeks the children asked if they could perform their rap in front of the mirror at the end of each session, with the mother and therapist serving as the audience, applauding them enthusiastically at the end. The children were doing well, and Mrs. Wilson, who reported feeling much less anxious, felt they had internalized the message in the rap and would know what to do if anyone threatened to touch them inappropriately. In the final session the family invited the team behind the mirror into the therapy room to be the audience for one final "rap," which the therapist videotaped so that the children could take home a recording and watch themselves "on TV." As the family left after their last session, the children were quietly rapping down the hall, while Mrs. Wilson lingered to express her gratitude for offering a creative approach to making sure that her children would never forget the important lessons in their rap. And that "(w)rapped" up their therapy!

Brief Clinical Vignette Two: Therapist-Created Hip-Hop: "Da Sword"

Mr. and Mrs. Silvio initiated therapy to help their 12-year-old son, Tony. Paulie Silvio owned a popular Italian restaurant, *Vesilvios,* which required him to work long hours. His wife Carmen was a teacher at Tony's private Christian school, where Tony had recently been expelled for fighting on the playground. This was quite embarrassing for Carmen. Tony had recently been diagnosed with ADHD, and had been started on a trial of medication. However, he still was not turning in his homework and his parents feared his impulsive behavior would result in another fight. The family were very religious and were dismayed that all their attempts to teach Tony right and wrong, and all their emphasis on Bible reading and attending church and Sunday school seemed to not have gotten through to Tony—at least in the area of not fighting.

It was very difficult to engage Tony the first few sessions; he sat quietly and would give only one- or two-word answers, and only when prompted by his father. In the third session the therapist decided to externalize the problem and asked Tony what, if he could name what got him in trouble, that name would be. Tony, suddenly alert, said, "I'll do better than that—I'll draw it!" He then went to the blackboard and drew a picture of the playground, with several figures playing football. When Tony finished, he pointed to a figure and described how that boy had ripped the ball out of his hands and shoved him to the ground. That's what had initiated the fight that resulted in his suspension. When asked what he would name that "thing" that got him to fight, Tony answered, "Mr. Devil," and he proceeded to draw a picture of a scary looking figure, and explain ways that Mr. Devil tricked him into fighting when he was provoked. Next the therapist explored the size of Mr. Devil and asked Tony to draw a mark on the board indicating how high Mr. Devil's influence was before coming to therapy (it was near the top of the board) and where it was currently (it was several inches lower) (see Shilts & Duncan, 2003; Sori, 2006a). The therapist then explored unique outcomes in the past—times when Mr. Devil tried to trick Tony into fighting, but Tony was able to resist. The therapist asked how he had resisted Mr. Devil's temptation in the past and requested that Tony and his parents notice times in the next week when Tony was able to resist Mr. Devil's attempts to get him in trouble.

This was a breakthrough, as each week Tony shared times he had resisted Mr. Devil and what he had done instead of fighting, as well as the few times when Mr. Devil still managed to trick him into fighting. The therapist joined with the Silvios around their religious beliefs. When Carmen reminded Tony that he could ask God for strength and that he had the "full armor of God," including the "sword of the spirit," the therapist took out a toy sword. She asked the parents to explain that verse to Tony, and then invited the parents to stand and Tony to kneel, while they "knighted" him with the sword—honoring him as a member of "God's army." First Paulie and then Carmen "knighted" Tony, while highlighting his strengths and courage and giving him their blessing. The therapist took pictures of Tony being knighted by each parent and another of him brandishing the sword in front of his drawing of Mr. Devil—pointing to his goal of diminishing the size and influence of this villain.

Over the next few weeks Tony continued to improve and avoid the influence of Mr. Devil, but was still having trouble turning in his homework. The therapist mused that Batman had a helper, Robin, and their enemy, the Riddler, also had a helper, Joker. She asked Tony if perhaps Mr. Devil had a helper, and Tony immediately went to the board and drew a picture he labeled as "Dr. Evil." This bad guy caused him to forget to turn in his homework and got him in trouble at school, which made him mad and less able to resist Mr. Devil's attempts to get him to fight when somebody said something "smart" to him. On Dr. Evil's shirt Tony drew a face with his name under it and an "X" through it, and said, "The X through my face means Dr. Evil doesn't want me to be happy."

The therapist asked the family what was different about times Dr. Evil did not trick Tony into forgetting his homework. After some discussion, they agreed that the homework got turned in if it was put in a special folder, and that folder was put on top of Tony's books in his book bag at night. With some prompting from the therapist, the parents reminded Tony that his weapon—the "sword of the spirit"—could also help him defeat Dr. Evil, and that they were on his side and so was God. Suddenly Tony jumped up and asked if the therapist would take a picture of him aiming the sword at his drawing on the board of Dr. Evil and Mr. Devil. He said he wanted to tape the picture to his homework folder to remind him every day to turn in his work.

This picture served as a reminder and helped Tony remember to turn in his homework. He continued to improve both behaviorally and academically as he was increasingly successful in defeating his giants. The tension in the home was greatly reduced as the parents learned more about ADHD and how they could understand and help Tony succeed. After discussing with the Silvios how some churches are using hip-hop to "take back" this medium as a way to empower young people and give them hope, the therapist suggested that perhaps Tony might want to write his own hip-hop for the last session. However, Tony, who was rather shy and introverted, declined. So in the last session the therapist asked permission to invite the team behind the mirror to come in for a special surprise. Using toy microphones, they performed this hip-hop, bouncing, snapping, and turning on each "chorus:"

Defeating the Giants Hip-Hop

Mister Devil made me fight at school
But I taught him he will not rule!
"Da sword...Da sword!"
He thought he'd make ME not smile,
But I learned to kick his butt a mile!
"Da sword...Da sword!"
Doctor Evil says homework stinks!
But he doesn't know what I really think!
"Da sword...Da sword!"
So these 2 guys, they think they're cool!
But they don't know that I WILL RULE!!!
"Da sword...Da sword!"
My secret weapon is my sword!
But they don't know I have my LORD!
"Da sword...Da sword!"
"Da sword...Da sword!"
DEFEAT!!!

Tony looked stunned at first to see these "professionals" rapping, beating, and breaking, but the whole family applauded wildly at the end, and asked for an encore. Tony was given a copy of the lyrics to remind him of the hard work he had done in defeating the influence of Mr. Devil and Dr. Evil. He bounced out of the room with his head held high and a huge grin on his face, clutching the lyrics.

Suggestions for Follow-Up

There are several ways to follow up this activity to punctuate change and the message in the rap. For example, if the therapist takes photographs of the family performing the rap, they could create a collage of the photos on a poster board and include a copy of the lyrics. As an alternative, the family could create a family mural drawing of them rapping on a large sheet of paper taped to the wall. In addition, children or adolescents could take any pictures taken during the course of therapy and make them into a picture book, using their own graffiti art to label the pictures or to express their experiences, thoughts, and feelings. All of these highlight progress and serve as visual reminders of the clients' experiences using hip-hop in therapy. These are all ways of creating visual representations of their joyful experiences that the family can take home and hang up to remind them of their work and the fun they had together.

The therapist might also suggest that the family invite extended family members to come into a session to watch a performance or they might be encouraged to perform the hip-hop at home for grandparents or other concerned family members.

Finally, if therapists are feeling like they have hit an impasse with young clients, or they need to jump-start their own creativity to use hip-hop, they can stand before the mirror and warm up with the following (see Handout 2.2):

Contraindications for Use

While hip-hop has become part of mainstream American pop culture, in recent years it has gotten a bad "rap" (pun intended!) because many use bad language and focus on topics such as materialism, sex, and drugs. Therefore, it is important to discuss with parents your goals for reclaiming hip-hop to give hope and to empower their children. It is also important to be informed about and sensitive to any cultural or religious beliefs that would make this activity objectionable to parents.

This activity often breathes life and joy into sessions and can be a wonderful method to have families experience pleasure together as they create and perform their hip-hop. However, it is not recommended for families who are experiencing a crisis, ongoing abuse, or are actively grieving.

References

Dermer, S., Olund, D., Sori, C. F. (2006). Integrating play in family therapy theories. In C. F. Sori (Ed.), *Engaging children in family therapy: Creative approaches to integrating theory and research in clinical practice* (pp. 37–68). New York: Routledge.

Freedman, J., & Combs, G. (1996). *Narrative therapy: The social construction of preferred realities.* New York: W. W. Norton.

Freeman, J., Epston, D., & Lobovits, D. (1997). *Playful approaches to serious problems: Narrative therapy with children and their families.* New York: W. W. Norton.

Gadsden, T. (2006). *Hip-hop in the church.* Presentation at Take Action, Arts with a Mission. Chicago, IL.

George, N. (1998). *Hip-hop America.* New York: Penguin Books.

Gil, E. (1994). *Play in family therapy.* New York: Guilford.

Gil, E., & Sobol, B. (2000). Engaging families in therapeutic play. In C. E. Bailey (Ed.), *Children in therapy: Using the family as a resource* (pp. 341–382). New York: W. W. Norton.

Irwin, E. C., & Malloy, E. S. (1994). Family puppet interview. In C. Schaefer & L. Carey (Eds.), *Family play therapy* (pp. 21–34). Northvale, NJ: Aronson.

LaChapelle, D. (Director) (2005). *Rize.* Los Angeles: Lionsgate.

Minuchin, S. (1974). *Families and family therapy.* Cambridge, MA: Harvard University Press.

Mitchell, K. M. (2003). *Hip-hop rhyming dictionary: For rappers, Djs and MCs.* Los Angeles: Firebrand Music.

Shilts, L., & Duncan, B. L. (2003). Integrating externalization and scaling questions: Using visual scaling to amplify children's voices. In C. F. Sori, L. L. Hecker, & associates, *The therapist's notebook for children and adolescents: Homework, handouts, and activities for use in psychotherapy* (pp. 230–236). Binghamton, NY: Haworth.

Sholtes, S. K. (2003). The use of consultants in play therapy: Narrative practices with young children. In C. F. Sori, L. L. Hecker, & associates, *The therapist's notebook for children and adolescents: Homework, handouts, and activities for use in psychotherapy* (pp. 225–229). Binghamton, NY: Haworth.

Simons, V. A., & Freedman, J. (2000). Witnessing bravery: Narrative ideas for working with children and families. In C. E. Bailey (Ed.), *Children in therapy: Using the family as a resource* (pp. 20–45). New York: W. W. Norton.

Smith, E., & Jackson, P. (2005). *The hip-hop church: Connecting with the movement shaping our culture.* Downers Grove, IL: InterVarsity Press.

Sori, C. F. (2006a). A playful postmodern approach to counseling children and families: An interview with Lee Shilts. In C. F. Sori (Ed.), *Engaging children in family therapy: Creative approaches to integrating theory and research in clinical practice* (pp. 117–137). New York: Routledge.

Sori, C. F. (2006b). Family play therapy: An interview with Eliana Gil. In C. F. Sori (Ed.), *Engaging children in family therapy: Creative approaches to integrating theory and research in clinical practice* (pp. 69–90). New York: Routledge.

White, M., & Epston, D. (1990). Narrative means to therapeutic ends. New York: Norton.

Williams-Alleyne, S. (1996). Insert. *The best of Sugar Hill Gang: Rapper's Delight* [CD]. Los Angeles, CA: Rhino Records.

Professional Readings and Resources

Fricke, J., & Ahearn, C. (Eds). (2002). *Yes, yes y'all: The experience music project oral history of hip-hop's first decade.* New York: DaCapo Press.

http://en.wikipedia.org/wiki/Hip_hop.

Light, A. (Ed.). (1999). *The VIBE history of hip-hop.* New York: Three Rivers Press.

Mitchell, K. M. (2003). *Hip-hop rhyming dictionary: For rappers, Djs and MCs.* Los Angeles: Firebrand Music.

Westbook, A. (2002). *Hip hoptionary: The dictionary of hip hop terminology.* New York: Broadway Books.

Bibliotherapy Sources for the Client

http://en.wikipedia.org/wiki/Hip_hop.

LaChapelle, D. (Director) (2005). *Rize.* Los Angeles: Lionsgate.

Mitchell, K. M. (2003). *Hip-hop rhyming dictionary: For rappers, Djs and MCs.* Los Angeles: Firebrand Music.

Handout 2.1: Hip-Hop "Rap" Sheet

Creating a Rap

Step One: Suggested Questions to Get Started

- Externalize: Name the problem.
- How is it influencing you?
- How does it trick or deceive you?
- When are times that the problem is not able to influence you?
- What do you do to resist it?
- What will it look like when the problem is no longer getting to you?
- Imagine yourself defeating the problem. What will that look like?

Note: You may want to write a rap that just expresses how you feel about something. The important thing is that it is meaningful to you.

Step Two: Drafting the Rap

Using answers to the preceding questions begin to write your rap. It can rhyme, but does not have to. Jot down any key words that come to you, and if you want some rhyme, see what words rhyme with those key words. You can use a rhyming or hip-hop dictionary if you would like. There is no right or wrong; this is your own rap. Do not worry about spelling or punctuation. The goal is to have fun and to express yourself in a creative way.

Step Three: Rehearsing

Read through your rap a few times, deciding on the rhythm (what beat you want), the tempo (how fast or slow you want it to be), and what words or parts of words you want to emphasize (either on beats 2 and 4 or beats 1 and 3). You may either memorize your rap or read it when you perform it. Some use props like plastic "microphones" to project their voice.

Next decide what types of movements you want to do while emceeing. They can be simple (like bouncing and snapping your fingers to the beat) or elaborate (even breaking). Practice these movements while emceeing several times until you feel comfortable.

You may want to emcee as a solo emcee, with family members, or with the counselor. Decide what each person will do. Someone might be a beat box maker, help by deejayin', or do breaking with you. Just so everybody has fun with it.

Step Four: Performing

To perform you have got to have an audience! This could be your therapist, family members, or friends you invite in to watch. If possible, record your hip-hop. Decide where you are going to perform, get all your props and people together, and do it! Sometimes it is good to emcee your hip-hop a few times until you are relaxed and flowing with the beat before you record it.

Handout 2.2: Sample Rap

Clinician's Rap*

So *when* you're *stuck* and don't know *what* to do
With that "*resistant,*" mute *kid* who's just a *lookin'* at you,
Ya can't *just* sit back! Ya gotta *meet* him where he's *at!*
So get *up* on your feet, start a *movin'* to the *beat!*
Ya gotta *ex*ternalize so you and *he* can be *wise*
As he i*den*tifize what's got him *par*alyzed
He'll come to *re*alize and then in*ter*nal*ize*
He got *ways* to def*eat* and an*ni*hilate that *Creep!*
Clinician's *Rap…Uh!*...Kid's *Rap…Uh!*
Clinician's *Rap…Uh!*...Kid's *Rap…Uh!*

*Accent beats 1 and 3 (which are italicized).

– 3 –

Creating a Narrative
A Storybook Activity Using a Cinematic Reference

Melissa L. McVicker

Type of Contribution: Activity, Handouts

Objective

In this chapter movies are used as an introduction to storytelling, wherein the therapist encourages the child to create and share stories that express personal narratives. Through the use of metaphors, the child's thoughts, feelings, and fears can be expressed indirectly to the therapist. This activity also creates a relaxing, playful environment that encourages dialogue and sharing between therapist and child. This is an excellent tool for joining with children and for assessment and goal setting, and is also adaptable for use throughout the various stages of therapy with children, as well as families.

Rationale for Use

Children coming to therapy for the first time may not know what exactly to expect from the therapist or therapy itself, and direct questioning about children's feelings and specific reasons for coming to therapy may add to their stress and anxiety about the therapy process. Entering a strange or unfamiliar environment can be intimidating for children, and it is the therapist's responsibility to establish a comfortable and supportive environment. Specifically, it is important for children to feel that their thoughts and feelings are important and should be shared. The aim of this activity is for the therapist and child client to have a dialogue in the therapy room through creating and performing a story that the child creates and performs.

In general, stories are a way for both children and adults to communicate and interact. Children enjoy hearing stories about other people or characters experiencing similar events that they have been through before (Berg & Steiner, 2003). Using a conversation about movies as an introduction to the story-creating process can serve as a familiar and fun way to begin the positive interaction between therapist and child and can decrease the child's resistance to initial sharing and discussing. Rather than having the child talk directly about himself, the therapist encourages the child to tell a story with the child's unique content, creativity, and imagination. This relaxed environment allows the child to share information indirectly. Thoughts, feelings, and fears can be expressed through the use of metaphors, with characters and plots revealing aspects of life and family experiences without the child directly stating them to the therapist (Gil, 1994).

Children may not be able to fully understand or clearly communicate their feelings, thoughts, or beliefs, but through the use of drawing, role-playing, and other variations of play, children can create and share stories that express their personal narratives (Dermer, Olund, & Sori, 2006). The problems the child may be experiencing become externalized in the story. Even the selection of puppets can have a symbolic representation, such as in size or associations with characteristics (i.e., a lamb as being vulnerable or a turtle suggesting shyness) (Gil & Sobol, 2000).

The story becomes a metaphoric representation of what the child is experiencing, revealing relationships, interactions, worries, stresses, and even possibilities. Perhaps the monster with 50 eyes appears in the story in situations where the child is feeling embarrassed. Through processing questions such as, "When would the 50-eyed monster appear? What would be going on when he would appear? How would you react to him?" the therapist expresses curiosity and encourages further description that may elicit meaningful, unconscious responses. The discussion, comments, and observations by the therapist can assist the child in finding alternative reactions or solutions to problems (or monsters), and enable the child to deal with stressors and overwhelming feelings (Dermer et al., 2006).

Theoretically this activity fits into the basic techniques of narrative therapy. The therapist maintains a curious stance about the story the child is telling and views the child as the expert and source of information for creating the story (Rambo, 2002). Narrative therapy also creates a unique interaction between child and therapist, with the child's knowledge and creativity given greater value, and the child in the position of the teller and the therapist as the listener (Simons & Freedman, 2000).

The therapist can begin a dialogue by encouraging the child to create and perform a story. This interaction can be beneficial in establishing a rapport and communication that will be conducive to continuing treatment. Also, by encouraging the child to be the active director and creator of the story the therapist confirms that the child is engaged and important to the therapeutic process. The story-creating process and performance promote continued discussion between therapist and child client, whether it is simply talking about playful topics or discussing more complex emotional concerns that are metaphorically represented in the story (see Sori, 2006).

Movies are used as a reference for this story-creating process and present a unique format to introduce the idea of storytelling. Deviating from traditional storytelling or literature, a context of "creating a movie" is promoted, leading the child to naturally visualize acting out the scenes while in the process of creating the story and "script." The reference to movies allows the child to draw on movie experiences and also includes the child's actual performance by acting out the story, just as would be done in a movie. This approach is a great way to attract a child's attention and promotes an atmosphere of creativity and fun, while introducing new variations of ways to tell a story. Referencing movies in this activity also may help to alleviate a child's initial anxiety or expectations about coming to therapy, since this is a medium that is familiar and entertaining to children.

Instructions

The activity can be used when the child first comes to therapy and can last from 15 minutes to the entire first session. Due to the level of cognitive functioning and use of metaphoric communication involved, this activity is suggested for children between the ages of 6 and 13. For younger clients who are not comfortable with or capable of writing dialogue, the activity would emphasize verbal discussion rather than written expression when adding dialogue for the characters in the drawings, or the therapist might write the dialogue down.

Materials for this activity include a large sheet of paper, markers, a (Polaroid or digital) camera, glue, stapler, and a variety of puppets. Also needed are the handouts at the end of this chapter (Handout 3.1: Movie Frame; Handout 3.2: First Page), both of which can be duplicated as necessary. Additional items could also include materials to decorate and personalize the storybook such as glitter, construction paper, stickers, etc.

Introducing the activity. The activity is introduced with a general discussion of the child's favorite movies and how the child most enjoyed watching movies, with whom, and where (at home, at a friend's house, in a theatre, etc.). To add to the movie atmosphere, younger clients could also be encouraged to pretend to drive to the movie theatre, and draw paper money and favorite snack items to buy at the pretend concession stand. The therapist then asks the child to draw a scene out of a favorite movie on the large sheet of paper, using the materials provided. The therapist and child discuss the specific movie and the scene the child selected to draw, including what the child liked about the movie, the character, or the setting. The therapist explains that a movie is like telling a story with a beginning, middle, and end.

The instructions are similar to those given for the family puppet interview (see Gil, 1994; Gil & Sobol, 2000; Irwin & Malloy, 1975). This story has to be original, so children should be told it cannot be a movie they have seen, like a Disney movie. The therapist instructs the child to now create his own movie story, including who the characters would be, the scene/setting, and what happens in the story. The child is told that the drawings will be like a "script" that can be acted out like in a movie. The child is encouraged to be creative and draw whatever comes to mind. The therapist explains that the large paper will be divided into four boxes—each for a different scene in the story. Specifically, the first box is for the beginning of the story, and the last box should show the ending of the story. The number of boxes in between the beginning and end can vary, according to the child and therapist's preferences and available time.

As the child draws, the therapist sits back quietly and does not attempt to engage the child in a conversation at this time, but simply observes the child's process as he or she creates the scenes. The therapist can be interested and curious in the development of the story, but should quietly observe the child's process in doing this activity, talking only in response to the child's prompts. It is important for clinicians not to be distracting by asking questions or trying to engage the child to talk or explain the story as it is unfolding (see Gil interview in Sori, 2006). Many children become quite absorbed in the creative process and asking them questions or engaging them in conversations as they are creating can take away from their internal process, which can prevent unconscious material from emerging. A therapist's attempt at conversation not only can interfere with this process, but also can influence the direction of the story, the drawings, and subsequent discussion. Unless the child initiates a conversation, little discussion should occur until after the drawings are completed. In addition, Gil (in Sori, 2006) emphasizes that therapists should focus on being fully present with the child and responding to the creation of the story and what is suggested (using the right brain), rather than focusing on what questions to ask when processing the activity (which would engage the left brain).

Processing the activity. After the child is finished drawing, the therapist can ask the child to tell the story through the characters. The child can be encouraged to "be" each character and talk through the character, as if the child *is* that character (Oaklander, 1988). The child can be asked to draw word bubbles to write in dialogue for the characters, similar to a comic strip. The child can also be encouraged to select puppets to represent the characters in the story, and to act out the story by talking through the puppets. This child may wish to assign roles and puppets to the therapist or other family members, or do all the "acting" himself or herself.

As the child becomes more comfortable with the therapist, the conversation can move from direct observation of the child's movie creation and performance to questions that allow for a better understanding of the child's perceptions, opinions, and thought processes. The following are sample questions to ask after the child is done creating/drawing the story (see Gil, 1994; Gil & Sobol, 2000; Sori, 2006):

- Who are the characters?
- What are the names of the characters?
- What does this character say?
- How do the other characters react to that?
- How do you think this character feels?
- Who can the main character trust?
- What is it about that person that makes him or her trustworthy?
- What is the main problem the character is having?
- How does the character solve the problem?
- What are other ways to solve the problem?
- What makes solving the problem difficult?
- Who can help him solve it?

- What would you do if you were in the same situation?
- Who can you get help from if you have a problem?
- What is your favorite part of the story?
- Is there anything else you would add to the story?
- What is the moral, or message, of this story?
- What title would you give this story?

It is vital when processing this activity that the therapist stays "in the metaphor" (Gil & Ashby, 2001; Sori, 2006). The questions should be related to what that specific character is saying and doing in a scene. For example, the therapist should not say, "Oh, so you feel scared to go to school," but instead say, "So the bunny is afraid to go to school because all the larger animals chase him on the playground." However, according to Gil (in Sori, 2006), when children are finished discussing the story, it is sometimes useful to ask them if there is anything about their life that is similar to the story.

Afterward, the therapist can take a picture of the child holding up the pictures, which can be used to create the storybook. Handout 3.1 at the end of this chapter can be duplicated, and each picture can be pasted inside the "movie frame." Handout 3.2 can be filled out and used for the first page of the storybook. The child then puts together the storybook using the drawings and additional materials and can design the cover for the book as well. The creative possibilities for putting together the storybook are endless, and can include a title page, list of characters, additional scenes, and even additional photographs, if desired. In addition, having children take the storybook home provides an opportunity for them to share their story more than once, and to show off what they completed in therapy (Berg & Steiner, 2003). Through discussion and retelling of the story, parents can further participate in the therapy process, and even act as characters in their child's movie.

Brief Clinical Vignette

Karen brought her 8-year-old son, Jacob, to therapy because he was having trouble in school. Karen reported he would throw tantrums during class and would get into physical altercations with his teacher and peers. Upon meeting the therapist, Jacob was visibly very shy and apprehensive about coming to therapy.

Starting out with a general discussion of favorite movies, Jacob and the therapist discussed how he most preferred to watch movies (with whom, at home or in a theatre, etc.), and what specific characters and movies he most enjoyed. The therapist then asked him to draw a scene out of his favorite story on a large sheet of paper. Jacob drew a "friendly monster," which he and the therapist discussed more in detail, including the qualities of the monster that the child liked and the monster's role in the story.

The therapist instructed Jacob to then create his own story, including who the characters would be, the scenes, and what happens in the story. The therapist encouraged Jacob to be as creative as he could, and reassured him that there was no right or wrong way to draw or create the story. The paper was divided into four boxes designated for a scene in the beginning, two for the middle, and one for the ending of the story.

Jacob was very eager to start the activity, and started by first creating a main character: a monster named "Fuzzy." Jacob and the therapist discussed and created details about the Fuzzy character, such as his favorite activities, what makes him happy, what makes him sad, where he lives, who he lives with, etc. Jacob stated that the story would be about Fuzzy, and how Fuzzy was feeling sad about not having any friends. In the first box, he drew a small monster with a frown on his face, on a playground by himself. As Jacob continued to draw the scene and add to the detail of the character, he also created word bubbles for the character. Next to Fuzzy's head, Jacob silently drew a word bubble, and wrote in "I'm sad."

In the second box Jacob said he would draw what Fuzzy does when he feels sad or upset. Jacob then added a larger monster on this page and called it "Fuzzy's mom." Jacob shared that Fuzzy could go talk to his mom when he was sad. He also shared that Fuzzy's mom felt sad when Fuzzy was sad, added Fuzzy to the second picture, and drew a sad face on both character's faces. In the word bubble above Fuzzy's mom's head, he wrote, "I'm sorry you're sad."

In the third box, Jacob drew the same two characters, but now hugging each other. He stated that Fuzzy's mom made Fuzzy feel better. Above Fuzzy's mom's head, he wrote in the word bubble, "It's okay. You can make other friends." Jacob also added smiling faces on both Fuzzy and Fuzzy's mom.

Jacob had been told that the last box was designated for how the story would end and, specifically, how he would know that the problem was solved. Jacob stated that Fuzzy would not be sad because he would have made friends with the new kid at school. Once again, he drew Fuzzy in the box. Next to Fuzzy, he drew a new character and named him "Bob." He stated that Fuzzy and Bob were best friends now, and that they had a lot of fun together. Jacob drew a basketball and skateboard in the scene. In the word bubble above Bob's head, he wrote "Fuzzy is my friend." And completing the scene, as well as the story, Jacob added "I'm happy" above Fuzzy's head and completed the picture by adding a big smile on Fuzzy's face.

The therapist then invited Jacob to select puppets to act as the characters he had created in the story. She asked Jacob to tell the story through the characters, using the drawings as a script. Jacob selected a puppet for the three characters, assigning the therapist to act as Fuzzy's mom. Using the puppets, Jacob then acted out the story he created, including instructing the therapist as to what her puppet was to say or do in that specific scene.

Once Jacob finished acting out the scenes with the puppets, the therapist and Jacob discussed some specific aspects of the story. Using the first drawing as a reference, the therapist asked Jacob what feeling "sad" meant and what Fuzzy does when he feels sad. Jacob added tears on the monster's face, responding, "He cries." The discussion continued to what Fuzzy's mom did to "make things better." Jacob replied (as the Fuzzy puppet) that she gave Fuzzy lots of hugs and also told Fuzzy he could make other friends. The therapist and Jacob also discussed what made Bob a good friend and what activities Bob and Fuzzy liked to do together. The therapist and Jacob continued discussing aspects of the story, with questions being directed about the puppets/characters themselves, in order to remain in the metaphor of the story that Jacob had created.

Afterward, the therapist used a Polaroid camera to photograph Jacob holding up the puppets. Jacob then cut out the four boxes and glued each box to a separate "movie frame" page (Handout 3.1). He decorated each one to his liking and stapled the pages together in order of the scenes. Jacob then created a cover page for his storybook, complete with his name and the title of his "movie." As the final touch, his photograph was glued on the cover page to serve as a fun reminder of the use of puppets as the characters, as well as his hard work creating the movie.

Following completion of the storybook, Jacob and the therapist then discussed the story and events, and any similarities or differences he saw in himself and the characters. Jacob stated that sometimes he also felt sad and would go to his mom for help. He also said that "it hurt" when people did not want to play with him. The therapist and Jacob discussed other possible solutions and reactions the characters could have, in addition to what Jacob might do, if he were the specific characters. Jacob stated that Fuzzy could have found something to do by himself, such as playing basketball or finding a toy. Jacob also shared that if he were another kid on the playground, he would "be nice" and ask Fuzzy to play with him. The therapist ended the session suggesting the possibility of doing this activity again in the future, to which Jacob excitedly replied that he would like to do so.

Through encouraging the creation of a movie and characters, the therapist was able to introduce Jacob to the therapy process through a means that was familiar and interesting to him. Since he was shy, he seemed more comfortable talking through the characters rather than directly to the therapist about himself. However, as the therapist continued to engage him in conversation about the movie and characters, Jacob seemed to be less hesitant in sharing, and began to move from a discussion about the movie to more dialogue about himself and his family.

The therapist found that doing this activity made this child feel more involved in the session, and encouraged a discussion about his problem. Creating a narrative through the use of the storybook and acting also established a more relaxed, nonintimidating environment that allowed the therapist to effectively join with Jacob and encourage future conversation in therapy. Also, having Jacob personalize the storybook and have the opportunity to "show" the movie (again) to his mother added to the therapeutic interaction.

Suggestions for Follow-Up

This activity is useful in introducing a child into therapy and beginning the dialogue between child and therapist. In addition, this activity can also be used in future sessions by continuing the development of the story to include current stressors or concerns the child may be experiencing. Discussion of the story that was created by the child can continue to include specific topics or issues, such as including a character who has to move to a new house, or how to deal with a school bully. The ongoing creation of the movie could also include the discussion of traits that allow the characters to be successful or overcome obstacles, or alternative choices that could be made to address the problems the characters are facing. Adapting or expanding to the story could allow child and therapist to brainstorm possible solutions to problems that may be applicable to the child's current stressors.

This activity is intended for the therapist and young client, but can also include other family members or additional children in the creative process. When including other children in this activity, it is important to emphasize turn taking and encourage each child's contribution in creating the movie and telling the story. If using this activity with a family, each member could decorate a "movie frame" page and once combined, the pages could begin a storybook that the family could continue to work on and create at home. The therapist may elect to put a parent in charge and observe the family process as the family creates the movie story and frames.

In addition, a family puppet interview could be used. Family members can select puppets and use them to create a story, and then act it out together (see Gil, 1994; Gil & Sobol, 2000; Irwin & Malloy, 1975).

Contraindications for Use

This activity is to encourage joining and creating an environment that is conducive to conversation and not as a means to squander therapy time. The therapist must balance the dialogue of imaginary or creative stories with information about the child's current situations and conflict. The child may enjoy the activity, but it is the therapist's responsibility to establish boundaries and expectations for therapy. This activity is intended to be a resource for creating and continuing dialogue—not as a routine, standard conversation for sessions.

As previously mentioned, some children may not have effective written communication skills, and in those circumstances a verbal modality would be more appropriate to use when creating characters' dialogue in this activity, or the child could dictate the dialogue and the therapist could write it in the bubbles for the child.

References

Berg, I. K., & Steiner, T. (2003). *Children's solution work.* New York: W. W. Norton & Company.

Dermer, S., Olund, D. O., & Sori, C. F. (2006). Integrating play in family therapy theories. In C. F. Sori (Ed.), *Engaging children in family therapy: Creative approaches to integrating theory and research in clinical practice* (pp. 37–65). New York: Routledge.

Gil, E. (1994). *Play in family therapy*. New York: Guilford.

Gil, E. (Producer), & Ashby, B. (Writer/Editor). (2001). *Family play therapy: Rationale and techniques*. [Motion picture]. (Available from Starbright Training Institute, P.O. Box 3050, Fairfax, VA, 22030).

Gil, E., & Sobol, B. (2000). Engaging families in therapeutic play. In C. E. Bailey (Ed.), *Children in therapy: Using the family as a resource* (pp. 341–382). New York: W. W. Norton.

Irwin, E. C., & Malloy, E. S. (1975). Family puppet interview. *Family Process, 14,* 170–191.

Oaklander, V. (1988). *Windows to our children.* Gouldsboro, ME: Gestalt Journal Press.

Rambo, A. (2002). The collaborative language-based models of family therapy: When less is more. In L. Hecker & J. Wetchler (Eds.), *An introduction to marriage and family therapy* (pp.149–171). New York: Haworth.

Simons, V. A., & Freedman, J. (2000). Witnessing bravery: Narrative ideas for working with children and families. In C. E. Bailey (Ed.), *Children in therapy: Using the family as a resource* (pp. 20–45). New York: W. W. Norton.

Sori, C. F. (2006). Family play therapy: An interview with Eliana Gil. In C. F. Sori (Ed.), *Engaging children in family therapy: Creative approaches to integrating theory and research in clinical practice* (pp. 69–90). New York: Routledge.

Professional Readings and Resources

Bailey, C. E. (2000). *Children in therapy: Using the family as a resource.* New York: W. W. Norton.

Freeman, J., Epston, D., & Lobovits, D. (1997). *Playful approaches to serious problems: Narrative therapy with children and their families.* New York: Guilford.

Gil, E. (1994). *Play in family therapy.* New York: Guilford.

Hecker, L., Wetchler, J., & associates (2002). *An introduction to marriage and family therapy.* New York: Haworth.

Piercy, F. P., Sprenkle, D. H., Wetchler, J. L., & associates. (1996). *Family therapy sourcebook* (2nd ed.). New York: Guilford.

Sori, C. F. (2006). *Engaging children in family therapy: Creative approaches to integrating theory and research in clinical practice.* New York: Routledge.

Sori, C., Hecker, L., & associates (2003). *The therapist's notebook for children and adolescents: Homework, handouts, and activities for use in psychotherapy.* New York: Haworth.

Bibliotherapy Sources for the Client

Baumgarnder, J. M. (1993). *60 art projects for children: Painting, clay, puppets, paints, masks, and more.* Largo, MD: Crown Books.

Dr. Seuss. (1996). *My many colored days.* New York: Random House.

VanFleet, R. (2000). *A parent's handbook of filial play therapy.* Boiling Springs, PA: Play Therapy Press.

Handout 3.1: Movie Frame

____

Title of Movie

Handout 3.2: First Page

Written, Directed, and Produced by:

____

Name of Child

– 4 –

The Future MySpace Page
Solution-Focused Adolescent Blogging

Adam S. Froerer and Sara A. Smock

Type of Contribution: Activity, Handout

Objective

Therapists can use the Future MySpace page activity to create change by using the client's language, focusing on positives and strengths, and maintaining a future focus that is consistent with adolescents' worldviews and interests. This activity could be useful in working with adolescents who are familiar with MySpace or other networking Websites. It can be used with virtually any presenting problem from depression or anxiety to physical challenges or family conflict. This activity may be helpful for the client and the therapist to join with one another, engage the adolescent in therapy, and use solution-focused brief therapy to help adolescents envision a future that is consistent with their goals and desires.

Rationale for Use

Since many clients use the MySpace social networking Website in their everyday lives, therapists can utilize language and activities that incorporate MySpace into therapy sessions to achieve goals and lasting change for their clients. This activity is designed for any client who is familiar with MySpace or those who are interested in creating a MySpace page. Therapists should be sure to get parental permission before providing any information to adolescents on creating their own MySpace page.

MySpace is a free Website where individuals create a profile and share photos and written entries with their friends and family (Wikipedia, 2007). MySpace can be found at www.myspace.com. After providing a valid e-mail address and creating a password, individuals are guided through the setup process. Once an account has been created, MySpace users can upload photos, download songs, write on message boards, join interest groups, and much more (http://www.myspace.com). MySpace has become a major outlet for teenagers to have an individualized place where their friends and family members can share comments and photos with each other. Many adolescents are familiar with and access MySpace regularly in order to connect and communicate with their peers. Most adolescents are well versed in cyberlanguage, and feel comfortable conversing about events through the Internet. However, adolescents are often reluctant to attend therapy and are regularly considered resistant in therapy (Ribner, 2000). Thus incorporating a common adolescent activity, such as MySpace, can help the therapist use the client's language in order for the client to make changes towards his or her desired life.

One way to engage adolescent clients in therapy is for the therapist to use the client's language; this is useful in joining with the client and helping to build rapport and credibility with him or her (O'Hanlon & Weiner-Davis, 1989). Solution-focused brief therapy (SFBT) is based on the principle that reality is created through language (de Shazer, 1994) and encourages the therapist to use the client's language as a way to join with the client and gain credibility (O'Hanlon & Weiner-Davis).

Additionally, SFBT utilizes future-oriented questions to help the client envision a problem-free situation and establish the solution. Future-oriented questions ask the client to think about the future when the problem will no longer be a problem. When the client describes this problem-free future, SFBT asserts that he or she has also described a solution to the problem (O'Hanlon & Weiner-Davis). Future-oriented questions also help produce the expectation that change is possible.

Since SFBT focuses on using the client's language and experience, using a MySpace activity with adolescent clients is a way that therapists can ask future-oriented questions in a manner that is relevant to young clients. By adapting future-oriented questions to MySpace, adolescent clients will feel as though the therapist is speaking their language.

In addition to providing a perspective for what the future will be like when the presenting problem is no longer a problem, this activity could be helpful for therapists in many other ways. By asking about how their MySpace page will be different in 2 years the therapist is simultaneously gathering information about the current situation and what the client considers to be the problem. Additionally, this activity allows the therapist and client to collaboratively establish goals based on the future MySpace page and to make plans and changes to accomplish the goals seen on the future MySpace page. This activity also provides an SFBT therapist with an opportunity to assign homework, which is an integral part of SFBT therapy (Gingerich & Eisengart, 2000). For example, the therapist can encourage the client to write entries for his or her MySpace page and bring them back to be discussed during the next session. Other homework assignments can include drawing pictures of what the future MySpace page would look like, making a list of links to be included on the page, making a list of comments that would likely be posted from friends and family members, or bringing lyrics or music that would be on the future MySpace page. These homework assignments are to be discussed in detail during the sessions. A compilation of the assignments can be kept in a notebook for reference by the adolescent.

The therapist can introduce a homework assignment by saying,

> For our next session I would like you to continue thinking about your future MySpace page that we started discussing today. Next time I would like you to bring a copy of an entry you imagine you would see on your MySpace page that would let you know that the depression you are dealing with now is no longer a problem.

Or, the therapist can say,

> Your homework assignment for this week is to think about music and lyrics that would be on your MySpace page 2 years from now. If you have a copy of the music or lyrics I would appreciate if you would bring it to our session. I would also like you to be prepared to discuss why this music would be on your page and how this music has been helpful to you in overcoming the challenges you are currently facing.

The handout at the end of the chapter provides clients with questions that can be considered when creating their future MySpace page. Although this activity can be used and adapted for many sessions, it is intended to be used in conjunction with other activities and interventions as part of an overall treatment plan.

Instructions

The therapist listens to the client to determine if using the example of MySpace fits with the client's language and experience. Once a fit is determined, the therapist introduces the MySpace activity by providing the future MySpace scenario. An example of how this could be done is:

> Suppose it is 2 years in the future and you are looking at your MySpace page you created about the previous 2 years of your life. You notice there are several entries covering the events of the previous 2 years. You also notice several pictures of these events. You see links to other Websites, and comments from friends who have viewed your page. As you are looking at the page, you

notice the problem you are dealing with now no longer present. As you look at your MySpace page, what is the first thing you notice that lets you know that the problem that has brought you to therapy is no longer a problem?

The client is given time to think about and report on the things he or she notices about the future MySpace page. As the client describes his or her page, the therapist follows up with clarifying questions. Additional questions that can be asked in this intervention are the following:

1. What does your MySpace page look like?
2. What is the general format of your MySpace entries? What opinions about things do you express on your page? What kinds of things do you say on your pages that you would not say in person?
3. What pictures or text entries do you see that tell you this is no longer a problem for you?
4. Who has access to view your page? Who does not have access to view your page?
5. Who has viewed your MySpace page and left messages that indicate that you have overcome this challenge?
6. How do those comments let you know that your friends have recognized that this problem is no longer a problem for you?
7. What does the caption of your page say? How does that title explain that you are different now from 2 years ago?
8. What were you writing about then that is different from what you would write about now?
9. The therapist can also ask exception questions, which are questions that focus on and look into times when the problem was not a problem. Exceptions may include a time when the client did not struggle with the problem or a time when the client was able to do something differently when faced with the problem (de Shazer, 1991). The therapist in this example could ask something like, "What do you notice on your MySpace page that is already happening?" This question implies that something is already the way the client would like it to be. Additionally, helping clients recognize exceptions to the problem helps them identify solutions.

Although this activity is introduced and begins during a session and the client is required to visualize the MySpace page, this activity can extend over several sessions and can provide an abundance of information for solutions for the client as homework assignments are given and discussed in future sessions, as described previously. Creating a future MySpace page is useful in joining with the client through language and provides valuable information in establishing solutions for adolescent clients.

Brief Clinical Vignette

Julie, an adolescent female, was brought to therapy by her parents. When asked why they had brought their daughter for therapy, her parents commented that she persistently misbehaved and they could not control her. Julie's parents continued by mentioning that they would ground Julie and take away her privileges to go out with her friends, talk on the phone, or use the computer when she acted up. However, recently when Julie was no longer allowed to hang out with her friends she began to show signs of depression, such as wanting to be alone more often, not wanting to spend time outside (something she used to enjoy), loss of appetite, and a general lack of energy. Because of this change in Julie's mood and previous behavior problems, Julie's parents referred her for therapy.

Early in therapy Julie expressed interest in communicating with her friends online via MySpace while she was expelled from school. She stated that this was the only way she felt connected to those she really cared about in her life. In attempting to use SFBT, the therapist wanted to ask future-oriented questions that would relate to Julie's interests. The therapist spent some time talking to Julie about why spending time on MySpace helped her to feel better about herself and less depressed. Julie commented that MySpace helped her feel like she was connected to her friends. Julie also stated that she liked to know what was going on with her friends and really liked when her friends left nice comments about her on her page. The therapist then transitioned by asking Julie questions about how her MySpace page had changed recently and what other changes she thought she would like to make on her page. The therapist then used the future MySpace intervention discussed earlier.

Julie mentioned that she had noticed that her friends had left comments about the pictures and entries Julie had posted of them at her 18th birthday party. When asked what some of the comments said, Julie mentioned that her friend Cassie said that she had a really good time at the party and that Julie was so cute. When encouraged by the therapist to discuss some of the other comments about the post and pictures, Julie stated that her friend Levi had left a comment about how much he liked Julie and how good she had looked at the party. Julie commented that she agreed with her friends and their comments about how cute she looked in the pictures. She mentioned that looking cute made her feel good about herself. When asked who else was in the pictures from MySpace, Julie discussed seeing a picture of herself with her mom. The therapist asked Julie how seeing this picture let her know that depression and disagreements with her parents were no longer problems for her. Julie stated that she and her mom were smiling and hugging one another. Julie continued by saying that she and her mom were able to spend time together without her mom yelling at her. Julie commented that the decrease in arguing was a big indication that she and her mom were getting along better. When asked what they would be doing instead of arguing, Julie mentioned that they would be spending time running together and shopping. Julie also mentioned that this would help her feel less depressed because she would know that her mom was happy with her. These things were indications to Julie that life had improved.

Julie described in detail how her life would be different 2 years from now and how it would be better. She talked about not needing to sneak around in order to fit in at school. She said that she was able to spend more time with her friends. The therapist continued by asking Julie questions about her MySpace page to generate more solution-oriented conversations. For example, the therapist asked, "How does your future MySpace page let you know that you have overcome the depression that you currently face?" Julie was able to discuss evidence of her better life by giving examples of photos and responses about her friends that she would have on her page. The therapist continued to ask additional questions about her page, such as "Who notices the most that you are less depressed?" and "What do the comments from your friends and the other people who have viewed your page say?" Julie stated that her best friend, Cloe, would notice that Julie had changed the most. Julie thought she would know that Cloe recognized the changes because of the responses Cloe left about their friendship and the fun things they had done together. Julie went on to describe how her other friends would have written funny stories about their time together and the things they had accomplished during the past 2 years. These comments and stories would also mention how happy Julie looked and how much they laughed together. Julie thought that when she laughed more often she would know that she was less depressed and less angry at her parents.

The therapist continued to ask Julie questions about the links on her MySpace page: "What links are included in your page and how would those links let you know you have overcome the depression you are currently facing?" Julie said she would have links on her future MySpace page about becoming a pharmacist because that is what she would like to do in the future. She mentioned that being a pharmacist would help her to feel successful and that she had done something worthwhile with her life. Julie said that she would know that things were better because these pharmacy links would be on her MySpace page. Julie also stated that she would have links from the university that she would be attending and her future sorority. Julie stated that the links on her MySpace page would be a very important sign that things were better and that she had made the changes that she wanted.

When the therapist checked in with Julie during later sessions Julie mentioned several times that the MySpace intervention was very helpful. She mentioned that it helped her feel more comfortable talking to the therapist and opening up about personal things. Julie also commented that it helped her think about how things could be different and helped her develop goals she really wanted to achieve. She mentioned that thinking about her goals seemed to help her feel better about her current situation. Julie also mentioned that the MySpace activity helped her realize that she had things to look forward to and friends who cared about her.

Suggestions for Follow-Up

The therapist can follow up with the future-oriented activity by assigning a homework assignment to complete a future MySpace page. Clients can be asked to continue thinking about the future page and what they would include on their future MySpace page that would indicate that the problem was no longer a problem. Again, Handout 4.1, which contains a list of possible topics to be included on the future MySpace page assignment, is included at the end of the chapter.

The therapist can also follow up by asking the client scaling questions (de Shazer, 1985) about the page. A scaling question asks clients to rate themselves (on a scale from 1 to 10) on where they feel that they are currently in relation to the issue being discussed (Berg & de Shazer, 1993). The rating is used to discuss what clients had done in order to be successful in obtaining their current rating. Clients are also asked to discuss what would be different when higher numbers on the scale were achieved and what would need to happen in order for the rating to increase. Examples of possible scaling questions could include: "On a scale from 1 to 10, where 10 is very *hopeful* that you can achieve the changes you see on your MySpace page, and 1 is the opposite of that, how would you rate yourself today, and why?" Or the therapist could ask, "On a scale from 1 to 10, 10 being your life the way you see it on MySpace, and 1 being nothing like that, where are you right now? What would it take to move up one number on the scale?"

Follow-up can also occur as this activity becomes a multisession intervention through homework assignments and in-session discussions. The therapist can adapt each session by discussing with the client any developments on the MySpace page that have taken place outside the session. As the client adds details to the page, discussions about how words, music, and/or photos help the client notice changes that have been made can encourage him or her to access resources and bring about lasting change.

The therapist can also follow up this activity by helping the client to begin establishing small, achievable steps to accomplish the changes seen on the future MySpace page. The therapist might ask, "What is the first thing that would need to be different that would lead to achieving the changes you see on your future MySpace page?" The therapist might also ask, "How will you know that you are moving in the right direction so that your life looks like what you see on your MySpace page?" In addition, the therapist can follow up in future sessions by returning to the metaphor of MySpace and discussing changes that have occurred since the future MySpace page was created that reflect life as seen on the page, and what the client has done to make these changes.

Finally, the therapist could follow up by having the client create an actual MySpace page. During sessions the therapist and client could view the client's page with specific intent to notice any items, entries, pictures, or music that could already be identified as exceptions or steps the client has taken toward future goals.

Contraindications for Use

With any clinical activity, the intervention should fit with the client. Some clients, including adolescents, may not use MySpace and thus the activity would not be appropriate. This intervention works best with any client who participates in online dialogue or uses online media. Additionally, actively psychotic clients should be treated for their psychosis before employing talk therapy or this intervention.

References

Berg, I. K., & de Shazer, S. (1993). Making numbers talk: Language in therapy. In S. Friedman (Ed.), *The new language of change* (pp. 5–24). New York: Guilford.

de Shazer, S. (1985). *Keys to solution in brief therapy.* New York: W. W. Norton.

de Shazer, S. (1991). *Putting difference to work.* New York: W. W. Norton.

de Shazer, S. (1994). *Words were originally magic.* New York: W. W. Norton.

Gingerich, W. J., & Eisengart, S. (2000). Solution-focused brief therapy: A review of the outcome research. *Family Process, 39,* 477–498.

MySpace (n.d.). Retrieved June 6, 2007, from http://www.myspace.com/.

O'Hanlon, W., & Weiner-Davis, M. (1989). *In search of solutions: A new direction in psychotherapy.* New York: W. W. Norton.

Ribner, N. G. (2000). *The first session with teenagers: A step-by-step guide.* San Francisco, CA: Jossey–Bass.

Wikipedia: The free encyclopedia (n.d.). Retrieved April 24, 2007, from http://en.wikipedia.org/wiki/MySpace.

Professional Readings and Resources

de Shazer, S. (1985). *Keys to solution in brief therapy.* New York: W. W. Norton.

Gross, E. F., Juvonen, J., & Gable, S. L. (2002). Internet use and well-being in adolescence. *Journal of Social Issues, 58,* 75–90.

Lipchik, E. (2002). *Beyond techniques in solution-focused therapy: Working with emotions and the therapeutic relationship.* New York: Guilford.

O'Hanlon, W., & Weiner-Davis, M. (1989). *In search of solutions: A new direction in psychotherapy.* New York: W. W. Norton.

Valkenburg, P. M., Peter, J., & Schouten, A. P. (2006). Friend networking and their relationship to adolescents' well-being and social self-esteem. *CyberPsychology & Behavior, 9,* 584–590.

Bibliotherapy Sources for the Client

Covey, S. (1998). *The 7 habits of highly effective teens: The ultimate teenage success guide.* New York: Simon & Schuster.

Facebook (n.d.). Retrieved June 6, 2007, from http://www.facebook.com/.

Illian, J. (2007). *MySpace, MyKids: A parent's guide to protecting your kids and navigating MySpace.com.* Eugene, OR: Harvest House.

MySpace (n.d.). Retrieved June 6, 2007, from http://www.myspace.com/.

MySpace Gateway (n.d.). Retrieved April 26, 2007, from http://MySpacegateway.com/.

Plummer, D. B. (2005). *Helping adolescents and adults to build self-esteem: A photocopiable resource book.* Philadelphia, PA: Jessica Kingsley.

Wikipedia (n.d.), http://en.wikipedia.org/wiki/MySpace.

Handout 4.1: The Future MySpace Page

Suppose it is 2 years in the future and you are looking at the MySpace page that you created about the past 2 years of your life. You notice that there are several entries covering the events of the past 2 years. You also notice several pictures of these events. You also see links and comments from friends who have viewed your page. As you are looking at the page, you notice that the problem you are dealing with now is no longer present.

Write an entry on your MySpace page as if it is 2 years in the future and the problem you are dealing with is no longer a problem. You may want to include things like:

1. What about your daily routine is different from what you are doing now?
2. What are things you have accomplished in the past 2 years that you are proud of?
3. What are things you have seen or done that indicate to you that things are better 2 years from now?
4. What is different about your relationships 2 years from now?
5. Whom are you close to that shows you that you have overcome the challenges you are facing now?
6. What goals have you achieved in the past 2 years?
7. As you think about yourself 2 years from now, how do you feel about yourself since you have overcome your current challenges?
8. Two years from now, how do you see yourself interacting with others since you have overcome your present challenges?
9. What would you like others to know about you now that your problem is no longer a problem?
10. What is a title for your entry that indicates that things are going better for you?

Bring your MySpace entry with you to our next session. Be ready to talk about what it was like to write this entry and anything else that will be helpful to talk about.

– 5 –

Educating Children about Parental Substance Abuse

Errol Rodriguez

Type of Contribution: Activity, Handouts

Objectives

The objective of these activities is to help children begin to express their feelings about their parents' substance abuse and addictive behavior and to increase their understanding of addictive disease. By educating and assisting children in the expression and identification of feelings associated with parental addictive behavior, the therapist has the opportunity to: (1) clarify feeling states, as children often feel confused about their parents' behavior; (2) educate children on the psychosocial effects of addiction; and (3) encourage children to return to age-appropriate developmental tasks.

By educating children about addiction and encouraging them to express their feelings associated with parental addiction, they learn about the disease process and their conscious and unconscious concerns. Many children report feeling afraid that something "bad" will happen to their parent but remain unaware of other feelings such as guilt, shame, and anger. By identifying these feelings and other irrational thoughts, children create emotional distance from their parents' behavior. This emotional distance, known as detachment, provides the necessary "breathing room" to process feelings without becoming overly involved in their parents' addictive behavior. It also prevents children from losing important connections to other sources of enjoyment (e.g., playing with peers). As an added benefit, children learn about the negative effects of addiction, which, in turn, may influence their own future choice to use or not to use drugs.

Rationale for Use

Over the last decade it has been widely accepted that the substance-abusing home environment is traumatic (Brown, 1988, 1991). Children who grow up in a home with parental substance abuse are at greater risk for developing emotional problems than those children whose parents are not struggling with a chemical addiction. As children adjust to the chronic nature of their parents' addictive disease, they learn to avoid the honest and spontaneous expression of feelings. Children may learn to avoid feelings from their nonaddicted parent, who may have unwittingly taught the child that to express his or her feelings may exacerbate the parent's addictive behavior (Rodriguez, 2005). Children may also learn to limit their demands for emotional and social support and, ultimately, lose touch with their own feelings and needs.

To begin an effective intervention, this treatment requires an intensive psychoeducational process to increase children's knowledge about addiction and address their underlying feelings and defensive reactions. The activities that follow are part of a larger systemic intervention for families recovering from addiction and can be integrated with most therapeutic strategies and modalities for children. This process includes education on the disease of addiction, the effects of substance abuse, and exploration of children's feelings and reactions.

Instructions

Addiction Education

This is an educational activity that requires children to participate in an interactive discussion with the therapist or group about addiction. For the purpose of discussion, a group model will be used to describe the activities. The children should sit in a classroom format or in a circle to facilitate discussion. The therapist will need a dry-erase board or any surface for writing and illustrating information. Once the children are adequately warmed up to each other, they are asked to identify images of a cigarette, marijuana, cocaine, alcohol in a glass, and heroin in the form of a needle. These images are drawn by the therapist and provide the stimulus for discussion. There are wonderful free educational resources available from the U.S. Department of Health and Human Services and the Substance Abuse and Mental Health Services Administration (SAMHSA)'s National Clearinghouse for Alcohol and Drug Information that can be substituted for or added to this activity. (The Website for this source is provided at the end of the chapter.)

Once the children identify all these images, they are asked to describe side effects from using each drug. Most children have witnessed their parent or others under the influence of drugs and can report observable effects such as a parent "being tired" from drinking alcohol, or "laughing a lot," or "feeling sick." Some children have witnessed or experienced other negative effects such as domestic violence, incest, or emotional and physical maltreatment. If using a dry-erase board, it is useful to write the children's descriptions under each drug and add any relevant side effects to increase learning. Handouts are given to each child for use as an activity during the session or as a homework assignment to be discussed in a following session. The handouts include a "Side Effect Word Search" (Handout 5.1) on the side effects of drug use and a "Feelings Word Search" (Handout 5.2) on common feelings children experience due to parental substance use. These handouts can be found at the end of the chapter.

The next educational activity raises their awareness of the nature of addiction. It is very important to explain to children that the disease of addiction and the effect it has on their parent is not their fault. Many children feel guilty about their parent's behavior. Hearing from a caring person that their parent's behavior is related to an illness they did not cause helps relieve their guilt. To help children understand their parent's behavior, the therapist will discuss addiction as a disease and include several key factors: (1) physical reaction to the substance, (2) difficulty discontinuing use, (3) denial, and (4) loss of control. The therapist will need to explain these concepts as clearly and playfully as possible. In general, children enjoy listening to stories told in a slow, animated tone, while emphasizing feelings. While sitting on the floor in a circle with the children, the therapist will introduce the topic of addiction in a way that builds curiosity. For example, the therapist could say, "How many of you like surfing the Internet? Today, I have a story to tell you about a boy named Bob who could not stop surfing the Internet. Guess what happened to him?" When the therapist uses questions and an animated tone, children generally respond positively.

It is quite useful to use a storytelling technique similar to that proposed by Gardner (1993) to highlight some of these factors. Instead of asking the child for a story, it is helpful to use items from the child's own life (e.g., candy, Internet, or video games) to create a playful story that is comparable to the obsessive quality of addictive behavior. For example, during an individual session, an 11-year-old boy listened to a story about a fictitious boy who loved to eat donuts. When he ate donuts, he felt happy; however, later he became very energetic and hyperactive. Despite getting in trouble at home and in school for his behavior, he continued to eat the donuts. After hearing this story, the boy enthusiastically volunteered that he eats candy every day and, although it makes him "hyper," he eats it anyway. He also added reluctantly that he "can't stop." He said, "I thought I could walk by the candy store and not feel like buying candy, but I did buy it." He wondered whether his love of candy was similar to his mother's love of alcohol. The point was made; that is, from this brief story, he was able to develop some understanding of the physical and psychological reactions from using drugs and the potential for loss of control. This story may lead to some insight about his mother's addictive behavior.

In order to further highlight these factors using storytelling, the therapist may use the analogy of an allergy. It is very useful to explain to children that the physical effects their parents experience from using drugs is similar to a person with an allergy. Many children have allergies to pollen, dust, and seasonal conditions, and they can understand the similarity. For example, a child who is allergic to pollen may feel ill after going to the park. Knowing this reaction is likely to occur may not have inhibited the child's wish to go to the park. In fact, the child may go to the park despite knowing these consequences. This analogy has striking similarity to a substance abuser's addictive behavior and may help children understand their parents' addictions. For children who are less able to use a storytelling format or for the therapist who feels less comfortable using storytelling, the following questions can be reproduced on a piece of paper and discussed in session:

1. Is there something you love to eat or an activity you love to do most of the time?
2. What is good about it?
3. What is not so good about it?
4. If you had to stop it now, how hard would it be?
5. What would you do to try to stop?

In the final activity, children will be asked to complete an art and writing task about addiction and its effect on their family life. Children are often confused about their feelings toward their parent who is using drugs. To begin a discussion of feelings at this point may be premature for school-aged children. Instead, it is often helpful to ask children to put their thoughts and feelings into art. This activity uses a narrative therapy technique called externalization. The goal of externalization in narrative therapy is to separate the person from the problem, to permit the problem to be viewed from a variety of perspectives and contexts, and to foster client agency over the problem (White & Epston, 1990). The externalization process includes using language that distinguishes the problem from the person, asking questions that map the influence of the problem, and exploring unique outcomes, such as times when the problem was less intense or absent. In short, externalization provides emotional distance from which the children can develop new meaning and understanding about addiction and their parent's behavior.

To facilitate this activity, the therapist provides the children with a sheet of paper and colored pencils and asks them to think about their families and how they have been affected by addiction. Allow the children time to reflect on their thoughts and then ask them to imagine what addiction might look like and then draw it. Most children are able to complete this activity with little assistance. Children may draw anything they imagine addiction to resemble. Some children have drawn monsters, demons, Martians, and stick figures with morbid detail. Once completed, ask the children to write a story about their drawing at the bottom of the paper or on the back. The therapist may use the following questions as prompts for those children who may have difficulty generating a story or as additional questions to expand a story:

1. What is it? What name could you give it?
2. How old is it?
3. Where did it come from?
4. What is it doing?
5. What does it want with your mother or father? With you?
6. What do you think it is going to do?
7. If you could say something to it, what would you say?
8. How does it affect you and others in your family?

9. What or who helps you cope when it is present?
10. When are some times and places when it is not around?
11. What is it like when it is not around?
12. Who or what helps you resist its influence?

These process questions allow children the opportunity to reflect on addiction and its impact on their family, take steps to release their feelings, and gain some sense of control. It also encourages them to consider what their life is like when addiction is not around. Some children, particularly younger children, may react emotionally to this writing activity. The therapist must remain aware of this potential and, if it occurs, consider relieving the child of the task and provide encouragement and support for the work completed.

It is very helpful to encourage the children to openly share their completed work. Children are usually ready to share their work and tell their story. It is through this sharing process that they become more aware of addiction and its effect in their life and in others' lives. In addition, they also begin talking about their experience to their peers. Not surprisingly, they all want addiction to "go away," but some of the children have unique ways of saying it, with profound emotion.

Brief Clinical Vignette

The following is a brief vignette of a group session utilizing these activities. The group membership consists of five children: Anna, age 7; Michelle, age 8; Michael, age 8; Raj, age 9; and Lisa, age 10. Each of these children had a parent who abused a substance within the last year, and they were aware of the parent's use. For each of these children, their nonusing parent initiated the clinical contact. Most of the children demonstrated some adjustment difficulties and manifested mild to moderate symptoms of anxiety and depression. All were fairly talkative, except for Michelle.

After a warm-up exercise that included tossing a small inflated ball around and responding to casual questions (e.g., "What is your favorite cartoon?"), the children were asked to assemble their chairs in front of a dry-erase board. The therapist drew images of drugs on the board and the children became very curious. Raj shouted, "That's a cigarette!" The other children remained silent but clearly attentive. The therapist acknowledged Raj's comment by stating that he was correct, and asked the other children what they thought were some of the other items. Anna responded first, but was unsure how to describe it. She said, "People smoke it too." Raj immediately said, "Marijuana." Lisa identified alcohol and cocaine, but no one identified heroin. This is not unusual. At this point, the group was interacting and working together. However, Michelle had not yet participated. Although she was clearly attentive, she appeared worried and anxious. As the session progressed, the children were asked to describe what someone looks like or acts like when he or she is drinking alcohol. Michelle finally engaged. She reported in a soft voice, "They look sleepy." Lisa asked her if she knew someone who drank alcohol and Michelle said her mother. Lisa responded by saying, "Mine too!" This connection helped Michelle feel more comfortable in the group. The therapist continued to inquire about observable side effects of using drugs and added other effects that the children did not know. Once completed, the dry-erase board was filled with images and descriptions of side effects from using drugs. Raj asked poignantly, "If drugs do all that, then why do people do it?" His question led nicely into the next set of activities, which were scheduled for the following week. The "Side Effect Word Search Handout" (Handout 5.1) and the "My Feelings Word Search Handout" (Handout 5.2) were given to each child, and the children were instructed to complete the assignments at home and bring the handouts with them the next week. Their parents were also reminded of the assignments and encouraged to help the children with the handouts.

The next session began with a light warm-up exercise and review of the homework. All of the children had completed their homework assignments and wanted to report the words they found. Each child was given a chance to read his or her words aloud. The therapist applauded each child's effort to complete the assignment, and reinforced the idea that all of the words were side effects of using drugs. The rest of the session was spent discussing Raj's question from the previous session. Raj asked why people use drugs if they cause side effects. To help the children understand the question, the therapist used a storytelling technique. The therapist created a story about a young boy who started playing video games and enjoyed it. Even during school, he thought about his video games and could not wait to get home to play. Eventually, his grades in school declined and his mother was upset that he focused more on his games than on his school work. Nonetheless, he found himself unable to stop thinking about playing his games and became very upset when she took his games away. This was an example of the "good feeling" and the obsessive quality of playing a video game and how it may negatively affect school performance and family relationships. After making the parallel to substance abuse, Lisa and Raj reported that they tried to take their parent's "alcohol" away, too. Raj even admitted that he tried to "hide a bottle" of alcohol once. Looking around the room, Anna and Michelle both looked stunned, and the therapist made a process comment to encourage discussion about these disclosures. Although the children were not able to comment with any significant detail, their nonverbal reactions gave the impression of commonality of experience.

The next activity in the same session required the children to draw an image of addiction and write a story about it. The most striking story came from Michelle. She drew an image of addiction that resembled a monster. It was a big, imposing monster with a large mouth and teeth. There were other people in the picture, but off at a distance. Her story described a monster who "ate" her mother, leaving her all alone. She was afraid that the monster had the power to "get her" too and vowed never to let "it get close enough." She stated very emphatically, "Give me back my mother and stay away from us!" When she read this in the group, she had everyone's attention. The group became silent and the therapist took a moment to process the experience. Michelle cried and Raj and Lisa comforted her. Anna stated that she "hate[d] addiction" and Michael nodded his head.

This brief vignette demonstrates the power of group work with children using sensitive, structured activity within a supportive environment. This work would not be possible without the support of the parents who bring the children weekly and who themselves are often in distress. It is most valuable to conduct this work within the context of individual and family therapy. These activities can be incorporated into existing family work when the therapist has identified an educational need for the whole family. This educational need may develop as a result of enduring family coping styles such as denial and enabling. These activities can be used with adults without modification and are most useful during the early to middle stages of family therapy. Once the family is able to openly discuss substance abuse without significant shaming, these activities may be introduced safely.

Suggestions for Follow-Up

Since this educational intervention is best conducted within the context of individual and family therapy, the therapist can continue to assist the child in understanding his or her emotional experiences from the parent's substance use. It is useful to revisit the art exercise periodically. Children generally enjoy drawing and it is a good projective measure of a child's emotional reactions to family dynamics. For example, a child who drew addiction as a demon may now draw it as a sick man, representing a possible psychological shift with his substance-abusing father. It is not necessary to have them create a new story about addiction each time, though it is useful in the short term. In individual and family counseling, the therapist can further monitor the child's defensive reactions and reinforce use of healthy coping strategies. It is not uncommon for the child who participated in these educational activities to clarify questions that his or her parent has about addictive behavior. For example, an 8-year-old boy explained to his mother, after she asked why her husband continues to drink despite the consequences, "Ma, dad is allergic to alcohol, so he gets sick. He just needs to see his doctor to feel better and to stay away from alcohol. But it is hard." His mother took a moment to smile from the simplicity of her son's response. She marveled at how much he had learned about addiction and his willingness to share it with her instead of crying and withdrawing.

Contraindications for Use

This intervention is excellent for latency-aged children who can grasp a simple, concrete explanation of addiction. However, children younger than 6 may be less willing to discuss their family experience openly and are less aware of a parent's substance abuse. These children could benefit from a general education on addiction. The art activity without the personal story may also be useful.

Finally, parents are encouraged to participate in the process by reviewing the handout and session material with their child. The therapist will need to evaluate safety issues and the appropriateness of engaging the substance-using parent in the process. Above all, the therapist must remain cognizant of the potential neglect and abuse of these children due to active addiction within the home and take all necessary steps to ensure safety.

References

Brown, S. (1988). *Treating adult children of alcoholics: A developmental perspective.* New York: Wiley.

Brown, S. (1991). Children of chemically dependent parents: A theoretical crossroads. In T. Rivinus (Ed.), *Children of chemically dependent parents: Multiperspectives from the cutting edge* (pp. 74–102). New York: Brunner/Mazel.

Gardner, R. A. (1993). *Storytelling in psychotherapy with children.* Lanham, MD: Jason Aronson.

Rodriguez, E. (2005, June). Revisiting the alcoholic family: An integration of psychodynamic and 12-step theory. *Counselor, 6,* 14–19.

van der Kolk, B. A., McFarlane, A. C., & Weisaeth, L. (Eds.). (1996). *Traumatic stress.* New York: Guilford.

White, M., & Epston, D. (1990). *Narrative means to therapeutic ends.* New York: W. W. Norton.

Professional Reading and Resources

Barber, J. G., & Gilbertson, R. (1999). The drinker's children. *Substance Use and Misuse, 34*(3), 383–402.

Black, C. (2003). *Straight talk from Claudia Black: What recovering parents should tell their kids about drugs and alcohol.* Center City, MN: Hazelden.

Brown, S., & Lewis, V. (1999). *The alcoholic family in recovery: A developmental model.* New York: Guilford.

Carmichael, K. D., & Lane, K. S. (1997). Play therapy with children of alcoholics. *Alcoholism Treatment Quarterly, 15*(1), 43–51.

Crespi, T. D., & Sabatelli, R. M. (1997). Children of alcoholics and adolescence: Individuation, development, and family systems. *Adolescence, 32*(126), 402–417.

Reinert, D. F. (1999). Group intervention for children of recovering alcoholic parents. *Alcoholism Treatment Quarterly, 17*(4), 15–27.

Bibliotherapy Sources for the Client

Bissell, L., & Watherwax, R. (1982). *The cat who drank too much.* Bantam, CT: Bibulophile Press.

Moe, J., Brown, C., & LaPorte, B. (1996). *Kids' power too! Words to grow by.* Stockholm: Imagine Works.

Substance Abuse and Mental Health Services Administration National Clearinghouse for Alcohol and Drug Information (http://www.ncadi.samhsa.gov).

Typoo, M. H., & Hastings, J. M. (1984). *An elephant in the living room: The children's book.* Minneapolis, MN: Compcare Publications.

Handout 5.1: Side Effect Word Search

Instructions: The following puzzle has 10 words that are some of the COMMON side effects from drinking alcohol and using drugs. See if you can find them all. Here are the words!

1. SAD	2. TIRED	3. DENIAL	4. ACT SILLY	5. SICK
6. ANGRY	7. HARD TO STOP	8. BREAK PROMISES	9. MEAN	10. ALLERGY

S	L	A	S	S	C	A	R	E	D	S	A	O
A	W	F	C	T	I	R	E	D	S	I	N	T
D	E	C	A	L	L	E	R	G	Y	C	G	K
A	C	T	S	I	L	L	Y	R	C	K	R	D
H	A	R	D	T	O	S	T	O	P	U	Y	M
D	E	N	I	A	L	Q	O	M	E	A	N	A
B	R	E	A	K	P	R	O	M	I	S	E	S

Handout 5.2: My Feelings Word Search

Instructions: The following puzzle has 10 words that are COMMON feelings children have as a result of their parent's alcohol and drug use. See if you can find them all. Here are the words!

1. SAD	2. SCARED	3. ANXIOUS	4. LONELY	5. GUILTY
6. ANGRY	7. ALONE	8. NUMB	9. CONFUSED	10. WORRY

S	L	A	S	S	C	A	R	E	D	N	A
A	L	O	N	E	I	R	E	D	S	U	N
D	E	C	A	L	L	E	R	G	Y	M	G
L	O	N	E	L	Y	L	Y	R	C	B	R
A	N	X	I	O	U	S	T	O	P	U	Y
C	O	N	F	U	S	E	D	M	R	A	Z
G	U	I	L	T	Y	W	O	R	R	Y	D

– 6 –

Do I Have to Give Rewards?
Nonastounding Ways to Recognize Children's Accomplishments

Elsa K. Weber

Type of Contribution: Activity, Handout

Objective

Children need and enjoy concrete recognition that they have met a challenge or done something well. It is important to recognize children's efforts and accomplishments in ways that go beyond materialistic rewards and reach toward constructive, engaging family activity. This chapter addresses that need in ways that are fun and easily accessible for parents and that build the parent–child bond.

Rationale for Use

Immediate verbal recognition of small attempts or successes may help a child to focus on and to take charge of developing useful habits, or to avoid inappropriate behaviors. Sometimes a more substantive response such as a smile or a pat on the back is appropriate. Small tokens can be tangible evidence of progress made. But the best "rewards" may sometimes be activities that recognize children's interests, contributions, or capabilities.

Children strive both for close relationships with adults who recognize and support them, and for autonomy/independence within the context of their own daily lives (Mahler, Pine, & Bergman, 1975). They want to be recognized as individuals with their own desires and needs, and they also want to be seen as competent (Erikson, 1963). This can manifest itself in terms of a child's ability and willingness to meet a parent's behavioral expectations and in a child's attitude toward academic achievement. Parents and children need to understand the child's accomplishments as natural progression toward competence and not simply as obedience or as adherence to a fixed standard. An emphasis on rewards can lead children to expect presents or material goods for being good or getting good grades, and keeps fundamental control of the child's behavior in the hands of an external authority. In contrast, recognition and encouragement for children's efforts and accomplishments should help them to see themselves as becoming valuable and competent (Dreikurs & Cassel, 1972). The goal is to support a developmentally appropriate increase in the child's own self-determination and control (Kohn, 1999). As a child begins helping out more, getting along better with parents or siblings, mastering nighttime fears, etc., the parent is released from coercive or palliative efforts, and this enables him or her to spend time engaging with or supporting constructive and creative activities with the child. Because a child can show better judgment, more disciplined study habits, or increased skill, he or she can be allowed more complex or responsible independent activities.

Explain why parents need this list. Ultimately, children just need to know that parents love them and value what they do. Some parents, however, may have difficulty finding ways to show their appreciation of children's accomplishments appropriately, when more than a "Good job!" is called for. They may have difficulty thinking of things to do with children, rather than for them. The list in the accompanying handout includes some simple recognitions, ranging from outright small prizes to more elaborate activity ideas. It is more suggestive than all encompassing, and it is organized into several parts. The ideas are inexpensive and can take place within the context of everyday life. They are special because of how or when they occur. The way an object or activity is offered will vary according to the specific accomplishment, what the child is ready to do, and/or the child's own desires or goals. Small tokens can often serve as pleasing markers for repeated small successes; however, they can easily become meaningless or boring, since they are often not directly relevant to the child's accomplishments or interests. Time spent in nonroutine pleasurable activities can be emotionally and intellectually stimulating and a real treat. Activities should match the child's specific interests or be something that the parent enjoys and would like to share. Many can be done either jointly or independently, according to a child's interests or capability.

The list is arranged in four sections: (1) small tangible items that can be used quickly and easily as immediate recognition of small steps to a goal, (2) activities to do at home, (3) places to go that are easily accessible, and (4) opportunities for planning.

Instructions

Consult with parents and/or children about their goals and their judgments of children's functioning within the family context or in school or other social contexts. It is important to discuss the child's developmental needs and capabilities and to be aware of the child's desires or goals as well as those of the parents.

Discuss the notion of recognizing specifically the child's positive actions or accomplishments with the parents. The conversation may encourage the parent to be more observant so as to "catch the child doing something well." Some parents may fear "spoiling" the child. This may be addressed through a discussion about the importance, for the *child,* of knowing that the parent sees her efforts or that he has not worked hard in vain.

The clinical vignette illustrates the use of several methods of keeping track of and appreciating efforts children (and adults) have made toward smoother family function. These include immediate marks on a chart, pleasant activities resulting from cooperation, and certificates recognizing specific capabilities. Handout 6.1 can assist the parent in understanding how to use the ideas for activities and how those can contribute to a richer family life. Handout 6.2 is a list of items and activities that can be used or that may engender additional ideas. Both handouts should be discussed with the parents, and perhaps with children as well, in an effort to determine which section or sections will be most useful. Follow-up sessions can then examine the level of success.

Brief Clinical Vignette

After a long week of work and school, Norma had Saturday to catch up with housework, and she found it a struggle. She tried to reserve Sunday afternoon and evening, when the children were with their father, to catch up on studying. Saturdays were particularly difficult because 7-year-old Joe and 4-year-old Elena wanted only to watch cartoons, yet they tended to argue and provoke each other constantly during that time. It seemed to Norma that she spent more time arbitrating than getting the wash together and over to the laundromat. By the time this process was finished, it was usually Saturday afternoon; other chores were still waiting and there was no time to do any kind of recreational activity. Elena was usually cranky and Joe complained that he was bored.

Saturday cartoons were the children's customary shows, and they were up at 7:00 a.m. sharp to watch. They were content to serve themselves cereal and watch by themselves for quite a while, allowing Norma the luxury of sleeping in a little. The children's favorite show came on at 8:00 a.m.

and finished by 8:30 a.m., at which time they usually began bothering each other. Cartoons were not yet over, though, and the children resisted mightily any request or demand that she made for quiet or help.

After considering many options, Norma decided that her best strategy might be to try to get the children involved in the housework so that the chores could get done earlier, leaving time for something more fun. She decided to suggest a change in the Saturday schedule. When she talked it over with the children, it became clear that they did not want to miss their favorite show, but that they did not really care about the ones that came after it. Norma explained that the wash had to get done on Saturday so that they would have clothes for the week. If it could get done in the morning, though, they would have time to do some other things. She asked the children what they thought they could do to help, and together they devised the following proposal for a Saturday morning routine.

Norma would get up at 8:00 a.m. and begin her morning work. At 8:30 a.m., Joe and Elena would turn off the TV and join in with specific chores. First, they would pick up any toys scattered in the bedroom they shared. Next, they would begin helping with family chores. Joe could divide the clothes into two loads: pants, dark socks, and heavy shirts in one and lighter clothing in the other. He could put the clothes into the two laundry bags that they usually filled. He could also gather together the detergent and other materials used for washing. Elena could gather all the towels from the bathroom and all the pillowcases from the beds and bring them to the pile. She could also find and collect all of the wastebaskets from around the apartment so that they could be emptied and the trash taken out.

Norma and Joe drew up a Saturday chore chart with everyone's name on it. They listed the laundry gathering and sorting, toy pickup, and trash basket gathering. They also listed the dishwashing and vacuuming that Norma wanted to get done on Saturday. They agreed that as each chore was finished, the person who did it could mark it off with a big D for "done." Elena chose a big red marker to attach to the chart. At the end of the morning, if all the chores had been accomplished, some special activity could take place in the afternoon. They planned that, among others, special activities would include making cookies (something Norma had been promising to let Joe help with for months, but never had done) and driving to a new playground that was a little too far to walk to. On the other hand, if the chores and washing did not get done by 1:00 p.m., there would be little or no time for a special activity. Norma was worried that she would be taking time away from other things she needed to get done, but decided it was worth a try anyway.

At first, things worked perfectly. Everything was finished in record time on Saturday. The children helped with two batches of cookies. Everyone, including Norma, was exhausted, but they had cookies for dessert at supper, and the pleasant day continued into the evening. Sunday's study session was highly productive. The children needed only a few reminders to keep up with the schedule and get chores done over the next several weeks. They took in a children's film festival at the library and enjoyed several afternoon outings. One beautiful weekend they spent all afternoon at the park.

By the end of spring, the system began falling apart. There was no more room on the chart and no time to make another one. Joe had T-ball practice at 11 a.m. on Saturdays. Elena had several weeks of early afternoon birthday parties. There was no time to do the wash beforehand, so it got pushed off until later in the day. Saturday outings began to be set aside. But Joe was pleased with the responsibility of finding *all* of the dirty clothing. He felt he was really strong when he successfully wrestled with the large laundry bags, getting them ready to go quickly. Elena decided she liked relining the empty wastebaskets with grocery bags and putting them back in exactly the right places. Norma was satisfied and made them each a certificate, "Top-Notch Laundry Sorter" and "Queen of Clean Wastebaskets." The morning provocation struggle was ended and they all looked forward to the fall, when they could redo the schedule and try some other types of family recreation.

Norma's goal of stopping annoying provocations on Saturday morning was accomplished. Saturday chores also became more manageable. The children's goals—having things to do on

Saturday afternoon—were also met happily, and their newly developed housekeeping skills were specifically recognized. Changes in the household schedule presented new challenges to be met.

Suggestions for Follow-Up

Follow-up conversations can focus on children's and parents' evaluations of the process. Have the goals been accomplished? Does each party feel some satisfaction? Does the child need continued or additional support with accomplishing what has been set out? Are there new ways in which parents and children can work together? How does the plan need to change to meet family transitions? Are there other small ways that the parent could be reinforcing the child on a daily basis? Does the child have any ideas of things that might be fun for him or her?

Contraindications for Use

Any of the suggested activities may be more or less appropriate depending on the age of the children involved. The approach requires sensitivity to children's developmental capabilities and aspirations. Parents with strong tendencies to overcontrol may tend to overwhelm child-conceived activities or critique child performance too harshly. Parents lacking confidence in their own or their children's capabilities may need extra encouragement to allow children to try new activities. In these cases, evaluation should focus on the child's need for appreciation or opportunities to try things out. Lastly, for smaller children, with small items, consideration should always be given to the size of any prize and the possibilities for choking.

References

Dreikurs, R., & Cassel, P. (1972). *Discipline without tears.* New York: Hawthorne Books.

Erikson, E. (1963). *Childhood and society.* New York: Norton.

Kohn, A. (1999). *Punished by rewards: The trouble with gold stars, incentive plans, A's, praise, and other bribes.* New York: Houghton Mifflin.

Mahler, M., Pine, F., & Bergman, A. (1975). *The psychological birth of the human infant.* London: Hutchinson.

Professional Readings and Resources

Damon, W., & Hart, W. (1988). *Self understanding in childhood and adolescence.* Cambridge University Press.

Deci, E. (1995). *Why we do what we do: The dynamics of personal autonomy.* New York: G. P. Putnam.

Nucci, L., & Smetana, J. (1996). Mothers' concepts of young children's areas of personal freedom. *Child Development, 67,* 1870–1886.

Nucci, L., & Weber, E. K. (1995). Social interactions in the home and the development of young children's conceptions within the personal domain. *Child Development, 66,* 1438–1452.

Bibliotherapy Sources for the Client

Ellison, S. (2005). *365 Days of creative play* (4th ed.). Naperville, IL: Source Books.

Ellison, S. (2005). *365 Smart after-school activities.* Naperville, IL: Source Books.

Farber, B. (Ed.). (1997). *The parents' and teachers' guide to helping young children learn: Creative ideas from 35 respected experts.* Cutchogue, NY: Preschool Publications.

Kaye, P. (2002). *Games with books.* New York: Farrar, Straus and Giroux.

Handout 6.1: To the Parent: Recognizing What Kids Are Doing Well

We want to recognize when children behave well, but it is not possible or advisable to give huge rewards every time. Nevertheless, children enjoy concrete recognition for a job well done. In the nonastounding list in Handout 6.2 you will find simple ways you can acknowledge what children have done. The suggestions may seem quite ordinary, but what makes them special is the ways you use them, and when. If you already do some of these things regularly, then your child will not consider them special. Choose something else. Be careful not to focus on the "performance" of an activity. Any of these activities could become chores instead of treats if you focus on "getting" or "doing" it right. Be ready to set aside some of your own expectations about neatness or completion. Let your child lead as much as possible. For little children, that may mean focusing only on the process. If you do not worry about having it "turn out right," the extra effort involved in a messy undertaking can be part of the pleasure, even for you. For older children, you may just need to be ready to help out.

Quick, easy, short ideas. If you want to mark many small successes, use tiny items to note them. These could even include sweet treats, though you will want to be careful of turning candy or food into comfort mechanisms. You can keep marks or certificates in a small folder or binder, or as a kind of diary. Some children will enjoy collecting tiny objects (be careful not to give smaller children items they may choke on). Your child will have a record of accomplishment to look at, and collections can be the basis for satisfying hobbies or further exploration later.

Things to do at home. Time to spend together is hard to find these days, but it is worth the effort. Joint parent and child activities can be a great opportunity. Intimate, one-on-one time with parents is often an elusive luxury for children and parents alike, and time in the kitchen or a workshop can serve as both a treat and a chance to experiment and learn. Younger children will enjoy helping out with real projects. Older children may want more and more responsibility within activities. Fooling around with games, language, music, or art without worrying about whether they are helpful for school is a fine way to relax. Children love to hear stories and sing songs, especially those about their own families. Remember that the goal is to enjoy it.

Places to go. Parents are often so busy that they tend to put off excursions; yet if your child successfully masters something new or helps with extra chores, that may free you up—actually or psychologically—to spend some time visiting an interesting place. Large museums may be more expensive and further away than you can manage often, but small places may be more available. Children often enjoy short, simple experiences as much as or more than elaborately planned ones because there is less to take in and more time to explore. Think about places that are interesting to your child and also about ones that you enjoy and would like to share. Within the available time let it be the child who determines how long she looks or which aspects he pays attention to. Allow time to linger.

Opportunities to plan. As children get older or surer of their abilities, they are ready for challenges to their individual competence. They are ready to do things on their own that were formerly done only with your help or company. Allowing a child to plan or do things shows that you recognize his individual personal areas of prerogative and choice, or her ability to act responsibly.

Remember: You can suggest something that you like, but choose activities with your child in mind, and what he or she will like. Very young children do not need fancy plans. Older children may want things a little more elaborate. If the child is really interested and wants to spend more time, allow it if you can. If not, be ready to let it go.

Handout 6.2: Simple Ways to Recognize Children's Accomplishments

General Type	Specific Ideas
Quick, easy, short ideas	Marks—checks, Xs, squares filled in on a grid, perhaps arranged in a special pattern that emerges
	A special stamp or pen to make the marks
	Stars or stickers—there are many kinds and little children love them
	Tiny toys that could become a collection—cars, animals, figurines
	Marbles
	Fancy pencils or pencil sharpeners
	Whimsical erasers
	Special bookmarks
	Key chains
	"Chits" (poker chips or any kind of small pieces that can be accumulated in a jar or box, including small denomination coins, perhaps leading to a larger item or activity)
	Buttons, ribbons or certificates—preferably home made
	Child's choice of items usually provided by adults—children's vitamins, breakfast cereal, special cup or bowl, special item of clothing
Things to do at home	Cook—a special dish or dessert (together, or child alone)
	Make art—Playdoh (specially scent or color it), finger paint, junk sculpture
	Craft projects—sewing, knitting, or simple wood work
	Make holiday decorations
	Build models—preprepared or fanciful approximations
	Plant a child's garden—a big pot or a small plot
	Play games—commercial, word games, card games, made up
	Tell stories—family history, favorite tales
	Put on skits, act out favorite stories with dress-up costumes
	Let children rearrange furniture to create play spaces
	Have a tea party
	Make a collage
	Make homemade tent
	Make music and dance—sing songs, play rhythms and dance to them, use real or made-up instruments
	Make a family picture album—look at pictures of family and friends together
	Make a home movie
	Allow extras—extra stories, extra time
Places to go	Take a walk—explore the neighborhood
	Find interesting houses, gardens, public buildings
	Visit a bakery or ethnic grocery
	Stop at garage sales
	Look for wildlife in the area—squirrels, rabbits, bugs, worms
	Look for flowers in the spring and smell them
	Go to the park or playground
	Run up and down hills you do not have at home
	Play games or toss balls. Get dirty without worry
	Have a scavenger hunt
	Go to the library
	Attend a planned story hour
	Look for and read books children like—fish, gardening, trucks, machines, etc.
	Get a child's library card
	Go to a favorite restaurant
	Go stargazing
	Go on a picnic
	Window shop: just look and talk
	Hobby store, pet store, fabric store, hardware store, auto parts store, green house, lumber yard, antique doll or train store, resale shop

(continued)

Handout 6.2 (*continued*)

General Type	Specific Ideas
	Go swimming
	Child-oriented film, arts, or storytelling festivals
	General public street festivals and outdoor concerts
	An individual visit with grandparents or other special older relatives or friends
	Formal places of interest:
	Local children's museum
	Zoo or aquarium
	Larger museum
	Forest or nature preserve
	Botanical garden
Opportunities to plan	What to eat for breakfast, lunch, dinner, dessert, snack
	Where to go for a special meal
	What to do for a birthday party
	What to do when a friend comes to play
	Family night or weekend activities
	A day on the town (which museum or play or show)
	A piece of vacation—which attractions
	Personalizing a bedroom or play space
	Assembling materials and designing an outdoor space in the yard
	Planning a garden spot

SECTION II: ADULT CLIENTS

– 7 –

Ready, Set, Goal!
Helping Families Come to Agreement on Therapeutic Goals

Patricia A. Robey

Type of Contribution: Activity

Objective

The objective of this chapter is to provide the therapist with a playful activity that may be used to help families come to agreement on therapeutic goals.

Rationale for Use

In his book *Choice Theory* (1998), Dr. William Glasser explains that all human behavior is motivated by our attempt to meet our basic needs. These needs include love and belonging, power, freedom, fun, and survival. However, the average person does not typically say, "Today I want to get some freedom." Instead, he or she will say, "Today I want to go outside and ride my bike." This second statement reflects the *internal picture* of what the person might do to feel free in the moment.

Dr. Glasser has created the metaphor of the "quality world" to describe the internal world that holds the pictures of the persons, things, ideas, and beliefs that are most important to us. "This small, personal world...is made up of a small group of specific pictures that portray, more than anything else we know, the best ways to satisfy one or more of our basic needs" (Glasser, 1998, p. 45).

Individuals consider only *specific* people, places, things, values, and beliefs to be need satisfying. Glasser contends that we put "pictures" of these persons and things into our quality worlds. Our behavior is driven by our desire to have these pictures, or what the pictures represent, which satisfies one or more of the basic needs. The quality-world pictures are a source of motivation and emotional energy. Sharing quality-world pictures provides an opportunity for connecting, goal setting, self-evaluation, learning, and fun.

Because quality-world pictures are the source of motivation for change, reality therapists try to move as quickly as possible from talk of problems to talk of desired outcomes. The desired outcome can be identified by accessing the pictures in the client's quality world. The therapist may ask, "What is it you hope to accomplish?" "Ideally, what would you like to see happen?" or "Describe how you would like your relationship to be."

Unfortunately, because quality-world pictures are unique to the individual, the answers to those questions may be as varied as the number of people in a family. In response to the question, "Ideally, what would you like to see happen?" Mom may say, "I want everyone to help me wash the dishes." Dad may say, "I want Mom to stop yelling." Teenaged son may state, "I want everyone to leave me alone." Little sister may say, "I want someone to play with me." Because of this conflict of wants, the therapist will ask the family to generate and share as many pictures as possible, including pictures for individual wants and for family wants. As Dr. Glasser states,

> To get along better than we do now with another person, we need to try to learn what is in that person's quality world and then try to support it. Doing so will bring us closer to that person than anything else we can do. (1998, p. 51)

When setting goals for family therapy, the therapist first identifies what each individual wants and then tries to find an area of overlap that all members can agree upon. The therapist should make sure that the goals are stated in positive and concrete terms—that is, something that should be done rather than something that should be stopped (Berg & Steiner, 2003). For example, the goal should not be for everyone to stop arguing. Instead, the goal could be for everyone to spend half an hour each day sharing their happy experiences from that day. Wubbolding (2000) defines the components of good goals as being simple, realistic, measurable, and immediately attainable. In addition, goals should be controlled by the individual, rather than contingent on the behavior of someone else ("I will do it if he or she does _____."). Finally, the therapist should ask for a firm commitment: "I will," not "I'll try."

Ready, Set, Goal! is a creative and playful activity that can be used in counseling to help identify both individual and family quality-world pictures and goals.

Materials Needed

Sturdy sheets of paper cut into large (12–14 in.) circles
Fine-tipped markers, colored pencils, crayons, or pens
Masking tape or tacks
Flip chart paper (optional: whiteboard and dry-erase markers)

Instructions

The following is a detailed description of how to utilize *Ready, Set, Goal!* with clients in therapy. Handout 7.1 at the end of the chapter offers readers a brief overview of the steps involved in this activity.

Ready: As with all therapy, the therapist begins by introducing himself or herself and establishing a relationship with the clients. As the therapist connects with the clients, he or she lets them know that he or she cares for the clients. The therapist lets the clients know that the therapist will listen to the clients' stories, attend to their needs, and help them make changes that will create better relationships. Through this behavior, the therapist puts the picture of himself or herself into the clients' quality worlds. When the therapist is important to the clients, the clients will trust the therapist to do what is best for them. Until this relationship is established, the clients may be reluctant to share their quality-world pictures because they fear that the therapist may criticize or ridicule what is so important to them (Glasser, 1998).

Set: Once the relationship has been established, the therapist will ask each member to *briefly* describe the problem. Usually this involves blaming and criticizing others for the problems. Ask other members to avoid interrupting and assure them that each will also have a turn to explain his or her point of view. This helps each member release some feelings of frustration and pain, and allows each person to feel that his or her complaint has been heard. It is important, however, that this does not go on for more than a few minutes, to avoid the session becoming an outpouring of blaming, complaining, accusing, criticizing, and threatening.

As soon as possible, the therapist should shift the focus from the complaint to the desired outcome of the therapy. The therapist will introduce the activity by stating,

> I can see that you all have a lot of ideas about what is wrong with your family, and you know what you *don't want* to see happen. Now I would like to shift gears a bit, and let's see what you *do want* to see happen in your family.

The therapist hands out a paper circle to each member of the family. Markers, colored pencils, etc. are offered so that each member can have a choice of colors for the activity. The therapist tells the family members,

> These circles represent your personal worlds. I would like you to write or draw on your world the things that you want that would make you happy for yourself and things that would make you happy to be with your family.

Sometimes this is difficult, as clients are most aware of what is painfully wrong. However, since the activity is focused on individual wants, clients soon are able to identify things that are important to them. If clients are stuck, the therapist can remind them of some things he or she learned about the clients during the early relationship-building phase of the counseling session.

As the clients write or draw their wants, they tap into their quality-world pictures and they usually begin to release some of the anger and hostility they were experiencing. The therapist should observe the members' response to the activity. Often, members are quiet and thoughtful, sometimes smiling, sometimes wistful (Gil & Sobol, 2000).

Goal: When the members have completed their task or the allotted time is over, the therapist will ask each person to share his or her wants. The therapist should advise other members that their job is to listen to and support the sharing, rather than criticize or judge:

> Now that you have had an opportunity to think of what is important to you, I would like you to share what you have written or drawn. Everyone will have a turn, so I will ask each of you just to listen now, without criticism or objection.

After all members have shared their worlds, the therapist will ask the family members to comment on the experience. If the family interaction is usually one of conflict, the therapist may guide the questions to the positive. "I noticed that you were quiet during this activity. I wonder how it felt for you to think about the things that are important to you?" "I noticed that several of you have pictures in common. What did you see?" The therapist should watch for connections between the wants, even if they are not readily apparent.

After the activity has been processed, the therapist takes the individual worlds and tapes or tacks them to the wall or whiteboard, on which a blank circle has been placed. The individual worlds should be placed in a circle around the blank circle, or may even overlap it a bit to show that the individual worlds contribute to the group world. The therapist says, "The center circle is your family world. Let's write here the things I heard you say that you all want." The therapist will write or draw the mutual wants in the family circle. Sometimes the therapist will have to be creative in identifying group wants. For example, "Everyone had ideas about how the family could be happy together. Can we all agree you would like to see the problem get better?" or "Can we all agree that you all would like to be happy?" "What would it look like if everyone was happy together? What would you be doing?"

When the family circle is complete, it has encapsulated the goals for the therapy. In this way, all family members have a say in what they would like to see happen. Because all members were involved, they are more likely to be active participants in the change process.

Brief Clinical Vignette

Beth (36) and Tommy (38) are a working-class Caucasian couple with three children: Stacy (13), Stephanie (11), and Susan (9). Beth had been in individual therapy for 6 weeks in an effort to deal with her depression. Beth explained that her life felt out of control since a house fire had demolished a large portion of the family's home. The family was living in the home while it was being rebuilt, which meant that the parents were sleeping on a foldout sofa in the living room while the three girls shared the only bedroom that had survived the fire. Because of problems with insurance, the family had been living in these close quarters for 8 months, and they had no idea when their home repair would be completed.

Beth reported that her relationship with her husband had lost all intimacy. Beth also said she felt exhausted all the time. Communication between the couple was based on their frustration about the rebuilding, concerns about the girls, and worries about money. Beth could not remember the last time the couple did something fun together.

Beth was also worried about the girls, who all seemed to have changed since the fire. Although they had not been home when the fire occurred, Beth felt that they had lost more than their things; they had lost their sense of security and safety. Stacy, who had always been cooperative and had been Beth's helper with the younger girls, began to stay away from home after school, often staying at a friend's house until 10:00 p.m., when she would return home and go directly to bed. Talking to Stacy, Beth said, was a series of Beth's questions about Stacy's activities, followed by Stacy's grunts, shrugs, or screams of "leave me alone!"

Beth's relationship with Stephanie had always been troublesome. "I just don't understand her," Beth said. Stephanie had allied herself with Tommy's sister Angie, much to Beth's chagrin. Angie, who had no children, welcomed Stephanie into her home and treated Stephanie like she was Angie's own daughter. This created conflict among Beth, Stephanie, and Angie.

Susan was Beth's "baby." The therapist observed that Beth's face softened when she talked about Susan, who would give Beth hugs and kisses and would curl up on Beth's lap in the evening. However, even Susan was having some difficulty. Susan's teachers reported that she would often daydream instead of doing her schoolwork. Susan would disrupt the class by talking to her friends or getting up from her desk during work time. Her grades had slipped from As and Bs to Cs and Ds. Beth wondered if Susan had ADHD.

When asked how Tommy's relationship was with the girls, Beth reported that he had always distanced himself from the entire family. Recently, Tommy had taken a second job, so he was usually away from the home until 11:00 p.m., when the girls were already in bed. When Tommy *was* home, he would spend most of his time on the computer, paying bills, or working on one of the many rebuilding projects.

After hearing of Beth's concerns about her relationship with her husband and children, the therapist decided that Beth's treatment would be most effective by addressing issues within the family system. The therapist asked Beth to invite her family to join her in therapy. Only Susan was enthusiastic about this idea, but all members agreed to come to the next week's session.

When the family arrived for the session, the therapist directed them to the family room, which was furnished with a sofa and several comfortable chairs. She noticed that Beth and Susan snuggled up with one another on the sofa, leaving a seat on the end that none of the other family members chose. Tommy sat across the room from Beth, Stacy sat to his left, and Stephanie took a chair that was separated on both sides from any family member. The therapist removed the extra chairs from the circle and sat next to Stephanie.

The therapist got the family *ready* for therapy by introducing herself to the family and explaining about confidentiality and the rules of family therapy. She told the family about her philosophy of counseling and how her role was to help them to figure out a way that they could all be happy and get along with one another better. She spent some time getting to know each member individually, asking about their interests, school or work, or friends. She noticed that Beth spoke first, followed by Susan, Tommy, and Stacy. Stephanie was the last and appeared the most reluctant to speak.

Next, the therapist began to set the stage for the work of therapy. She asked the family members to briefly explain what they thought the problems were with the family relationships. Not surprisingly, each member blamed the others for the problems. The therapist listened respectfully, acknowledging how painful the situation was for everyone.

The therapist then told the family,

> I can see that you all have a lot of ideas about what is wrong with your family, and you know what you *don't want* to see happen. Now I would like to shift gears a bit, and let's see what you *do want* to see happen in your family.

She asked each member to choose a colored circle and some markers. "These circles represent your personal worlds," she said. "I would like you to write or draw on your world the things that you want that would make you happy for yourself and things that would make you happy to be with your family."

Soon the family members were engaged in the activity. Susan asked Beth for help spelling some of her words, and Beth, who was busy with her own circle, suggested that Susan draw instead of write. Stephanie had also chosen to draw.

When the therapist noted that the activity was beginning to slow down, she said, "I know that you may have some more things to add, and feel free to add them as you think of them. For now, though, I would like to hear about what you have written or drawn."

Susan was the first to share her world. She had drawn a picture of all family members standing in a row, with Beth first, then Tommy, then the girls in order of their ages. She had also drawn a cat, her school, her bike, and a picture of herself swimming. The therapist asked her to elaborate on her drawings to get a sense of what was important. In particular, the therapist asked Susan to describe what her family would be doing if she could arrange their time together. Susan said they would be at Disney World, eating, having fun, and going on rides.

Next Beth shared her pictures. Beth wished that the family would talk to one another, would have dinner together, and could go on a vacation. The therapist asked Beth how she would feel if the family did those things. Beth said she would feel peaceful, loved, happy, and comfortable instead of anxious and worried.

Stacy had drawn pictures of her friends and school. She drew herself in her own bedroom, without the other girls. Her picture of the family was in a big house, with everyone in his or her own space. She said she wanted to be left alone sometimes with no one nagging her or getting in her things. The therapist asked Stacy if she had an idea about what she might like to do with her family. Stacy shrugged. Rather than press her, the therapist decided to wait until the processing time to see if she could make a connection between Stacy's wants and those of the rest of the family.

Tommy wrote that he wanted money, the house fixed, more free time, golf, vacation, and sleep. He said that most of these wishes would be good for the family as well as for him. The therapist asked how the family would benefit if he had what he wanted. Tommy replied, "I wouldn't be so grouchy, for one thing. Probably we all would be happier if the house was fixed and we weren't on top of each other all the time."

Stephanie had written her aunt's name and listed a few friends. Most of her world was covered by pictures of animals. Stephanie loved animals. She had a cat, a dog, rabbits, and a hamster at home. She also helped take care of her aunt's horses. When asked about her wish for the family, she said she wished they could have a horse and that everyone would cooperate and take care of it.

While the therapist was listening to the family, she had been noting some similarities in their wants for themselves and their family. The therapist was now ready to help the family set the *goal* for the therapy and for their lives.

The therapist had tacked a large circle on a corkboard that was hanging on the wall. She asked each family member to tack his or her circle adjacent to the large circle. The therapist said,

> While you were sharing about the important things in your worlds, I noticed several things and wishes that you have in common. What I would like to do now is to take your separate worlds and make one big world for your family. First, I would like to ask each of you to tell me what you noticed about what you and your family have in common.

The therapist allowed some quiet time for the family to consider this. Because the members had not used the same language in defining their wishes, the commonalities were not readily apparent to them. Finally, Tommy said, "Well, I think we all want the house to be fixed." The therapist checked with the family members, who all agreed. She wrote "house fixed" on the family circle. Then she asked, "If the house was fixed, what would that mean to the family?" The family indicated that there would be less fighting, more peace and quiet, everyone would enjoy being home together, and probably would be able to have more fun. The therapist wrote these wants on the circle, too.

The therapist continued looking for similarities in wants, being careful always to note what impact the want would have on the family system. Finally, the family circle had a large list of goals for the family, including having the house fixed, happiness, peace, cooperation, fun, no fighting, playing together, vacation together, and having personal space (see sample in Handout 7.2). The therapist congratulated them on how many goals they had generated. She read them back and then encouraged the family, saying "I think these are workable goals. What do you all think?"

Though some members appeared skeptical as to whether the family could actually be like they wished it to be, they did seem to feel optimistic that some changes could be made and that their relationship with each other could be improved. Beth said, "Well, it is nice to think that everyone actually wants to get along. I was beginning to lose hope."

The therapist closed the session by summarizing the strengths she observed in the family:

> What I see is that you all care about one another and want yourselves and your family to be happy. The fact that you all agreed to come here tonight tells me you are willing to do what it takes to make that happen. I am looking forward to working with you on your happiness journey, and I feel confident that you can make it to your goals!

The therapist then gave the family a homework assignment that was related to their goal of having time together: to choose two days that they would have dinner together and to take time during dinner to share something good that had happened during the day. They were to report on this when they came to the next session. Note that the therapist limited the plan to only two days, which was a realistic goal.

As therapy continued, the therapist introduced the family members to the concepts of choice theory and taught them about the caring and deadly relationship habits (see Handout 7.3: "Habits That Can Build or Destroy Relationships"). She demonstrated how the family meeting and solving circle could be used when the family was in conflict. The family continued in therapy for 3 months, at which time they felt they had what they needed to manage their relationships and discontinued therapy. The therapist invited them to call her if necessary.

During this time Beth continued her individual therapy. Her depression improved as the problems within the family were reduced. Beth reported that everyone was getting along much better at home and that she was considering going back to school to study accounting.

Suggestions for Follow-Up

Ideally, the family members would be involved in creating a plan for how to get what they have identified that they want. However, there often is not enough time at the end of the session to create a plan. Planning may be the focus of the next session. For example, the wish for fun generated by the family was vague. In the following session, the therapist might ask the family to define fun further. If they were having fun together, what specifically would they be doing? Where would they be? Who would be with them? Would this cost money?

If there is not enough time for the family to create a plan, homework may be assigned. Homework should be simple, attainable, measurable, and something that each person can do himself or herself (Wubbolding, 2000). The solution-focused homework of catching someone in the act of doing something good would be an example of an effective assignment that almost anyone could do (Berg & Steiner, 2003).

In following sessions, the therapist would continue to keep the focus on what the clients are doing to meet the goal, how their relationship is improving, and what is successful. Reality therapists believe that it is good to teach their clients choice theory, so this will also be part of the agenda for follow-up sessions. In this way, the process is demystified and clients are given a model for understanding one another, which they can use to improve their relationships for the rest of their lives.

The family can be taught to manage family problems through a family meeting or "solving circle" (Glasser & Glasser, 2000). When the family has a problem that influences the relationship, a member can request a meeting of the solving circle. The "circle" is a metaphor for the relationship and when the family is working within the solving circle, they are working within the context of the relationship and for the sake of the relationship, rather than for the sake of each individual. Within the circle only caring habits are used. If the family cannot agree to focus on what is best for the relationship, the circle is broken for that time and they must arrange an appointment to meet again when each is willing to focus on the relationship rather than on himself or herself.

Contraindications for Use

If the family shows a great deal of conflict, the therapist may want to set limits on what the clients should draw. "Remember that these are positive pictures. So rather than draw a picture of your family disappearing, you could draw how your life would be better if you had more time alone." As an alternative, the therapist may choose to do the activity in individual sessions prior to setting the goals for the group.

References

Berg, I., & Steiner, T. (2003). *Children's solution work.* New York: W. W. Norton.

Gil, E., & Sobol, B. (2000). Engaging families in therapeutic play. In C. E. Bailey (Ed.), *Children in therapy: Using the family as a resource* (pp. 341–382). New York: W. W. Norton.

Glasser, W. (1998). *Choice theory: A new psychology of personal freedom.* New York: HarperCollins.

Glasser, W., & Glasser, C. (2000). *Getting together and staying together: Solving the mystery of marriage.* New York: HarperCollins.

Wubbolding, R. (2000). *Reality therapy for the 21st century.* Philadelphia, PA: Brunner-Routledge.

Professional Readings and Resources

Crawford, D. K., Bodine, R. J., & Hoglund, R. G. (1993). *The school for quality learning.* Champaign, IL: Research Press.

Erwin, J. (2004). *The classroom of choice.* Alexandria, VA: Association for Supervision and Curriculum Development.

Glasser, W. (1992). *The quality school.* New York: HarperCollins.

Glasser, W. (1998). *Choice theory: A new psychology of personal freedom.* New York: HarperCollins.

Glasser, W. (2000). *Counseling with choice theory: The new reality therapy.* New York: HarperCollins.

Glasser, W. (2000). *Every student can succeed.* San Diego, CA: Black Forest Press.

Ludwig, S. A., & Mentley, K. W. (1997). *Quality is the key: Stories from Huntington Woods School.* Wyoming, MI: KWM Educational Services.

Myers, L., & Jackson, D. (2002). *Reality therapy and choice theory: Managing behavior today, developing skills for tomorrow.* Lanham, MD: American Correctional Association.

Wubbolding, R. E. (1988). *Using reality therapy.* New York: Harper & Row.

Wubbolding, R. E. (1998). Client inner self-evaluation: A necessary prelude to change. In H. Rosentahl (Ed.), *Favorite counseling and therapy techniques* (pp. 197–198). Washington, DC: Taylor & Francis.

Wubbolding, R. E. (2000). *Reality therapy for the 21st century.* Philadelphia, PA: Brunner–Routledge.

Bibliotherapy Sources for the Client

Buck, N. S. (2000). *Peaceful parenting.* San Diego, CA: Black Forest Press.

Glasser, W. (1998). *Choice theory: A new psychology of personal freedom.* New York: HarperCollins.

Glasser, W., & Glasser, C. (2000). *Getting together and staying together: Solving the mystery of marriage.* New York: HarperCollins.

Wubbolding, R. E., & Brickell, J. (2001). *A set of directions for putting and keeping yourself together.* Minneapolis, MN: Educational Media Corporation.

Handout 7.1: The Ready, Set, Goal Process

Ready	The therapist joins with the family, creating a working atmosphere of caring and trust.
Set	The therapist sets the stage for goal setting, by briefly discussing problems and then asking clients to identify what is important to them and what they would like to see happen.
Goal	The therapist looks for the commonalities in the clients' wants, asks about the meaning behind the wants, and lists the wants/goals on which the family agrees.

Handout 7.2: Sample Goals from Tommy and Beth's Family

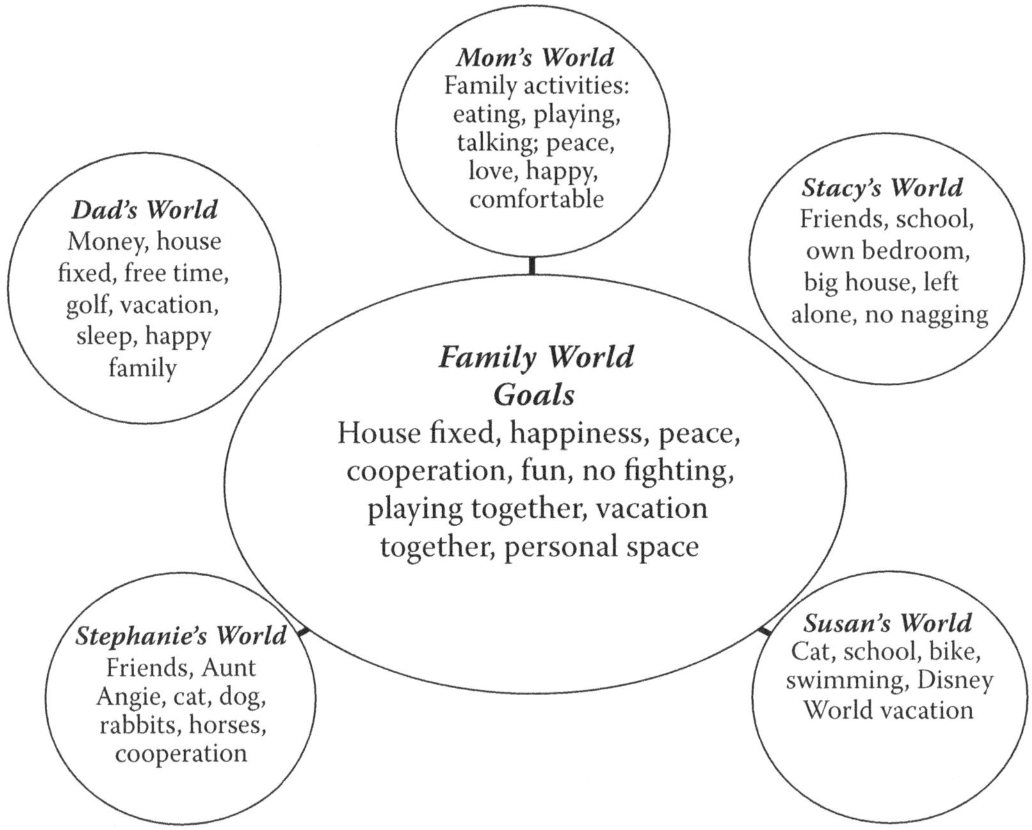

Handout 7.3: Habits that Can Build or Destroy Relationships

Caring Relationship Habits	Deadly Relationship Habits
Listening	Criticizing
Supporting	Blaming
Encouraging	Complaining
Respecting	Nagging
Trusting	Threatening
Accepting	Punishing
Negotiating disagreements	Bribing or rewarding to control

Source: Glasser, W., & Glasser, C. (2000). *Getting together and staying together: Solving the mystery of marriage.* New York: HarperCollins.

– 8 –

The Repetitive Listing Technique
A Homework Task Assignment

Mark S. Carich and Margaret R. Kohut

Type of Contribution: Homework, Activity

Objective

The purpose of this activity is to facilitate change in a client's internal thought patterns that lead to undesirable and otherwise problematic behavior. Repetitive listing is a cognitive–behavioral intervention that requires the client to continuously write specific statements a predetermined number of times. To date, this technique has not been well established in the literature except briefly by Carich (1990). The initial idea for using this intervention as a therapeutic task evolved from a workshop called "Eliminating Self-Defeating Behaviors" given by Terry Waldren in 1985. Prior to Waldren's presentation, the task was referred to as "repetitive listing" by Cudney (1975) and later Chamberlain (1982). The technique can be used with almost any mental health client; although it was originally developed for incarcerated individuals, time and experience indicate that a majority of nonincarcerated psychotherapy clients—adult and juvenile—can benefit from this technique. For example, this technique can be of great benefit with clients who are depressed, clients with low self-esteem, clients who suffered some sort of trauma in their lives, clients with problems in anger management such as domestic abuse clients, and clients with various anxiety, phobic, and panic responses.

Rationale for Use

Suppose that when you were a child, your teacher had you write "I will not push girls down on the playground" 100 times; the same principle applies in the repetitive listing technique (RLT). This technique is cognitive–behaviorally based in that it requires the client to use cognitive experiential dimensions as well as behavioral dimensions. Thought processes are stimulated in the client via his or her internal statements, or self-talk. The behavioral rationale for using this technique consists of the physical activity of repetitive writing. Therapeutic change occurs by learning to extinguish undesirable behaviors that have caused negative consequences in the client's life, and replacing these behaviors with appropriate, healthy behaviors. This change occurs through repeatedly writing pattern interruption statements and by writing pattern developmental statements. A pattern interruption statement is any sequential set of behaviors that stop, or interrupt, problem behaviors. Pattern development is the initiation of a new pattern of behavior that replaces the problematic behavior. This change occurs through the repetitive writing of pattern interruption statements and pattern developmental statements.

Keeney (1983) described "change" as drawing a distinction or creating a difference in the client's behavior. Change involves patterns of interruption and pattern building or development (O'Hanlon, 1982; Yapko, 1988). More specifically, pattern interruption is selected to extinguish or make extinct an undesirable behavior. It dissociates, disconnects, neutralizes, or deletes previously learned associations or patterns of behavior. Pattern development is used to teach the client to incorporate new, desirable behavior. Through pattern development, newly acquired behavior is put into action as the client writes statements that facilitate the learning of new behavior. To create change, both patterns complement each other; one decreases undesirable behavior and one helps clients to develop healthy new behaviors. Thus repetitive written statements may facilitate either of these patterns, depending upon the consequences the client is experiencing. If the client wishes to extinguish behavior, then the repetitive statement is a pattern interruption. If the client initiates new behavior because of the repetitive statement, then pattern development occurs. At times, either pattern may bring about both extinction and learning.

Pattern interruption statements are usually phrased in the negative, while pattern development statements are phrased with positives, occasional negatives, and activities containing many active verbs. Developmental patterns then replace problematic behaviors. A repetitive statement can consist of patterns of interruption or development, or both. In this situation, the desired outcome determines the type of pattern. For example, the repetitive statement "I choose to say no to drugs" is a combination of pattern interruption (taking drugs) and pattern development (I have a *choice*). Examples of pattern interruption include "I choose not to drink alcohol," "I choose not to feel cravings when I'm offered drugs," "I choose not to act on my sexual fantasies about children," I choose not to feel anxious when talking to women," "I choose not to feel insecure and nonconfident," "I choose not to blame others," "I choose not to overeat when bored or stressed," and "I choose not to smoke cigarettes."

Examples of pattern developmental statements include "I choose to feel confident and secure;" "I choose to relax by taking deep breaths and remembering pleasant scenes;" "I choose to take responsibility for my actions;" "I choose to replace smoking by relaxing, holding a pencil, and feeling confident about being cigarette free;" "I choose to think positively and feel confident;" "I choose to see myself as confident and see secure scenes when I'm feeling anxious;" "I choose to change any deviant sexual thoughts or fantasies;" and "I choose to eat more slowly and feel fuller with each bite." Again, note the all-powerful word "choose." With each repetition, the client realizes that he or she is in control of actions and thoughts.

The content of a statement may consist of any rational belief, a corrected irrational belief, a corrected cognitive distortion, and a futuristic goal or behavior (thoughts, emotions, and behavior). The client delivers statements with confidence. The therapist's expectations imply that the client will successfully complete the assignment and benefit greatly from doing the homework.

If the client fails to believe in the positive gains and effectiveness of the assignment, it will have limited, if any, therapeutic value. Referring back to the previous example of a naughty child writing on the blackboard 100 times, this is *punishment*. Thus, it is imperative for the therapist to construct a positive, appropriate context prior to using this intervention. The client must be "sold" on the potential benefits of writing repetitive statements rather than viewing the homework as punishment. This is a way for the client to choose to give up dysfunctional behavior that carries negative consequences and choose to learn new, positive behavior. When using the RLT with clients, the therapist should emphasize the importance of deleting old, dysfunctional behaviors and replacing them with new, healthy ways of behaving. Emphasis is also placed on the concept that one way to successfully change negative behavior is by rewriting internal "scripts." Repetitive listing is a form of reprogramming the client's "self." The introduction of the client to this technique and its rationale should be carefully timed when the client is receptive to making permanent changes in his or her life.

Repetitive writing has been successfully used with clients who are in recovery from chemical dependence and with incarcerated criminal offenders (Kohut, 2006). In these cases, the therapist helped clients to begin writing a daily journal of their thoughts, feelings, and beliefs. If a client was experiencing psychological cravings for alcohol, he or she wrote in the journal "I don't need to drink to cope with stress and unhappiness." The client was tasked to write this pattern interruption statement, filling at least two pages of the journal. In the alternative, the client was tasked to write a developmental pattern statement: "I am confident in my ability to deal with my feelings when I'm sober." The rationale for successful use of this technique with long-term criminal offenders is more difficult for several reasons: Inmates with lengthy sentences or life sentences often see no reason to change their behavior and become "prisonized" to cope with long-term life incarceration. Keeping journals and writing to obtain pattern development is much more effective with inmates who have relatively short sentences and hope for parole (Kohut).

As a homework task, RLT is very useful in the treatment of mood disorders. With depressed or dysthymic patients, the client and therapist first identify the client's internal self-talk about issues common to depression (e.g., shame and guilt, feeling helpless and hopeless to bring about change in their lives, anhedonia, sleep and appetite disturbance, inability to concentrate, and suicidal ideation that does not involve an active plan for suicide that would require an immediate intervention). Pattern interruption statements for depressed clients might include "I choose not to blame myself for my father's suicide," "I choose not to avoid social functions that I previously enjoyed," or "I choose not to believe that I can't change how I view the world and my place in it." Asking clients to repeatedly write these phrases in a journal after a therapy session targets the client's primary manifestations of the diagnostic criteria for major depression. Pattern development statements may include "I have the power to change many things about my life," "My father's decision to kill himself had nothing to do with me," or "I enjoy working in my spring flower garden."

Following this vein with affective disorders, RLT is an excellent homework task for clients suffering from an anxiety disorder. The more pattern interruption phrases that are chronicled daily in the journal, the less dread the client feels about anxiety-producing situations related to problems such as phobias, agoraphobia, panic attacks, obsessive–compulsive disorder, post-traumatic stress disorder, and acute stress disorder. The pattern interruption phrases break the cycle of the client's anxiety-producing self-talk and irrational beliefs. For example, a client with a clinically incapacitating fear of spiders might write, "I choose not to stay in the house every day because there will be spiders outside" as a pattern interruption statement. The same client might write, "There are spiders outside, but they are not going to hurt me" as a pattern development statement to ease an irrational fear of spiders.

Clients with personality disorders do fairly well with the RLT if they are motivated to change their interactions with others. Motivation, or *mindfulness,* is crucial with personality-disordered clients (Sperry, 2003). Their internal chaos and dysfunction may not allow them to form the self-discipline to use a journal, *honestly* target their pattern interruption self-talk, and form healthy pattern development statements. These clients may also lack the patience for repetitive listing. Paranoid, borderline, and narcissistic clients will resist accepting accountability for their own actions, choosing to blame others for "misunderstanding" them and lying about them. If a therapist determines that the RLT is not helpful for these patients, the task should be abandoned.

Finally, this technique is useful in the treatment of juveniles who have been diagnosed as having oppositional defiant disorder (ODD) or conduct disorder (CD). Since one of the focuses on the rehabilitation of juvenile offenders is on developing empathy, vulnerability, and morality (Bernstein, 1996), RLT can be used to extinguish undesirable patterns of behavior and teach new developmental patterns. Regardless of the type of criminal offenses and/or oppositional behavior that juveniles exhibit, relearning acceptable social behavior becomes easier when a juvenile "soaks up" new information through repetitive listing. Children diagnosed with ODD can be coaxed into compliance with RLT by utilizing prosocial statements in a nonpunitive context. It is most effective if the therapist develops a rapport with ODD adolescent clients that demonstrate a *cooperative relationship* between the therapist and the client.

Children diagnosed with ODD or CD are much more likely to develop basic empathy and morality according to society's expectations within this context of trust. Conduct disordered children will be more comfortable in revealing their vulnerability and become more willing to change their response to authority figures when they have a strong therapeutic alliance with the therapist. If the therapist is not overtly telling them how to behave as an authority figure, the ODD or CD child has no one to defy or fight with for dominance. For example, an ODD juvenile who is involved in the juvenile justice system for hacking into a government computer system would likely respond well to the therapist who says, "You should not have done what you did, but you must be really smart with computers. Can you explain to me what hypertext is?" This could go far in gaining the client's trust; the RLT homework task of developing and writing a pattern development statement in this example might be, "I choose to use my computer knowledge to help people and businesses work better."

Materials Needed

Paper; pencil or pen

Instructions

The design and implementation of repetitive listing is not difficult. The procedure consists of five basic steps:

1. Define the client's problem behaviors in very precise terms.
2. Select therapeutic goals as well as specific goals of the RLT homework task. This includes the selection of a specific pattern modality upon which to base the intervention (O'Hanlon, 1982, 1987; Yapko, 1988). A pattern modality refers to the basic patterns involved in every change process. These patterns occur in any successful therapy and are synonymous to enabling objectives that state how a task will be used to help the client achieve therapeutic goals (O'Hanlon; Yapko). For example, if a client's therapeutic goal is to remain abstinent from alcohol, the selected pattern, or enabling objective, would involve repetitive writing of the chosen phrase when the client has an urge to drink. Recognizing his or her urge to drink and then using RLT to cope with the urge is a part of the client's change process.
3. This step is the creation of an appropriate therapeutic frame that consists of both metaphors used by the therapist and the client's personal frame of reference to describe the problem behaviors. Keeney (1983) claimed that any intervention is packaged, placed, or framed by communication and context created by the therapist and the client. The frame or package of the intervention consists of providing a rational definition of the client's problems. Part of the therapeutic frame consists of selecting a specific statement or statements that logically relate to the desired goal. For example, if the therapist is working with a chronic sex offender, the repetitive phrase, "I do not have the right to force women to have sex with me" suggests the desired outcome of treatment. The therapist should also outline the parameters, or rules, of the homework assignment, such as the number of times the word or phrase must be written or the number of pages produced, and the date the homework is due. This helps ensure compliance and cooperation by the client.
4. This step is the delivery of the homework assignment to the therapist (Carich, 1990). It is important that the therapist maintain confidence that the client will complete the homework in a genuine and acceptable manner. The expectation that something important will happen in the client's life facilitates a self-fulfilling prophecy by the client.
5. The last step is monitoring the client's response, progress, and outcome of the homework task. Any response by the client is utilized towards achieving therapeutic goals. For example, a client diagnosed with antisocial personality disorder who is able to repetitively list victim "harm" statements, such as "I harm others when I steal from them," has taken a step towards achieving the goal of increasing victim empathy.

Clinicians who have successfully used RLT with clients often wonder how long they should use this therapeutic tool. There is no "set in stone" answer to this question; it can only be emphasized that the technique should be used until the patient changes the undesirable behavior or until it becomes clear to the therapist that this technique is not helpful to the client. In this case, another therapeutic approach should be considered and implemented.

Clinical Vignettes

Robert, age 17, was diagnosed with schizophrenia at age 12. He reported having auditory hallucinations of his deceased lover, who had committed suicide a year ago. In these hallucinations, Robert's former lover commanded him to commit suicide so that she and Robert would be together in the afterlife. Robert was compliant in taking antipsychotic medication; he did not present as currently psychotic. He understood that the hallucinations were not real but they were troublesome for him because he blamed himself for his lover's death by not understanding that she was suicidal. Robert partially understood that *he* was the source of the hallucinations, not his deceased lover. His guilt issues were therapeutically resolved via writing a good-bye letter to his former lover. To extinguish his pseudohallucinations, Robert was instructed to write repeatedly, "I choose not to hear Laura's voice" and "I choose not to harm myself" on several pages, front and back, as a pattern interruption statement. Robert produced a pattern development written statement: "I am only responsible for my own actions."

Robert and the therapist agreed that he would write the pattern interruption statements 50 times per day. The therapist then assessed how Robert responded to the technique; Robert indicated that writing the statements 50 times helped him come to believe their truth. Robert and the therapist agreed that Robert would now write his pattern development statement 50 times per day. He reported to the therapist that repeatedly writing the pattern development statement every day gave him something positive to do and to focus on emotionally. Since Robert brought his journal with him to his twice-weekly therapy sessions, the therapist could see that he complied with the RLT homework task. At this point, Robert and the therapist developed a list of other distressing behaviors and beliefs, and he selected the next pattern interruption statement of "I choose not to isolate myself at home." Robert continued to use the RLT homework task with each of his clinically significant negative self-talk. The changes made in Robert's emotional state were attributed to a combination of successful RLT, individual therapy, and medication.

Another example of RLT involves Jack, age 41, a chronic substance abuser who had served time in prison; Jack was on parole for drug trafficking. He feared that he would return to using drugs and alcohol. Most of his crimes involved substance abuse; he was involved in drug trafficking to support his own addictions. Jack identified two problem areas: his persistent desire to use substances and his response to peer pressure to use. To facilitate change in both areas, Jack was asked to write in his journal four to five pages each with these statements: "I choose not to use drugs" and "I have the power to say no to drugs and alcohol." The first statement is a pattern interruption phrase, while the second is a pattern development statement. Jack's initial response to RLT was skeptical; he questioned whether this homework would help him abstain from drugs and alcohol. He also stated that he did not like to write, and that the RLT homework task sounded "boring." He agreed to try RLT and determine if it was helpful for him. Being on parole, Jack said, required him to fully comply with treatment goals and techniques. The therapist explained that the RLT was *not punitive* in nature, and that it was his choice to decide what interventions were helpful for him in staying sober.

The following session, Jack reported feeling "relieved." He completed the RLT homework, and whenever he felt tempted to drink or use drugs, he wrote both statements in his journal; he wrote the statements more often than he initially had agreed to do. Jack stated that he took his journal with him to daily Alcoholics Anonymous meetings and told others about the RLT. One member chastised him for using anything other than the AA "Big Book" in his recovery; Jack reported that he responded calmly that he reads the Big Book every day and that if he wanted to use the RLT to help him abstain, that was his business.

Jack believed that the RLT homework was helpful to him at this time, but he was uncertain about its effectiveness for him over the long term. He and the therapist discussed his irrational beliefs about using drugs and drinking, and Jack agreed to continue the task until he had developed pattern interruption statements and pattern development statements for each irrational thought that led to relapse in the past. Once that treatment goal was accomplished, the therapist explained, Jack could use RLT anytime he felt the need to do so.

During the course of therapy, Jack reported increased feelings of self-worth because of confidence in his choice to personally direct his behavior rather than react to peer pressure. When Jack was released on parole, one of his conditions of parole was that he would provide random urinalysis. He was tested eight times in one year, and he was "clean" each time. He was able to manage the stress and challenges in his life without using drugs and alcohol.

Of course, the real test of the effectiveness of the RLT can only be measured when the client is exposed to the previously problematic behaviors. For example, a client with anger management problems uses RLT by writing, "Screaming and honking my horn won't move traffic any faster" (pattern interruption statement) and writing, "I will use my stress relief techniques" (pattern development statement).

Suggestions for Follow-Up

In both these vignettes, periodic follow-up would focus on whether or not the behavior changes experienced by the clients were lasting or if they were fleeting. Jack was on parole. Inmates and parolees often say and do what they believe is expected of them to secure or maintain their release. "Tell them what they want to hear" is part of inmates' code of behavior (Kohut, 2007). Re-offense would certainly be an indicator that the client failed to internalize the phrases used in the RLT homework tasks or was indeed simply telling the mental health professionals what the client believed they wanted to hear. Jack's parole officer should not relax his or her vigilance on Jack's potential to return to drug offending.

Robert suffered from schizophrenia; as long as he took his antipsychotic medication and kept using the RLT that had helped him previously, his prognosis is good. However, a major difficulty in working with schizophrenic clients is that they tend not to be compliant in treatment over the long term and symptoms reoccur. Follow-up with Robert should focus on treatment compliance as a whole.

Clients with mood and/or personality disorders and juveniles diagnosed with CD or ODD can continue using RLT as long as they believe it helps them. Clients suffering from depression tend to be faithful in continued use of RLT since they are usually motivated to bring about life changes. With substance abusers, relapse prevention is a perpetual challenge; if they make the choice to drink and use drugs again, they tend to stop even attempting to become abstinent (Kohut, 2006). The RLT is not effective as a stand-alone treatment for substance abuse or dependence; to be successful, it must be combined with therapy interventions such as group treatment, individual treatment, a 12-step program, or inpatient hospitalization.

On the other end of the effectiveness spectrum, juveniles with ODD or CD may comply initially with a variety of treatment tasks, including RLT homework, but they do not do well after treatment. Once they are off the "radarscope" of the juvenile justice system, they tend not to follow up with learned therapeutic interventions and are likely to re-offend (Kohut, 2007).

One method of assisting a client to internalize the RLT concepts prior to the end of treatment is to have the client stop the task, and then assess the client's mood and behavior. If symptoms return fairly rapidly (within 2–3 weeks prior to discharge), it is likely that the pattern development statements were not fully internalized. Other methods include role-playing where the therapist describes a problematic behavior and the client assists him or her in devising pattern interruption and development statements; if the client is able to do this, it is likely then that he or she has internalized the RLT concepts.

The RLT should never be the sole homework task within the client's treatment plan. Other tasks such as practicing stress and anger management, educational reading material, and completing relevant workbooks are all effective homework tasks that can be combined with therapy and increase the possibility of genuine internalization of the RLT concepts.

Contraindications for Use

Typically, the RLT homework task is not effective with actively psychotic patients or with clients who are not motivated to comply with the task. It can work well with depressed, suicidal patients who are stable enough to actively work towards behavioral change. These clients must be monitored continuously for suicidal behavior. This technique is only useful with the treatment-compliant patient and should be used in conjunction with other types of therapeutic interventions. The RLT should not be used as the sole form of therapy; it must be incorporated into the client's overall treatment plan as a homework task and an intervention (Haley, 1967, 1973, 1976; O'Hanlon, 1987; Yapko, 1988). The technique is meant to access and use as many experiential domains as possible (cognitive, emotional, behavioral, social or interpersonal, spiritual, biopsychosocial, and contextual).

Noncompliance with one or several forms of treatment (RLT, therapy, and medication) most likely means that either the client is unmotivated with any form of treatment or the treatment plan does not adequately address the client's needs and should be revised. One way to increase a client's motivation is for the therapist to compliment and otherwise notice that the client has made some positive differences in cognitions and behaviors. Of course, RLT is contraindicated for any client who simply finds no benefit from the technique; the client and the therapist together can discuss and implement new strategies for treatment of the client's presenting problem.

Conclusion

The relevant literature supports the repetitive listing technique as a way to help a client alter problematic behavior through pattern interruption and pattern development. The technique is especially helpful with those who are sincere in wanting to change inappropriate behavior and develop healthy, acceptable behavior. The RLT can be used for in-patient psychiatric patients, outpatient mental health patients, juveniles, and incarcerated offenders with equal effectiveness.

References

Bernstein, N. (1996). *Treating the unmanageable adolescent.* Lanham, MD: Roman and Littlefield.

Carich, M. S. (1990). Utilizing task assignments within Adlerian therapy. *Individual Psychology, 46*(2), 217–224.

Chamberlain, J. M. (1982). *Eliminate your SDBs.* Provo, UT: Brigham Young University Press.

Cudney, M. R. (1975). *Eliminate self-defeating behaviors.* Kalamazoo, MI: Life Giving Enterprises.

Haley, J. (Ed.). (1967). *Advanced techniques of hypnosis and therapy.* New York: Grune & Stratton.

Haley, J. (1973). *Uncommon therapy: The psychiatric techniques of Milton H. Erickson, M.D.* New York: W. W. Norton.

Haley, J. (1976). *Problem solving therapy.* San Francisco, CA: Jossey–Bass.

Keeney, B. P. (1983). *Aesthetics of change.* New York: Guilford.

Kohut, M. R. (2006). *ITT Technical Institute criminal justice course 436: Crime and substance abuse.* Indianapolis, IN: Pearson Custom Learning Solutions.

Kohut, M. R. (2007). *ITT Technical Institute criminal justice course 439: The juvenile justice system.* Indianapolis, IN: Pearson Custom Learning Solutions.

O'Hanlon, W. H. (1982). Splitting and linking: Two generic patterns in Ericksonian therapy. *Journal of Strategic and Systemic Therapies, 1*(4), 21–25.

O'Hanlon, W. H. (1987). *Taproots: The underlying principles of Milton H. Erickson's therapy and hypnosis.* New York: W. W. Norton.

Sperry, L. (2003). *Handbook of diagnosis and treatment of DSM-IV-R personality disorders.* New York: Brunner–Routledge.

Waldren, T. (1985). Eliminating self-defeating behavior workshop. Lubbock, TX.

Yapko, M. D. (1988). *When living hurts: Directives for treating depression.* New York: Brunner/Mazel.

Professional Readings and Resources

American Institute for Cognitive Therapy. www.cognitivetherapynyc.com.

Criminal and addictive thinking. (2002). Center City, MN: Minnesota Department of Corrections and the Hazelden Foundation.

Flora, R. (2001). *How to work with sex offenders: A handbook for criminal justice, human service and mental health professionals.* Binghamton, NY: Haworth.

National Association of Cognitive Behavioral Therapy. www.nacbt.org/.

Pallone, N. (Ed.). (2003). *Treating substance abusers in correctional contexts: New understandings, new modalities.* Binghamton, NY: Haworth.

Scharf, R. (2007). Psychotherapy. Microsoft Encarta. Redmond, WA: Microsoft Corporation.

Bibliotherapy Sources for the Client

Cash, A. (2002). *Psychology for dummies.* Hoboken, NJ: Wiley.

Chamberlain, J. M. (1982). *Eliminate your SDBs.* Provo, UT: Brigham Young University Press.

Johnston, J. (2003). *The complete idiot's guide to psychology.* New York: Alpha Books.

Wikipedia, the Free Encyclopedia (2007). www.wikipedia.com. Cognitive behavioral therapy.

– 9 –

The Sexual Beliefs Checklist

Michelle T. Mannino[*] and Teresa L. Young[†]

Type of Contribution: Activity, Handout

Objective

The objective for this activity is for heterosexual, lesbian, and gay couples presenting with sexual concerns to explore sexual myths to which they may subscribe. The goal is to expose possible limiting factors that may be affecting the quality of the couple's sexual relationship. It is hoped that, after identifying various sexual myths, discussions will take place regarding where the couple received the messages that contributed to the erroneous beliefs. Further discussion will ultimately lead therapists and clients to narrate a preferred sexual future for the couple.

The objectives are as follows:

- To identify sexual myths subscribed to by each individual in the relationship
- To compare and contrast the responses between the couple
- To begin a dialogue between individuals in the relationship regarding sexual expectations or beliefs
- To identify the possible sources of the sexual beliefs (e.g., "Where did you learn that sexual activity always includes vaginal intercourse?")
- To identify which myths the couple deems as a problem and determine which are most problematic
- To identify the possible impact the sexual belief is having on the couple's relationship (both sexual and nonsexual)
- To have clients discuss how they would rewrite the myths to better fit their relationship
- To move clients into discussion regarding their preferred sexual futures that includes articulating what they *want* sexually versus what they *do not want*

Rationale for Use

This activity is greatly influenced by a social constructionist framework. Social constructionism, sometimes referred to as the postmodern movement, refers to the idea that individuals use language to construct meaning in their lives. A fixed, universal reality is considered an illusion, as an individual is thought to actively participate in the creation of his or her perceived reality. Western culture is saturated with sexual "realities" and ideals that often become the scripts that one follows. As such, when individuals do not live up to these cultural expectations, they may perceive themselves as failures. Doan states that "the definition of abnormality is being made on the basis of deviation from a socially constructed grand narrative that represents what our culture determines 'should' be the case, rather than on the basis of actual experiences and behaviors" (2004, p. 153). This realization affords clients an exciting opportunity to make what they always believed *should* be in their sexual lives what they *want* it to be.

---

[*] denotes equal authorship
[†] denotes equal authorship

One of the most pervasive sexual myths is that sex equals intercourse. In other words, individuals and couples often believe that (1) intimate activity that does not involve vaginal intercourse (for heterosexual and lesbian couples) or anal intercourse (for gay couples) is not really "sex," and (2) all intimate activity should and must lead to intercourse. There are various problems with the "sex equals intercourse" myth. Primarily, this myth serves to limit the vast possibilities for sexuality and intimacy. Couples may not even consider or explore other means of sexual expression such as oral stimulation and sensual touch. Furthermore, Tiefer discusses the burden that is placed upon men and women when they endorse the myth that penile erections are "the essence of men's sexual function and satisfaction" (2004, p. 363). The belief that a woman cannot be sexually satisfied without vaginal penetration leads to unnecessary performance pressure on men. It may also burden women in that they may be intimidated to vocalize other sexual interests that do not involve intercourse for fear that they might be rejected. Identifying the sexual myths that a couple endorses allows them greater freedom to explore the way that they would like their sexual relationship to be.

This idea—that people have the ability to "write" their preferred sexual stories and edit them as they go along—is concordant with what O'Hanlon (2004) refers to as "possibility therapy." Possibility therapy asserts that the past is influential, but does not ultimately cause one's behavior in the present. Individuals have choices about the direction their lives will take. O'Hanlon states that "people are influenced by their sense of what is possible for their future" (p. 2). As one talks about sexual myths and explores new ways of thinking about one's sexuality, new possibilities have the potential to become new realities.

Finally, for those couples who have not had open conversations regarding their sexuality, discussing the sexual myths may afford them the opportunity to begin this dialogue in a safe, therapeutic atmosphere. Additionally, couples will often find it easier or more natural to tell their partner what they *do not* enjoy or what they want them to *stop* doing instead of telling them what they *do* enjoy or what they want them to *start* doing. Individuals may also make the assumption that their partner will automatically know what is pleasing (Lankton, 2004). However, individuals are not mind readers and can greatly benefit from having honest dialogue with their partner regarding sexual desires. Upon deciding which sexual myths are adversely affecting the relationship, the couple may then come together to decide how they want to "rewrite" the myths. This presents an opportunity for the partners to share what they want instead of commenting on what they do not want.

Instructions

The sexual beliefs checklist can be used with any couple who would like to discuss their sexual relationship. It might be particularly beneficial in instances when the therapist recognizes that certain sexual cognitions or scripts are limiting the couple's sex life or causing distress. It is recommended as an activity during a session; it should be completed with both partners in the room together, but filled out separately. Prior to presenting the handouts, the therapist may briefly explain the purpose of the activity to the couple. The following is a sample statement:

> I thought it might be helpful to look at some of your beliefs about sex since you mentioned that this is an area of concern in your relationship. I have a handout that I'd like each of you to take a minute to fill out individually, and then we'll come together to discuss your answers. The handout has a list of statements about sex and sexuality. You will check whether or not you agree with the statements. Try to be as honest as possible and not to worry about your partner's answers. You'll each have the opportunity to share and explain your responses. This will serve as a good starting point for our discussion.

After the couple has finished, you can inform them that the handout they just completed was actually a list of commonly endorsed sexual myths. To normalize the task, you should mention that most individuals agree with some of these statements and that it is not important how many answers the partners got "right" or "wrong." Ask the couple to indicate what statement caught their eye or where they would like to begin. It is not necessary to go in any particular order or to get through the entire checklist in one session. It is actually recommended to focus on one to three statements per session in order to have a thorough, in-depth discussion. Progress is not necessarily made by "getting through" the statements; rather, progress is indicated in that the couple is having new conversations. Some questions that may spark conversation include:

- Where were these ideas presented to you? Where did you receive these messages?
- How did the family you grew up in influence these ideas?
- How does your culture, race, ethnicity, or religion have an impact on how you feel?
- What societal expectations regarding being male or female have guided your way of thinking?
- How do these beliefs impact your relationship with your partner?
- For which items do you notice you have different responses?
- How do you handle disagreements about these areas of your sexuality?
- What does it mean to you that you have disagreements in these areas?
- If you could change these statements, how would you make them different?
- For which items do you notice you have similar responses?
- How do your similar ideas positively affect your relationship and your sex life? How so?
- What does it mean to you that you have similarities in these areas?

Some clients may find that they have very similar responses, while others may find that they have very different responses. It is important to emphasize that couples who have more similar responses are not necessarily at an advantage to those who have more differences and vice versa. It may be helpful to have a conversation regarding the items in which the couple has the highest consensus and the items in which they most strongly disagree. This will promote a sharing of ideas so that the partners can begin to deepen their understanding of one another's experiences.

While these conversations are intended to enhance intimacy, speaking about differences may also produce anxiety and tension. In such circumstances, the therapist can ask each partner to elaborate and discuss the meaning behind the differences. For example, if a couple disagrees about the statement that "women should refrain from vocalizing their sexual desires," the therapist might ask each partner to discuss what deeper meaning the disagreement plays in the relationship. In this example, the partner who feels that he or she should be able to vocalize his or her sexual desires may feel powerless in other areas of the relationship. As such, the disagreement represents feelings of inequality. The therapist can then process these emotions with the couple to facilitate further understanding and to create an environment of emotional safety.

Many clients will discover or have a hunch that the list of statements involves sexual myths. In our experience, the discussion was not hindered by a client asking, "Aren't these all common myths that I'm supposed to disagree with?" In this instance, it is fine to joke with your clients by saying something like, "I guess I can't pull one over on you!" You can then ask if it would be all right to discuss the statements anyway. It might also be beneficial to let your clients know that recognizing that something is a myth does not make one immune to endorsing it. In other words, a client may be able to say, "I know this one is false," but may have feelings or display behaviors in accordance to the myth. Also, it may be appropriate to let your clients know that ascribing to a myth does not make a person foolish or naïve. A brief conversation regarding how these myths are engrained in our culture may lessen this sense of embarrassment.

Clinical Vignette

Background of Couple

Donna and Charlie, ages 32 and 36 respectively, sought couples counseling because after 10 years of marriage they felt more like friends than lovers. At the beginning of their relationship, Donna reported that they had made love several times a week, whereas at the time of therapy they were only intimate twice a month. Both considered that parenting their two small children, ages 2 and 5, could be a factor in the decline of intimacy. Donna initiated therapy, indicating that their lack of sexual activity was making her feel "unattractive" and "unwanted." Charlie reported that he had not lost attraction to Donna, but that the long hours at the office were to blame.

The couple shared the mutual goal of "resparking" sexual interest. However, whenever Donna and Charlie began discussing the matter during a session, a fight would ensue. Most fights involved the "blame game" during which Donna would accuse Charlie of not finding her attractive because he did not initiate sex. When she initiated sex, Donna found it insulting that Charlie would at times turn her down. She also mentioned that during foreplay, she felt as though Charlie was only touching and kissing her in order to get her aroused for intercourse. Charlie would blame Donna by arguing that he wished she could be more spontaneous. Charlie also stated that he was frustrated that Donna could not consistently achieve orgasm via intercourse.

Use of Activity

The therapist gave Donna and Charlie each a copy of the handout. She let them know that it might be beneficial to begin having conversations regarding their general sexual beliefs. After they completed the checklist, Donna stated that she knew that the answers should be false, but that she still felt like some of the areas were a problem in their relationship. The therapist stated that Donna was correct in that the statements were indeed common sexual myths and complimented her on her honesty in recognizing that she may indeed endorse some of the beliefs.

Donna reported that she had left statement number two (that men are always ready for sex) blank. The therapist asked her why she had not responded to that item. Donna stated that she knew the answer was false, but that she also felt that Charlie should want sex when she was "in the mood." She described feeling "embarrassed" and "self-conscious" when he would turn her down. Charlie responded that he genuinely felt too tired or overwhelmed by work and that it had nothing to do with his attraction to her. He also pointed out that there were times when Donna had turned down his advances. Donna acknowledged that at times she, too, felt "too exhausted" to have sex. She began to wonder aloud if she might actually endorse myth number two. The therapist asked Donna where she might have learned that men are always ready for sex. Donna spent several minutes reflecting on how men are portrayed in the media as always wanting sex.

The discussion turned to Charlie's answers. He explained that he agreed with number seven (that the purpose of foreplay is to help a woman become aroused). Donna reacted strongly, saying, "This is what I was talking about. Whenever we are fooling around I get the sense that Charlie is rushing it and only kissing me so that we can have intercourse." Charlie responded, "You're always complaining that we don't have enough sex. Now you're saying there isn't enough foreplay." The therapist asked, "Now that we have heard some complaints regarding what you don't want, could you both tell me what you *do* want regarding foreplay?" Donna explained that she likes to think of foreplay not as a "means to an end" (e.g., intercourse), but rather as an enjoyable act in of itself. She asked Charlie if he could take more time kissing her without checking to see if she was aroused. Charlie was excited to feel that he finally knew what Donna wanted. When asked what he needed from Donna, Charlie indicated that he would like to know that what he is doing is pleasurable. This way, he would not feel as though he needed to check for himself, making Donna feel as though he was only interested in intercourse. Donna agreed, stating that she would try to be more vocal about her satisfaction.

In subsequent sessions, Donna and Charlie discussed other myths, including Donna's belief that a man should initiate sex and Charlie's beliefs that sex is only enjoyable when it is unplanned and that a woman should orgasm via vaginal intercourse.

Suggestions for Follow-Up

It is suggested that the therapist encourage his or her clients to continue their discussions regarding sexual beliefs outside therapy. It is hoped that this open dialogue will generate new possibilities within the couple's sexual and nonsexual relationship. The therapist can check in with the clients regarding any changes that they have noticed since their initial discussion. The therapist can also encourage "couch sessions" after sex to further encourage more open communication regarding sexual issues.

Contraindications for Use

Therapists need to be aware of clients' cultural beliefs when deciding to utilize the sexual beliefs checklist. It may not be appropriate to challenge or expand myths that go against one's cultural beliefs when both partners indicate that the belief does not harm the relationship. Therapists must also generally use caution to not impose their own sexual values via this activity. This may easily happen if both partners endorse a belief that goes against that of the therapist. A therapist in this situation can gather information about how this belief affects the relationship; however, upon discovering that the couple is content with the belief and its impact on the relationship, the therapist should not insist that the couple change their way of thinking. Questions in the sexual beliefs checklist can be modified or eliminated to fit the clients' values.

Finally, this activity is appropriate for use with heterosexual, lesbian, and gay couples. Please refer to letter following the title of each handout. Handout 9.1A is for heterosexual couples, Handout 9.1B is for lesbian couples, and Handout 9.1C is for gay couples.

References

Doan, R. E. (2004). Who really wants to sleep with the medical model? An eclectic/narrative approach to sex therapy. In S. Green & D. Flemons (Eds.), *Quickies: The handbook of brief sex therapy* (pp. 151–170). New York: Norton.

Lankton, C. (2004). Shining light on intimacy and sexual pleasure. In S. Green & D. Flemons (Eds.), *Quickies: The handbook of brief sex therapy* (pp. 45–67). New York: Norton.

O'Hanlon, B. (2004). Come again? From possibility therapy to sex therapy. In S. Green & D. Flemons (Eds.), *Quickies: The handbook of brief sex therapy* (pp. 1–14). New York: Norton.

Tiefer, L. (1994). The medicalization of impotence: Normalizing phallocentrism. *Gender and Society, 8,* 363–377.

Professional Readings and Resources

Green, S., & Flemons, D. (Eds.). (2004). *Quickies: The handbook of brief sex therapy.* New York: Norton.

Kleinplatz, P. (2001). *New directions in sex therapy: Innovations and alternatives.* New York: Guilford.

Leiblum, S. R. (2006). *Principles and practice of sex therapy* (4th ed.). Philadelphia: Brunner–Routledge.

Bibliotherapy Sources for the Client

Heiman, J., LoPiccolo, J., & Palladini, D. (1988). *Becoming orgasmic.* New York: Prentice Hall.

Joannides, P. (2004). *Guide to getting it on.* Waldport, OR: Goofy Foot Press.

Handout 9.1A: The Sexual Beliefs Checklist

Following is a list of statements regarding sex and sexuality. Read the statement and decide if you agree or disagree. Place a checkmark in the appropriate box.

Sexual Belief	Agree	Somewhat Agree	Somewhat Disagree	Disagree
1. Sex should always include intercourse.				
2. A man should always be ready for sex.				
3. A woman should be able to achieve orgasm via vaginal intercourse.				
4. A woman should refrain from vocalizing her sexual desires.				
5. It is the man's responsibility to initiate sex.				
6. "Good" sex always ends in an orgasm.				
7. The purpose of foreplay is to help a woman become aroused for intercourse.				
8. Sex has to be spontaneous to be enjoyable.				
9. A "real" man can "go all night."				
10. Sex is less exciting the longer a couple is together.				
11. A woman should always be ready and available for sex.				
12. A man should refrain from vocalizing his sexual desires.				
13. A woman should be able to have multiple orgasms.				
14. Vaginal orgasms are better than clitoral orgasms.				
15. Erotica and pornography should be enjoyed by men but not women.				
16. A couple should not talk about their sexual needs and desires "outside the bedroom."				
17. To be a "good" lover a person must be turned on by multiple means of sexual expression (i.e., oral sex, anal sex, swinging, threesomes, sex toys, fetishes, etc.).				
18. A person should fantasize only about his or her partner during lovemaking.				
19. If a man or woman is in a relationship, he or she should not masturbate.				
20. If a couple loves each other, "good" sex should come naturally.				

Handout 9.1B: The Sexual Beliefs Checklist

Following is a list of statements regarding sex and sexuality. Read the statement and decide if you agree or disagree. Place a checkmark in the appropriate box.

Sexual Belief	Agree	Somewhat Agree	Somewhat Disagree	Disagree
1. "Good" sex always ends in an orgasm.				
2. "Good" sex involves one partner taking on a butch role and the other a fem role.				
3. Sex has to be spontaneous in order to be enjoyable.				
4. Women should refrain from vocalizing their sexual desires.				
5. One partner should always be responsible for initiating sex.				
6. Sex should always include vaginal penetration.				
7. Kissing and touching should lead to other forms of sex.				
8. Women should be able to achieve orgasm via vaginal penetration.				
9. Sex is less exciting the longer a couple is together.				
10. Women should always be ready and available for sex.				
11. The older women become the less sex they have.				
12. Women should be able to have multiple orgasms.				
13. Having children reduces sex drive.				
14. If a woman does not become easily lubricated, she is not turned on by her partner.				
15. Erotica or pornography is always harmful to a relationship.				
16. A couple should not talk about their sexual needs and desires "outside the bedroom."				
17. To be "good" lovers women must be turned on by multiple means of sexual expression (i.e., swinging, threesomes, sex toys, fetishes, etc.).				
18. Women should fantasize only about their partner during lovemaking.				
19. If a woman is in a relationship, she should not masturbate.				
20. If a couple loves each other, "good" sex should come naturally.				

Handout 9.1C: The Sexual Beliefs Checklist

Following is a list of statements regarding sex and sexuality. Read the statement and decide if you agree or disagree. Place a checkmark in the appropriate box.

Sexual Belief	Agree	Somewhat Agree	Somewhat Disagree	Disagree
1. Sex should always include anal intercourse.				
2. Men should always be ready for sex.				
3. Men should be able to achieve orgasm via anal intercourse.				
4. Men should refrain from vocalizing their sexual desires.				
5. One partner should always be responsible for initiating sex.				
6. "Good" sex always ends in an orgasm.				
7. The purpose of foreplay is to help a man become aroused.				
8. Sex has to be spontaneous to be enjoyable.				
9. "Real" men can "go all night."				
10. Sex is less exciting the longer a couple is together.				
11. The larger the penis, the better the lover.				
12. The older men become, the less sex they have.				
13. A "good" lover is able to have sex multiple times in a row.				
14. All men enjoy erotica and pornography.				
15. A couple should not talk about their sexual needs and desires "outside the bedroom."				
16. To be a "good" lover a man must be turned on by multiple means of sexual expression (i.e., oral sex, anal sex, swinging, threesomes, sex toys, fetishes, etc.).				
17. Men should fantasize only about their partner during lovemaking.				
18. If a man is in a relationship, he should not masturbate.				
19. If a couple loves each other, "good" sex should come naturally.				
20. Fatherhood reduces sex drive.				

– 10 –

Writing a Letter to Your Sexual Self

Tiffani S. Kisler and F. Scott Christopher

Type of Contribution: Activity

Objective

Writing a letter to one's sexual self is a useful technique for addressing issues of sexuality such as sexual identity, sexual history, sexual functioning, and sexual satisfaction and dissatisfaction. The objective of using the sexual self letter is to enable clients to address sensitive topics and begin a discussion of aspects of their sexuality. Specifically, the purpose of this activity is for clients to be able to express their feelings about their own sexuality and work through issues as they relate to the client's sexual self. This activity is open ended so that clients may take any direction they choose with their letter. For example, clients could potentially focus on anatomy, physiology, sexual attitudes, sexual satisfaction, sexual enjoyment, sexual dissatisfaction, interactions with their partner, past abuse, or current victimization experiences. Moreover, the therapist can use this letter to gain insight into how the client sees his or her sexuality by the focus of the writing (reproductive, pleasure, pain, infidelity, guilt, anxiety, etc.).

In addition, the letter to one's sexual self may provide clients with an opportunity to express and explore relational, social, and cultural contexts for their expression of sexuality. Clients can gain insight into the dyadic nature of their sexual issues. Alternatively, clients can be encouraged to challenge their own beliefs about sexuality and expand their comfort level by engaging in a discussion of a range of sexual concerns. Recognizing that there are alternative sexual belief systems to those expressed in one's letter can facilitate therapeutic insight.

Rationale for Use

Sexuality is a sensitive and often private matter, and aspects of sexuality can often be very difficult for clients to discuss. Individuals' discomfort regarding their sexuality may prevent an open dialogue from occurring when therapeutic issues exist. Moreover, many clients are unaware of ways to express feelings because they have not developed a language to discuss issues pertaining to their sexuality, sexual functioning, sexual preferences, and sexual satisfaction or dissatisfaction, to name a few. In other cases, sexual issues can be difficult to disclose because they are so emotionally charged. This can include problems of sexual dysfunction, sexual abuse, sexual victimization as an adult or a child, or sexual difficulties in a relationship.

Clients may develop a sense of secrecy about their sexuality difficulties that consequently contributes to feelings of guilt and shame. In fact, clients may have been raised in families where it was forbidden to discuss sexual issues. These prohibitions may make it difficult to take the first step to address issues of sexuality and sexual functioning by initiating a conversation with a therapist in a face-to-face interaction.

Operating from a narrative perspective and influenced by social constructivist schools of thought, problems are seen as the performance of oppressive, dominant stories or knowledge (Foucault, 1980, 1984; White & Epston, 1990). Specifically, the writings of French philosopher

Michel Foucault exposed how there are certain stories about life perpetuated as "truths" by the dominant culture that maintain a society's power structure and eliminate alternative accounts of the same event. People evaluate themselves (i.e., what it means to be successful, worthwhile, attractive, well functioning) against a standard set by those who are considered to hold expert power in society (i.e., doctors, clergy, celebrities, therapists, politicians). Individuals in society who hold power control the social discourse and determine what knowledge is held to be true, while the beliefs and voices of others are marginalized. This so-called knowledge can result in the labels people are identified with, such as "sick," "mentally ill," "dysfunctional," and "perverted," to name a few. Narrative therapy examines oppressive factors and aims to liberate people from forces of oppression.

According to a narrative perspective, there is no one set reality; stories are constructed in the interactions between people, and if stories can be constructed, they can be reconstructed (see White & Epston, 1990, for a review). Basically, people give meaning to their lives by plotting their experiences into stories. However, often people hold narrow and self-defeating views of themselves and the world around them. Moreover, people often fail to attend to experiences that are counter to the dominant story they hold. Narrative therapy attempts to reexamine the stories that form the basis for the way people live their lives and aims to help people rewrite their stories by including previously neglected bits of vital information that contradict the dominant narratives they have been using to give meaning to their experiences (Freedman, Epston, & Lobovits, 1997; White & Epston, 1992).

Issues of sexuality are largely influenced by beliefs in the dominant culture (i.e., homosexuality as a mental illness prior to 1973), and as cultural and societal beliefs change, so do our constructions of sexuality in terms of what is acceptable, what is "normal," what is "functional," and what is satisfying, dissatisfying, or deviant. At the same time, it is important to note that there are legal and moral strictures on sexual behavior in our society. Many of these focus on individuals' use of manipulation and force to achieve sexual goals on others who are either unwilling or unable to give their consent. Examples of this include child abuse and sexual assault. These legal and moral strictures are important for the protection of society and therapists are ethically and legally bound to operate within these strictures.

Taking influence from a narrative therapeutic perspective, the sexual self letter can be a starting point to have clients begin to rewrite the story of their sexuality and break free from the potentially oppressive forces constructed by society's beliefs about sexuality within the limits already described. To further this aim, the letter to one's sexual self can become a form of externalizing so that the focal point of the discussion is the letter rather than the client. This distance can help initiate discussions that can lead clients to explore their sexuality from a safe and less vulnerable place. As clients address issues of sexuality while writing and rewriting their stories, they can liberate themselves from oppressive forces such as feelings of secrecy, guilt, anger, and shame.

Instructions

As a way to introduce this activity it may be helpful to begin with some variation of the following preface. "Talking about issues relating to one's sexuality can sometimes be difficult to initiate. One method that has been helpful to enter into this dialogue is to begin by writing a letter to your sexual self." While some individuals like to begin by writing a letter, others prefer to chart their sexual history, or sexual self, into a life story that places their experiences, attitudes, beliefs, and values within a context. The instructions for this activity are as follows:

> Write a letter to your sexual self. The letter can take any form you like and may be handwritten or typed. Aim for it to be at least three pages in length, but you can make it as long as you wish. If you would like potential ideas of where to begin your letter you may use the sexual self handout to guide the process [see Handout 10.1 at the end of this chapter]. In some cases,

individuals may prefer to verbally share the "sexual life story" of their sexual self rather than writing a letter. The timeline for your "life story" is open; you can choose to begin your story at childhood and tell up through the present time, or you may opt to focus on a specific period in life (i.e., adolescence, adulthood, postmenopause, etc.), a relationship with a particular partner, or a specific sexual experience. Choose the option that you feel most comfortable with and believe will best suit you. Feel free to let your feelings and ideas flow. Do not worry about grammar, spelling, punctuation, or structure. This is not a "graded" assignment, but one that will allow you to begin to share your thoughts, feelings, and experiences.

Brief Clinical Vignette

Lauren (36) presented for therapy reporting "relationship issues" with her husband, Michael (34), of 10 years. Lauren attempted to get Michael to agree to go for couples therapy. Michael, however, repeatedly refused, believing that Lauren was the one who needed help. Upon meeting with the therapist, Lauren reported that "communication" and "intimacy" were the couple's main concerns. With further exploration, Lauren revealed that she and her husband had not had sexual intercourse in 4 years and were currently sleeping in separate bedrooms. Lauren reported that the separate bedrooms were not planned but evolved out of the need for a restful sleep. Michael often snored loudly and Lauren was a light sleeper. At this time, the therapist explored with Lauren how she would like her sexual relationship with her husband to be, assessing for aspects of her relationship that she would like to have stay the same and aspects that she hoped would change. During this process, Lauren reported that she wanted to have a more physically and emotionally intimate sexual relationship but did not know how to achieve it. Lauren reported being in a rut, and the thought of getting out of the rut caused more anxiety than keeping the routine. Lauren had difficulty talking with Michael about sexual issues, and she did not talk to her female friends about sexual issues either. She reported feeling very anxious when talking about this subject. The therapist asked Lauren if she would be interested in expressing some of her feelings in writing as a way to begin a dialogue about her sexual concerns and feelings. Lauren agreed to write a letter to her sexual self.

The following session Lauren returned with her letter. The therapist explored what the process of the letter writing was like for her. Laruen reported at first that it took her a long time to get started on the writing. She said she felt embarrassed addressing issues that she had not expressed before. After Lauren began writing, she said her emotions and the words kept flowing, resulting in a five-page letter. Lauren reported that the assignment was actually very cathartic for her. The therapist asked Lauren her preference as to who would read the letter. Lauren reported that she would like the therapist to read the letter.

The therapist noticed different themes throughout Lauren's letter. It began by focusing on issues of anatomy, specifically referring to health issues and problems of infertility. Part way through the letter, the tenor changed to one of frustration. In the letter, Lauren revealed her feelings regarding a major event that took place 4 years in the past when, as a result of cervical cancer, Lauren was told that she would not be able to have children. While Lauren was successfully treated for the cancer (there has been no evidence of it returning), it was not long after this that Lauren and Michael moved into separate bedrooms. In her letter, Lauren voiced anger at the cancer as it drove a wedge between herself and her husband.

Lauren went on to discuss confusion about her sexual expression now that children were out of the picture. Lauren was raised a strict Catholic, and deep down she still had some residual feelings that sex was for procreation, and outside of that purpose Lauren experienced guilt. In the letter, Lauren also reported concern that being intimate with her husband would only be a painful reminder that they are childless and will not be able to have children of their own. Lauren apologized in the letter for letting her husband down and expressed extreme disappointment at not being able to fulfill her role as a wife. She identified that in a way she was punishing herself by remaining distant from Michael, believing she did not deserve closeness from him. Lauren reported fear that her anxiety about discussing her feelings about their sexual relationship could ultimately lead to losing her husband. She wanted to share her feelings but lacked a language common with her husband and did not feel comfortable to begin doing so. Lauren identified the belief from childhood that "you don't talk about sexual issues." The power of the secrecy contributed to feelings of guilt and shame and kept her isolated from her partner.

After processing the letter with the therapist, Lauren came to the conclusion that the secrecy of her feelings in the marriage was isomorphic to the secrecy about sexuality from childhood. After sharing the letter with the therapist, Lauren thought it might be a good idea to break the cycle of secrecy and share the letter with her husband. Lauren reported feeling more comfortable opening up the conversation as a result of having the letter as an entry point.

Noticing a change in Lauren, Michael joined couple's therapy at session three. At this point, with the comfort and support of the therapist, Lauren shared her letter to her sexual self with Michael in session. The following sessions were used to address feelings about sexuality, anxiety, infertility, roles as a spouse, and sexual expression. The sharing of the letter led to an open dialogue about their relationship, which allowed them to begin to process their sexual feelings, communication, infertility issues, and roles within the marriage. As they began sharing with each other, they felt more connected and began to move their relationship in a direction they both wanted it to go. The couple reported feeling closer than they ever had before at termination and were enjoying a very satisfying and intimate sexual relationship.

Suggestions for Follow-Up

The letter to one's sexual self can highlight various themes, such as experiences of childhood sexual abuse, problems of sexual functioning, sexual dissatisfaction, or sexual victimization, which may be important to address throughout the course of therapy. The letter can also be used to identify positive aspects of one's sexual self and sexual relationships. The highlighted themes can guide the course of treatment through the creation of therapeutic goals. Moreover, the therapist may also use the letter to introduce topics into therapy. Throughout the course of therapy, as issues are addressed, the letter may be referred back to as a way to track change.

Throughout the course of therapy, clients can be encouraged to rewrite the story of their sexuality by rewriting their letter to their sexual self. Hence, the letter can also be used as a catalyst for change by querying clients about what direction they wish their letters would take. At later points in the course of treatment, a subsequent letter can be used to mark progress, and this second letter can be used for comparison to the original letter. This can help both the client and the therapist track the therapeutic progress as the client moves forward.

Furthermore, clients may choose to write different letters as other aspects of their sexuality are addressed, and as a way to hallmark their work on new therapeutic goals and subsequent progress. As a final step, the client and therapist may compare the initial and the final letters and discuss the process of how the letters evolved throughout the course of therapy.

Although not presented in the preceding vignette, this activity can also be used for couples wherein both partners participate in writing separate letters to their sexual self, which can then be processed during conjoint therapy. In addition, throughout the course of therapy, the couple concurrently may choose to write new letters to their sexual selves within their relationship. These new letters can provide a vision for how the couple would like to see their future sexual relationship.

Contraindications for Use

Some clients may be too uncomfortable to put their feelings about sexuality into writing. Issues of privacy may also arise, and clients may not feel safe to write the letter due to a lack of privacy. Moreover, this may not work for clients who have difficulty writing or expressing themselves in writing. Care should always be taken to ensure that a client is not illiterate before suggesting this activity.

In instances of severe sexual abuse or in cases of individuals with trust issues, it may be too painful to put down feelings in written form, or it may make the client feel too exposed or vulnerable. In this case, one may modify the task by having clients share a verbal story of their sexuality rather than writing a letter.

References

Foucault, M. (1980). *Power/knowledge: Selected interviews and other writings.* New York: Pantheon.

Foucault, M. (1984). *The history of sexuality.* Great Britain: Peregrine.

Freedman, J., Epston, D., & Lobovits, D. (1997). *Playful approaches to serious problems: Narrative therapy with children and families.* New York: Norton.

White, M., & Epston, D. (1990). *Narrative means to therapeutic ends.* New York: Norton.

White, M., & Epston, D. (1992). *Experience, contradiction, narrative, and imagination.* Adelaide, Australia: Dulwich Centre.

Professional Readings and Resources

Christopher, F. S. (2001). *To dance the dance: A symbolic interactional exploration of premarital sexuality.* Mahwah, NJ: Lawrence Erlbaum Associates.

Dolan, Y. M. (1991). *Resolving sexual abuse: Solution-focused therapy and Ericksonian hypnosis for adult survivors.* New York: Norton.

Glass, S. P., & Coppock-Staeheli, J. (2003). *Not "just friends": Rebuilding trust and recovering your sanity after infidelity.* New York: Free Press.

Harvey, J., Wenzel, A., & Sprecher, S. (Eds.) (2004). *The handbook of sexuality in close relationships.* Mahwah, NJ: Lawrence Erlbaum Associates.

Leiblum, S. (Ed.) (2007). *Principles and practices of sex therapy.* New York: Guilford.

McCarthy, B., & McCarthy, E. (2003). *Rekindling desire: A step-by-step program to help low-sex and no-sex marriages.* New York: Brunner–Routlege.

O'Hanlon, W. H., & Bertolino, R. (2002). *Even from a broken web: Brief, respectful solution-oriented therapy for sexual abuse and trauma.* New York: Norton.

Peluso, P. R. (Ed.) (2007). *Infidelity: A practitioner's guide to working with couples in crisis.* New York: Routledge.

Rosen, R. C., & Leiblum, S. R. (1995). *Case studies in sex therapy.* New York: Guilford.

Savin-Williams, R. C. (2001). *Mom, dad, I'm gay: How families negotiate coming out.* Washington, DC: American Psychological Association.

Tiefer, L. (2004). *Sex is not a natural act & other essays.* San Francisco: Westview.

White, M. (1995). *Re-authoring lives: Interviews and essays.* Adelaide: Dulwich Center Publications.

White, M., & Epston, D. (1990). *Narrative means to therapeutic ends.* New York: Norton.

Wincze, J. P., & Carey, M. (2001). *Sexual dysfunction: A guide for assessment and treatment.* New York: Guilford.

Bibliotherapy Sources for the Client

Davis, L. (1990). *The courage to heal: A guide for women and men survivors of child sexual abuse.* New York: HarperCollins.

Davis, L. (1991). *Allies in healing: When the person you love was sexually abused as a child.* New York: HarperCollins.

Grubman-Black, S. D. (2002). *Broken boys/mending men: Recovery from childhood sexual abuse.* Caldwell, NJ: Blackburn Press.

Lew, M. (2004). *Victims no longer: The classic guide for men recovering from sexual abuse.* New York: Harperc ollins.

Love, P. (1995). *Hot monogamy: Essential steps to more passionate, intimate lovemaking.* New York: Plume.

Pitman, F. (1989). *Private lies: Infidelity and betrayal of intimacy.* New York: Norton.

Schnarch, D. (1997). *Passionate marriage: Sex, love and intimacy in emotionally committed relationships.* New York: Henry Holt & Company.

Westerlund, E. (1992). *Women's sexuality after childhood incest.* New York: Norton.

Handout 10.1: Sexual Self Handout

This handout can be used as a guide to begin addressing different areas of your sexuality. These are only suggestions; feel free to use them if you are having problems beginning your letter. You may also find that they help you with different parts of your letter. Choose only the topics or sentence stems that seem relevant to you. Again, feel free to create your own as well if that is more helpful.

The first time I remember talking about sexuality was...

I learned about sexuality from...

My attitude towards sexuality is...

My first sexual memory was...

I first became aware of sex when...

I became aware that I was different from others when...

Talking about sex is hard because...

No one knows this happened to me...

I've kept this private my entire life...

The first time it happened...

I feel uncomfortable talking about...

I feel really comfortable talking about...

I enjoy it when...

The best part of my sexual relationship with my partner is...

I feel very satisfied when...

I feel good when I...

In the future I would like to...

I wish my partner would...

I feel uncomfortable with...

I am ashamed of...

I have never shared with anyone...

I wish I could talk about...

I began having trouble when...

I wish I could tell my partner...

I wish I could ask my partner for...

I would feel "normal" if...

I wish I knew more about...

It is hard for me to trust because...

I feel vulnerable when...

SECTION III: COUPLES

– 11 –

The Couples Relationship Quiz Show

Kimanne Foraker-Koons and Shannon B. Dermer

Type of Contribution: Activity, Handout

Objective

The objectives of this activity are congruent with the basic "floors" of John Gottman's sound relational house (2004). According to Gottman, the foundation of a happy, stable relationship is to have current knowledge of a partner's life, increasing positive feelings toward one another, and understanding a partner's dreams and expectations for both their relationship and their lives. The activity, *The Couples Relationship Quiz Show,* can be used to assess the amount of knowledge a couple has about one another, assist the couple in identifying and expressing affection and respect, begin to access relational expectations and life dreams, and infuse fun into the couples counseling process.

Rationale for Use

According to John Gottman's (1999) research on relationships, a strong relational friendship creates the foundation of a happy, stable relationship. The Gottman method of couples therapy stems from the sound relationship house (SRH) theory (Gottman, 2004). The SRH theory compares relationships to the structure of a house, with the foundation based on love maps, fondness and admiration, and turning toward a partner, rather than distancing. The midsection of the house is based on positive sentiment override, managing solvable problems, accepting perpetual problems, and honoring each other's dreams. The pinnacle of the relational house is creating shared meaning.

When people collect knowledge about their partners, this creates a *love map* of the partner's internal world (Gottman, 1999, 2004). Updating knowledge about a partner's friends, likes and dislikes, frustrations, hobbies, goals, dreams, and fantasies creates a more complex, current map. Imagine trying to use a map that had limited information like only interstate highways listed on it or a map that was created in 1950 and outdated—it may be useful in some ways, but the driver is also going to take a lot of wrong turns. For a strong relationship, each member of the couple needs to have a current, complex map.

A couple's knowledge about one another can be assessed through pencil-and-paper instruments (see Gottman, 1999, for examples). However, utilizing a playful, interactive approach over traditional approaches has several advantages. First, assessing couples through an experiential activity allows therapists to observe couple interaction in addition to assessing the level of knowledge that each person has about his or her partner. Second, because of the interactive nature of an activity versus a paper-and-pencil assessment, it is more easily employed as an intervention. Therapists can interrupt unhelpful interactions and direct couples to interact in more useful ways during the activity. Third, the activity brings fun and humor into the session. Overall, playful techniques open the door to increased joining between therapist and clients, infuses fun and positivity into sessions that may have been previously marked by negativity, and allows for simultaneous assessment and intervention.

Instructions

The activity, *The Couples Relationship Quiz Show,* is designed to emulate a game show and is used to assess a couple's love maps and to increase their knowledge of one another if their love maps are outdated. In order to allow time to explain the game, play it, and process the game, the therapist may want to schedule a longer session than usual. The actual game should last approximately 30 minutes.

The therapist serves as the emcee of the game show and the clients act as the contestants. If possible, the therapist should be standing at a podium with the couple seated in front of the therapist. This gives the activity a game show feeling typical of a television quiz show. In addition, the activity could be videotaped and played back in future sessions to point out positive aspects of the couple's relationship, as well as areas for growth.

The game should last around 30 minutes, during which time the couple is asked a series of questions (listed in Handout 11.1 at the end of this chapter). The first client to raise his or her hand and answer the question correctly is given two points. After he or she answers correctly, then the second person is given a chance to answer the question and earn one point. If the first person answers incorrectly, then the second person is given a chance to answer the question for two points. After each question is answered, the therapist encourages a brief discussion of the answers. The game ends when all of the questions have been answered or when time runs out.

During the activity the therapist should note briefly on the handout any questions he or she wishes to discuss after the activity or in subsequent sessions. Besides noting the content of answers during the game, the therapist should pay attention to body language and emotions that may be invoked during the game. These can be useful observations to reflect back on when processing the game.

Brief Clinical Vignette

Joe and Julie sought couples counseling because they said they were living together as "roommates." They had been married 10 years and had two children, ages 4 and 5. The couple lived in the same household, but acted more like business partners whose job it was to raise children than like spouses. The couple stated they had lost touch with each other due to daily stresses and strains of life.

Joe and Julie reported that, before, they had argued frequently, but in the last 2 years, instead of arguing with each other, they had distanced. When Julie brought up a topic that might develop into an argument, Joe retreated to the recreation room and watched television. The couple reported that they rarely kissed or hugged, and they had not had intercourse in over a year.

Despite the distancing from one another and the decline in physical affection, it was obvious in sessions that Joe and Julie still had fondness and affection for one another. They described the beginning of their relationship with fondness and humor. When Julie cried in session Joe would reach out to hold her hand, and when Joe's feelings seemed hurt, Julie put her arm around him. Both stated that they wanted to stay married and that they loved each other, but they were not sure how to get past old relational wounds. In addition, they did not know how to break out of the pattern of distancing from one another when they got upset.

After three sessions the therapist decided to use an experiential intervention, *The Couples Relationship Quiz Show.* During the previous sessions, the couple exhibited friendship and had a playful manner in which they communicated effectively. The sessions had been relatively serious, but it was apparent to the therapist that the couple had a good sense of humor and would most likely participate in the game. At the fourth session the couple agreed to play a game to see how well they knew each other.

The therapist first explained the rules of the game to the couple. Then the therapist stood at the podium, asked questions from the handout, and watched to see which person raised his or her hand first to answer the questions. There was not enough time to ask all of the questions on the handout, so the therapist selected a series of questions to assess the couple's cognitive love map and their expectations and dreams. For example, questions such as "Who is your partner's best friend?" and "Name three things or issues your partner has been concerned with this month" were meant to assess how much current knowledge the couple had about one another. Questions such as "Describe your partner's idea of a romantic date" and "What is your partner's idea of 'financially stable?'" are meant to assess dreams and expectations. The therapist helped the clients discuss their answers and how they felt about the game.

Joe and Julie obviously really enjoyed playing the game. They were serious about answering the questions and were playfully competitive. Both were mildly surprised at how much the other knew, allowing both partners to recognize that their relationship was not as "broken" as they had first thought. Both simple and more complex questions opened space for the couple to reminisce about life events or their relationship. For example, asking a question about pets led Joe to share a story about when they went with their children to pick out the family dog. Even when one partner answered a question correctly, asking the other partner to comment whether the answer was correct or not led to interesting conversations. For instance, when Julie was asked about three things or issues that she thought concerned Joe that month, she identified issues that Joe had indeed been concerned about. Nevertheless, when Joe was asked to comment on Julie's answer he remarked that while these were issues he was concerned with, there were other issues that weighed more heavily on his mind. He stated that one of the things he had been worrying about is that Julie no longer found him attractive. Julie was surprised because she associated their sexual problems with her own worries about her body, depression, and frustration. She had not considered that her husband would start to worry about his own level of attractiveness.

After completing the quiz show, the therapist processed the game and answers with the couple. The therapist asked a series of questions about the process of the game and about the content of the answers. Some examples are:

1. What did they like or dislike about the game? How did they feel about competing against one another?
2. Were they surprised by any of the answers? If so, what were they surprised by? How were the answers different from what they thought they should be?
3. Did each think the partner would do better or worse than he or she did?
4. Were the answers different from a year ago, or even from when they first met? If different, how did the partner come to change his or her view?
5. If changed, how did they feel about the change? What did they like about the change? What did they not like about the change? How did they think the change came about? How did the partner feel the change had impacted the relationship? Had any of the changes had an impact on other family members? If so, who was affected and what type of impact had it made?

The goals of the game, which were successfully met with this couple, were to explore and/or improve the levels of Gottman's (2004) sound relational house to (1) assess the couple's cognitive love map and update or increase their knowledge about one another, (2) increase their fondness and admiration for one another, (3) increase positive feelings toward one another, (4) help them to understand each other's dreams and expectations, and (5) help them create shared meaning.

For Joe and Julie, the therapist was able to observe that they had strong cognitive love maps. In addition, reminiscing and recognizing how much they did know about each other helped increase their fondness for one another. In subsequent sessions, some of their commonalities and differences in expectations, based on how they answered certain quiz questions, were discussed, as well as how these dreams and expectations related to issues they felt they could not resolve. The game served as a fun assessment and set the stage for intervention in later sessions.

Suggestions for Follow-Up

The basic goal of the game is to focus on the lower level of Gottman's (1999) relational house (numbers 1 and 2). However, the rest of the levels of the relational house may be more thoroughly explored while processing the game and in subsequent sessions. The game itself is not meant to go into the upper levels of the sound relational house in depth, but the activity does open the door to further discussion of these topics.

There are several follow-up suggestions following this game. Immediately following the activity, the therapist should process what it was like to play the game, the accuracy of the answers, whether or not the couple were surprised by any of the answers, and what they enjoyed about the activity. The therapist can also trace the development of the relationship by discussing with the couple how some of their answers to the questions may have changed over the course of their relationship. For example, what they consider romantic may have changed dramatically from when they were first dating.

Clients should also be asked, after the game is completed, if there are topics that were brought up during the activity that they would like to discuss further. Finally, if the therapist was able to videotape the session, he or she may want to play back particular parts of the tape in subsequent sessions and ask the clients to comment on the content or process of the clip. Depending on how they did during the game, the couple can be encouraged to discuss their answers at home and the therapist can give a copy of the questions used in the session.

Contraindications for Use

There are certain circumstances in which the game should not be used with clients. Therapists should avoid using this game if there is recent history of violence in the relationship, or with couples who use the game as a means for showing contempt for their partners. Contempt is physical or verbal communication that conveys disgust for the partner. This may be expressed through sarcasm, name calling, eye rolling, mocking, and hostile forms of humor (Gottman, 2000). The game should not be used if the therapist suspects that competition would be used as a way to display contempt or "superiority" over the other partner.

References

Gottman, J. M. (1999). *The marriage clinic: A scientifically based marital therapy.* New York: W. W. Norton.

Gottman, J. M. (2000). *The seven principles for making marriage work.* New York: Three Rivers Press.

Gottman, J. S. (Ed.). (2004). *The marriage clinic: Casebook.* New York: W. W. Norton.

Professional Readings and Resources

Johnson, S. M. (2004). *The practice of emotionally focused marital therapy: Creating connection.* New York: Brunner/Mazel.

Bibliotherapy Sources for the Client

Gottman, J. M. (2000). *The seven principles for making marriage work.* New York: Three Rivers Press.

Gottman, J. M. (2002). *The relationship cure: A 5-step guide to strengthening your marriage, family, and friendships.* New York: Three Rivers Press.

Handout 11.1: The Relationship Quiz Show[*]

Instructions: The therapist should select questions that are appropriate to the clients. The game should last around 30 minutes, during which time the couple is asked a series of questions. The first client to raise his or her hand and answer a question correctly is given two points. After the first to raise his or her hand answers correctly, then the second person is given a chance to answer the question and earn one point. If the first person answers incorrectly, then the second person is given a chance to answer the question for two points. After each question is answered the therapist encourages brief discussion of the answers. The game ends when all of the selected questions have been answered or when time runs out.

1. Who is your partner's best friend?
2. Name your partner's favorite type of pet.
3. What was your partner's best day at work this year?
4. What was your partner's worst day at work this year?
5. Who is your partner's favorite person at work?
6. Who does your partner consider a problem at work?
7. Name three things or issues your partner has been concerned with this month.
8. If your partner had $100 that he or she could spend freely, what would he or she spend it on?
9. If your partner were to go back to school tomorrow, what would he or she study?
10. If your partner won a dream trip, where would your partner want to go?
11. If your partner had a free evening to do what ever he or she wanted, what would that be?
12. What is your partner's favorite food?
13. What is your partner's favorite channel to watch on TV?
14. You and your partner must leave your home during an emergency evacuation. What would be the one item (do not include his or her wallet or purse) your partner would choose to take?
15. If you and your partner were going to a holiday party, what would your partner say he or she would like to see you wear?
16. You are making your partner's favorite meal; what would that meal be?
17. Name a scary moment for your partner.
18. What does the phrase "that's hot" conjure up in your partner's head?
19. What is the first "thing" your partner would buy if he or she won the lottery?
20. List three ways you and your partner would spend the big lottery winnings.
21. What would your partner consider to be the "best" possible holiday?
22. What family member is your partner's least favorite and why?
23. What family member is your partner's favorite and why?
24. My partner thinks it is funny when I...
25. What would be your partner's thought on the "best movie ever seen"?
26. What is your partner's most cherished possession?
27. Name your partner's most recent goal in life.
28. What is one goal your partner has already reached in life?
29. Name one food dish that your partner makes that you dislike, but eat anyway.
30. Name one food dish you make that your partner loves to eat.
31. What is one act of kindness your partner did this week?
32. Name your partner's favorite singer or musical group.
33. Describe your partner's idea of a romantic date.
34. What did your partner wear to bed last night?
35. What are three priorities in your partner's life?
36. What is your partner's idea of being "financially comfortable"?

[*]Adapted from Gottman, J. M. (2000). *The seven principles for making marriage work.* New York: Three Rivers Press.

– 12 –

"May I Have This Dance?"

Shannon B. Dermer, Jill Matson, and Catherine Ford Sori

Type of Contribution: Activity, Handouts, Homework

Objectives

The purpose of this activity is twofold: First, it provides therapists with a unique method to assess a couple's relationship, and second, it can be used to increase proximity and foster intimacy in couples who may be distant or disengaged. This is done through the use of music and dance movement. No special training in music or dance therapy is required for clinicians to utilize this activity.

Rationale for Use

As anyone who counsels couples knows, couples therapy sessions may be tense for both clients and therapists. Couples may become locked in rigid patterns of interacting and reacting that can escalate and leave all parties feeling emotionally drained and physically exhausted. Traditional talk therapy can be tedious and ineffective when couples engage in verbal assaults that include blame, defensiveness, pursuing, or distancing, and many therapists flounder when treating these couples (see Doherty, 2002). At other times, sessions are characterized by one partner dominating the session, while the other sits silent and sullen. Changing these patterns can seem as difficult as getting tigers to change their stripes! Sometimes our best efforts fail, and we need to break those entrenched patterns by doing something different.

Couples' relationships have often been described in the literature as a "dance." This term is often used as a metaphoric representation of a couple's stylized, cyclic, and repetitive patterns of interacting (e.g., Lerner, 1985, 1989; Minuchin, Nichols, & Lee, 2007). According to Middelberg (2001), "Dance is a term that is commonly used in systemic couple therapy to refer to the repetitive sequence of interactions or vicious cycles between partners" (p. 341), and it is quite visible in the family therapy literature (Pistole, 2003). In one of her popular "dance" books, *The Dance of Anger,* Lerner (1985) wrote that couples' "dances" involve circular interactions where "the behavior of one partner maintains and provokes the behavior of the other" (p. 56). This metaphor brings to mind an image of a couple dancing repetitive interactions in a pattern that both provokes and maintains their behaviors (Pistole).

Similarly, Middelberg (2001) discusses five common metaphoric couples' dances. They are the (1) dance of conflict, where couples regulate their anxieties about intimacy by blaming and attacking one another; (2) dance of distance, where both partners distance due to a low tolerance for intimacy or conflict; (3) dance of pursuer/avoider, a common pattern wherein one partner pursues intimacy while the other avoids it; (4) dance of overfunctioner/underfunctioner, which appears when one partner assumes the role of parent or caretaker, while the other acts childish or under responsible; and (5) dance of triangulation, which occurs when a couple regulates their intimacy by focusing on a third person.

The activity described here is an experiential intervention that utilizes music and dance movement in order to engage partners' senses while physically and emotionally helping them to connect.

In addition to being a powerful intervention, the use of dance is a reminder to the therapist to assess common patterns in relationships and the stylized "dance" unique to each couple. Dance is an assessment tool, an intervention, and a metaphor easily incorporated into therapy. Although the activity could be integrated with almost any theory, in this chapter the rationale for *May I Have This Dance?* is based on structural and experiential theory and concepts.

Incorporating Dance in Couples Therapy

While much has been written on using dance therapy with individuals and groups, there is a paucity in the literature on incorporating dance in couples therapy. Yet dance offers couples a unique, experiential method of addressing common couple issues. Dancing has elements of playfulness, freedom, and joy (Hawkes, 2003), and many of these qualities are sadly lacking yet sorely needed in couples therapy. The playful quality and vitality of dance can help counterbalance the difficult and challenging work of talk therapy (see Mills & Daniluk, 2002).

The simple act of getting out of the chair and moving one's body implies movement and change. Dance can liberate people from the physical and mental restriction of their seat in therapy and free them from having to find words to express all their problems and emotions (Mills & Daniluk, 2002), promoting a mind–body connection. This movement has both intrapsychic and intrapersonal benefits for partners. Individuals become more aware of their physical self in space (their posture, the ease or awkwardness of their movements) as they move to the music. They also become aware of their partner's physical presence as they experience moving together, finding their rhythm, and attuning to each other. While dancing, couples move from the intellectual realm to one that encompasses the senses and helps them create an experience together that may allow them to gain insight into their problems and alter their old patterns. Music has long been known to promote positive moods, and music can express what words cannot. There can also be a spiritual element in music and dance, which couples can experience together.

While the metaphor of dance symbolizes a couple's sequences of interaction, illustrating how partners prompt and respond to one another, a couple's dance literally brings those patterns to life in the therapy room. When a couple dances, the fundamental nature of the relationship comes to light because of the visual, kinesthetic, and kinetic characteristics of dance (Watanabe-Hammond, 1990). As couples are invited to dance in session, the preceding patterns (or "dances") become visible.

Dance can be used both literally and figuratively to help clients understand the complex, recursive nature of marital interactions. Like two dancers, if the movements of a couple are not in sync they may end up "stepping on each other's toes." This activity, through music and dance, is designed to help couples having trouble with emotional and physical intimacy to express positive feelings for one another. Once couples are able to experience one another more openly and honestly, the therapist can begin to challenge the problematic ways they interact. Dance, in couple therapy, provides partners with an opportunity to nonverbally express their feelings for one another through the rhythm and lyrics of music, as well as through the physicality of dancing.

Fit of dance with experiential family therapy. Experiential therapy emphasizes the feeling side of human nature that includes creativity, spontaneity, and the ability to play (Nichols & Schwartz, 2004). The foundation of therapy in the experiential model is in valuing experiences for their own sakes. Experiential therapy focuses on being able to express one's emotions openly and honestly within the context of the family (see Satir, 1988; Whitaker & Blumberry, 1988). The goal is to help individuals uncover their honest emotions, and then help them to forge more genuine family ties out of this enhanced authenticity (Nichols & Schwartz, 2004).

According to Hawkes (2003), dancing advances a sense of aliveness as the body moves and comes to life, and this can unblock emotions, expressions, and gestures. Dancing promotes vitality, which should be an essential objective in therapy—"to be as alive as possible, with all that we are and can be. And what has more vitality than dancing?" (Hawkes, p. 300). Pistole (2003) emphasized that dance can provide an emotional outlet to express everything the heart is capable of feeling, including passion, ecstasy, desires, and various moods.

Dance allows clients to "access nonverbal levels of functioning...and opens up issues concerning the other, including meeting/leaving, guiding/following, deciding/trusting, and so on" (Hawkes, 2003, p. 288). Many have lost touch with their own internal states and need to block out others in order to be aware of their own feelings. When clients dance, they move "out of their heads" (Mills & Daniluk, 2002, p. 83), away from cognitive defenses, as they attune to their own physical sensations and to their partner's physical presence. Hawkes believes that the use of dance and music allows access to other levels of consciousness and can free people to become aware of and then express unconscious aspects of both their individual experiences, as well as their relationship. This occurs when clients first connect to their own bodily sensations, and then connect to the physical proximity of their partner. Dance can increase an awareness of both the physical person of the self ("their muscle tone, posture, balance, axis, resistance, etc.," Hawkes, p. 293), as well as the couple's physical interaction (the feeling of leading or of responding to being guided).

Hawkes (2003) remarked how clients have described dancing with an attuned partner as a kind of magical experience, especially the joy of flowing together. In describing the excitement clients experience in dancing and moving together, Hawkes points out that they can understand one another at a deeper, subsymbolic level. She states, "This excitement can then revitalize other aspects of their lives" (p. 297).

Dance can be used to increase physical proximity in couples, which can be helpful in couples who present with sexual issues. Beyond that, there is an erotic aspect to dance that is more subtle and can be useful to open conversations about the difference between a "sexual" and a "sensual" relationship (see Hawkes, 2003, p. 298). There is a sense of aliveness, awakened senses, stimulation, and excitement when one dances in close contact with another (Hawkes), and each partner's reactions, emotions, memories, and thoughts about this contact can be quite useful in opening communication about erotic or sexual issues, and as to how attuned couples are to one another.

While utilizing dance in therapy might appear to be challenging, it can infuse pleasure and joy into sessions (Mills & Daniluk, 2002). Mills and Daniluk listed several themes that emerged in their study on the experience of dance therapy for women who were sexually abused as children. These themes were (1) a reconnection to the body, (2) permission to play, (3) a sense of spontaneity, (4) a sense of struggle (with being observed or looking foolish), (5) a sense of intimate connection to others while dancing, and (6) a sense of freedom to move, to change, and not to talk, since dance gave them an alternative way to process material and become aware of underlying feelings. Many of these themes reflect goals of experiential therapy and can be applied to the use of dance in couples therapy.

Fit of dance with structural family therapy. Therapists who use structural family therapy with couples often focus on the boundaries between individuals and subsystems, as well as patterns of complementarity between partners that have become rigid (i.e., pursuer–distancer or over-responsible–under-responsible patterns). Structural techniques include joining, creating intensity, using enactments, and unbalancing the system (Minuchin & Fishman, 1981). One common goal in working with couples is to change rigid complementary patterns to alter the structure of the family and promote healthier family functioning (see Minuchin & Fishman; Minuchin et al., 2007). In structural family therapy terms, dance can be seen as a type of enactment that reveals the interactional pattern (or "dance") of the couple. As in a structural enactment, the role of the therapist is to observe how partners approach one another (noting any resistance, such as one partner literally "dragging his or her feet"), interact (verbally and nonverbally) while dancing, make eye contact, and depict boundaries as they regulate personal space and negotiate their physical contact. All this provides important information that the therapist may or may not choose to comment on, and offers an opportunity to unbalance the system (Minuchin, 1974) by encouraging a change in some aspect of the couple's dance.

When a couple dances together there is an implicit suggestion that "it is no longer necessary to carry everything alone" (Hawkes, 2003, p. 292). One person is not carrying all the weight, but has a partner; this can lead to a sense of "lightening" of the load. A discussion on this topic can be helpful to break rigid patterns seen in couples with polarized over-responsible/under-responsible roles.

Couples can be encouraged to talk about each of their experiences in leading and following. Hawkes (2003) suggests exploring if one partner can lead without controlling everything. Can one follow without being too passive? These questions are excellent for exploring gender issues, the importance of balance between being active (leading) and passive (following), (recognizing that everyone benefits from being each at times), as well as the importance of each partner being both "decisive and receptive" (Hawkes, p. 292). This is useful to increase adaptability to move couples from rigid complementary roles to a relationship that is more symmetrical (see Minuchin, Lee, & Simon, 1996; Minuchin & Nichols, 1993; Minuchin et al., 2007).

Instructions

Before introducing this activity the clinician should carefully select the song or songs to be used. Songs should be chosen to fulfill a purpose or therapeutic goal, such as promoting intimacy or expressing love (see Handout 12.1 at the end of this chapter for a list of selected songs according to therapeutic topics). The therapist may introduce the activity to the couple at the beginning of a session by saying that they are going to do something different in session. At other times it may be useful to use this activity to breathe life into a heavy or stalled session. In either case, therapists may briefly explore any feelings and past experiences a couple has with dancing, and then find out if they are familiar with the selected song and if they have any positive or negative feelings about it (see Handout 12.2). Next, therapists should direct the couple to stand in the middle of the room and ask them if they are willing to slow dance. After dimming the lights the therapist begins the song and quietly takes a seat in the peripheral vision of the couple. As the couple dances, the therapist takes note of the couple's physical and emotional responses.

Role of the therapist. The therapist guides the couple in the dance activity and creates an atmosphere of safety by being someone on whom the clients can rely (Gorham, 1995). Therapists should observe the clients' verbal and nonverbal interactions and be ready to intervene if necessary (Gorham). Since some couples may have difficulty dancing while under the gaze of the therapist (Hawkes, 2003), clinicians may want to be subtle while observing the dancing couple.

Use of talk. It is important for therapists to provide the structure for a dance activity, to carefully select appropriate music to advance therapeutic goals, and to shape the experience for the clients (see Gorham, 1995). In discussing the work of Middelberg and Wood (1991), Gorham lists three ways to utilize talk with dance in therapy, and these readily apply to couples dance: (1) dancing without talk, 2) dancing with talk after, and (3) dancing with talk on top. In dancing without talk the focus is on the nonverbal activity, and the therapist does not process the activity afterward (Gorham, 1995). This would allow couples to focus on the music and the sensation of moving together, with no pressure to process the activity afterward. This can be useful when dance is first introduced in a couple's session. In dancing with talk after, the couple still does not talk during the dance, but afterward the therapist may discuss each person's experience and share observations. Finally, dancing with talk on top occurs when clients talk with each other or the therapist while doing the activity. Like a structural enactment, this allows the therapist to guide the process to advance therapeutic goals and to discuss any images, thoughts, or emotions as they occur.

Self of the therapist issues. Therapists also should recognize their own reactions to a couple's dance. As this intervention is experiential, the therapist's reactions to the couple's dance are important, and he or she can acknowledge these emotional reactions to their dance in order to process them with the couple. The therapist's observations of how the couple danced (their physical proximity, who took the lead, etc.) are very important to comment on as well, since these observations are indicative of the structure of the relationship. For example, if one partner dominates the dance while the other quietly follows, the therapist can make hypotheses that there is a significant gap in hierarchy in the relationship or complementary patterns have been exaggerated.

Processing the activity. After the song has ended, the therapist and couple spend about 30 minutes processing their reactions to this activity. Sample questions (see Handout 12.2 at the end of the chapter) include:

- What was it like to slow dance together? What were your reactions?
- What was your comfort level, and did it change as the dance progressed?
- What did you notice about your partner? (physical self, looks, scents, etc.)
- What thoughts and feelings came to you as you danced?
- What were your reactions to the music? To the lyrics of the song?
- Who had the harder time with this?
- Did this bring back any memories?
- How do you feel now after dancing, and how is that different from how you felt before the dance?

The couple and therapist discuss their various reactions and the therapist allows them to express their emotions and thoughts regarding the experience of the dance and the music. After discussing and exploring the couple's reactions, the therapist suggests they end the session with another dance. The song for the second dance can be the same one or something different. Again, the couple dances while the therapist observes them from the side of the room. Once the song has ended, the therapist waits for the couple to stop dancing. The couple is then asked to think about and discuss their reactions to their dance over the next week. The therapist also invites the couple to bring in songs that they find meaningful and important to them.

Dance can be used at different stages of therapy. In the beginning of therapy, dance can be used as an assessment tool and to introduce couples to being physically close in session. In initial sessions, dance can be a gateway for couples to reconnect. In the middle stages of therapy dance can be used to invite couples to experience what it is like to reconnect and relate in different ways. In later sessions dance provides couples the opportunity to consolidate what they have learned and how they have reconnected.

Dance as homework. The therapist may also recommend that a couple dance as homework between sessions. For example, therapists may suggest that a couple dance to a particular song as a prelude to sex. By setting the stage with soft lights and candles, dance can be a way to increase eroticism and sensuality as the couple flows together in close physical contact. Therapists may also suggest that a couple dance together as a way to feel closer, calmer, and more relaxed before discussing a difficult topic. Finally, dancing can be prescribed as a nonverbal way for a couple to reconnect after a disagreement.

Brief Clinical Vignette

John, 52, and Judy, 51, were a Caucasian couple married for 8 years. John had been married once before and Judy twice before. They both had advanced degrees and were successful in their professional careers, and both had adult children from previous marriages. They sought therapy because they felt they were "drifting apart and wanted to learn how to communicate better."

The couple associated their difficulties with extremely busy work schedules and incongruence in their sexual needs. Judy's sexual desire had decreased over the years and she preferred to have less intercourse and more nonsexual ways of expressing affection. At the time of the consultation, the couple had not had intercourse in almost a year. Judy had been experiencing menopausal symptoms that included a complete loss of sexual desire. During a sexual assessment the couple reported that they used to have sex approximately once a week. The therapist discussed with the couple the possibility that Judy's antidepressant medication, relationship issues, and/or menopause might be contributing to changes in sexual desire.

When John and Judy sought therapy for their dissatisfaction with their marriage they had become stuck in a pursuer–distancer pattern, although they shifted roles. John avoided conflict by refusing to engage in discussions or arguments with Judy. Judy would pursue John with her concerns, and, when John would not engage with her, she would then retreat and withdraw.

The decrease in physical contact and sexual affection, their stressful schedules, and differences in sexual desire resulted in the couple being stuck in a cycle of rejection, distancing, and pursuing. John, frustrated by not having sex as often as he would like, continually tried to be what he thought was romantic in order to make the likelihood of sexual interaction more likely. On the one hand, Judy wanted to be emotionally closer to John and engage in more nonsexual physical affection. On the other hand, Judy interpreted any attempts John made to touch her or be romantic as him pressuring her to have sex. John admitted that he touched her or tried to do what he thought were romantic things both because he loved her and because he was hoping it would lead to sexual activity. Both felt frustrated and lonely, but still expressed a strong desire to work on their relationship.

Although both Judy and John wanted to feel closer to one another, they had difficulty operationally defining what their relationship would look like when they felt closer. The therapist decided that the couple needed a way to get emotionally and physically closer without feeling either pressured or rejected. The therapist decided to begin and end the third session with having the couple dance to two songs: an instrumental song and a song with lyrics that might be meaningful to the couple. By having the couple dance, the intensity would be raised and it would provide John and Judy with the opportunity to bridge the gap between them. It would also help to break the pattern of pursuer–distancer.

When the couple entered the room to begin their session they noticed that the lights were dimmed and that the center of the room had been cleared. The couple was informed that the session was going to be a little different this time. They would continue to discuss the issues that brought them to therapy, but the session would start with some dancing to set the mood to talk about communication and intimacy. It was explained that communication comes in many different forms, including music and dance. To help them relax and reduce any "performance" anxiety, the therapist led them briefly in a deep-breathing exercise (e.g., Hecker & Sori, 2007).

The couple was then asked to stand in the middle of the room and to put their arms around one another. Two songs would be played; the first was an instrumental, "Memory" (Weber, 1983, track 9, performed by Guy Maeda), and the second song was Anne Murray's "Could I Have This Dance?" (1994, track 14). They were instructed not to talk during the first dance and to just pay attention to the music and what it was like to dance with each other. This was to help them attend to one another, experience their physical proximity, and to facilitate a "flow" state (see Csikszentmihalyi, 1990) with the music and movement. While dancing to the second song the couple was encouraged to talk about what it was like to be dancing with one another.

At first the couple seemed somewhat embarrassed and slightly reluctant. The therapist encouraged Judy to put her arms around John's neck, and John was asked to put his arms around Judy's waist. As soon as the music began they started to sway and slow dance. As the music progressed the couple moved closer and John whispered into Judy's ear. They giggled at the beginning of the song and then became quieter as the song continued. By the end of the song, their eyes were closed and they seemed to be much more relaxed. They continued to dance to the second song and hummed along with the tune, but did no talking. When the song ended the couple slowly stopped dancing and then sat down across from the therapist.

After the dance, the therapist and couple discussed what this dance experience was like for approximately 30 minutes. In an enactment, the couple was asked to face one another and talk about their reactions to dancing with one another. John and Judy started reminiscing about the last time they had danced many years ago at a friend's wedding party. They both stated that they missed dancing together.

In addition, they processed what it was like to dance during session. Judy shared with John that she enjoyed dancing with him, but felt he had diminished the experience somewhat by not following the rule of not talking during the first dance. John explained that he did not mean to upset Judy by talking and joking. He also expressed how wonderful it felt to be close to her and how he wished they could be close more often.

Before the end of session the therapist invited the couple to dance again, but asked them not to talk during the dance, in order to increase the intensity of the dance and have them experience it more fully. By asking the couple not to talk, the therapist acted as the director in order to restructure the organization of the couple's subsystems. As they came together in the center of the room they were much closer than during the initial dance at the beginning of session. They danced with their arms wrapped around one another, eyes closed, and cheek to cheek. Once the song ended they slowly opened their eyes, and their bodies lingered together for a few moments before they turned toward the therapist. As they faced the therapist they held hands and smiled, and commented on how relaxed they both felt and how much they enjoyed dancing together. The therapist and couple agreed that they would continue to "dance" in future sessions. Judy and John added that they looked forward to learning to "dance" more often and in ways that were more satisfying.

The therapist welcomed the couple into the next session by having them turn toward one another in their seats. She directed the couple to talk together about what it meant to each of them to be intimate. After a conversation in which both were encouraged to share openly and to listen without retreating, the therapist pointed out that they were free to create a new dance together. She decided to have the couple dance to the song, "The Very Thought of You," recorded by Rod Stewart (2002), to focus on their love and their desire for more romance in their relationship. The therapist directed the couple to dance without speaking in order to raise the intensity in session. Since they were not allowed to speak while they danced, they began to take on different roles. John did not talk and make jokes this time, but instead held Judy close and looked into her eyes. Judy smiled dreamily and allowed him to lead her in the dance, where they swayed and moved in synchrony.

After the song ended, John and Judy sat to process the dance for about 30 minutes. During the debriefing, John and Judy were markedly more relaxed and at ease. They held hands as they sat, and smiled at one another a great deal. They sat with their knees touching one another. The therapist asked them what it was like to dance after actually listening to one another. John squeezed Judy's hand when he told her he did not realize before how much it hurt her when he would make jokes and try to make her feel better. He also told her how, although he had the best of intentions, the role he had been playing as the laid-back jokester had really been hurting her. Judy responded to John with tears in her eyes and said she just wanted him to talk to her and acknowledge what she had to say. She said she did not want to always be the one who brought up issues and was upset. She told John that she wanted to be able to laugh as well.

Following this session, the therapist would periodically utilize the intervention of the dance, both in session and as homework, in order to allow John and Judy to explore different roles within their relationship. While the intervention of the dance increased the intensity and proximity between the two, it also allowed John and Judy to experience some of their innermost emotions in the presence of one another. Judy and John became aware of the roles they each played in their relationship, and how they had learned these roles from their families (see Minuchin et al., 2007). Judy began to talk to John about how she would feel rejected when he ignored her. John began working on engaging in discussions and even arguments with Judy, instead of withdrawing. They reported feeling as if they were making progress, and also happily shared they had had sex—following a dance! They ended their termination session with a final dance (to Rod Stewart's "That's All"), which concluded with a gentle and lingering kiss.

Suggestions for Follow-Up

May I Have This Dance? is a technique that is used in session and involves the therapist and clients debriefing following the dance experience. As an experiential technique used within a structural framework, it is important that emphasis is placed on the couple's experience and ability to express their emotions honestly, openly, and safely within session. It is also crucial that focus is placed on how the actual dance portrays the structure and boundaries around and within the couple's relationship. It is a powerful experience for couples to dance within session, but it is even more profound when couples can begin to become aware of how they dance together (e.g., who does and does not lead, who keeps his or her distance, etc.) and how this illustrates the pattern of their relationship, and to recognize possible new ways to "dance" together.

Therapists can utilize metaphors in accordance with the literal use of dance and music. For example, metaphorical discussions can be generated about how the couple dances or what kind of music they make together. There are two ways therapists can utilize metaphors in couple's therapy. One way is by paying attention to the spontaneous, spoken metaphors that couples share in session. Another way is by paying attention to possible metaphors the couple might relate to, according to what therapists learn about them in session (Kopp, 1995; see Minuchin et al., 2007). By having couples literally dance and listen to music in session, therapists can utilize the metaphors of dance and music with them since they will relate to it through the actual activity.

The literal utilization of dance in sessions can also be used throughout therapy in order for the couple to talk about the experience of being physically intimate. Dance can be used both literally and figuratively to help clients understand the complex, recursive nature of marital interactions. Like two dancers, if the movements of a couple are not in sync they may end up "stepping on each other's toes." The therapist can also help the couple discuss what intimacy means to each and how they can find ways to be more intimate with one another, by discussing what it means to be physically and emotionally intimate.

Giving the couple a photograph of their dance "frame," pose, expressions, etc. can provide them with a concrete image of their relationship and can be useful in future sessions to discuss many of the issues discussed in this chapter earlier. Clients can begin to explore what they notice about their pose; what each was thinking, feeling, longing for, etc.; and what, if anything, they would like to change about their "dance" or their relationship.

Partners can also experiment with freestyle dancing, where they share a space, but move as "individual improvisers" (Pistole, 2003, p. 236). This can be useful in strengthening interpersonal boundaries and promoting autonomy in a couple who is too close, and in helping free individuals to be more expressive.

Therapists can discuss common complementary patterns in couples (e.g., pursuer–distancer, over-responsible, under-responsible; see Middelberg, 2001), encourage couples to identify their own predominant "dance," and then to create actual dances that depict their patterns of interactions. This can be followed with a description and performance of the couple's "ideal dance."

While some couple dances result from efforts to regulate their anxiety about intimacy, other dances may result from family and cultural influences that lead to a couple's distinctive style of interacting (Middelberg, 2001). Each partner can be encouraged to quickly and explicitly depict the "dance" of his or her family of origin, which Watanabe-Hammond (1990) calls "family dances" (also see Pistole, 2003, p. 236). Therapists can ask questions similar to those used in family sculpts. These might be questions regarding the tempo, style, or type of movement in the family dance, as well as questions about family members' facial expressions, hand placements, attitudes, and emotions (Watanabe-Hammond). Once these old family patterns are in conscious awareness, clients can then demonstrate their current family dance using movement, rhythm, and tempo to experientially illustrate couple and family interactions. This material can be useful in family of origin work with the couple. Clients can then discuss how each brought in elements from his or her family of origin dances, and be encouraged to portray how this has influenced the development of their own couple's dance (Watanabe-Hammond; also see Minuchin et al., 2007). A final follow-up activity might be to then have the couple explore how they can incorporate elements from both partners' family-of-origin dances into their own ideal couple's dance (Watanabe-Hammond).

Contraindications for Use

Although having partners dance in session can be useful for many couples, this type of activity is not appropriate for all clients. Incorporating dance and music into couples therapy requires therapists to join with the couple and have a thorough understanding of each person's view of the presenting problem and an initial assessment of the couple's relationship. Couples must be assessed for physical and emotional abuse or violence before implementing this intervention in therapy, since it requires couples to be physically close and it is imperative that clients feel safe. Therapists can utilize this intervention after the first session in order to be sure it fits with the couple's style. Some couples may not be open to or comfortable with interventions that require physical activity such as this, and some may be physically unable to dance. Therapists should also ask clients if this activity fits with their specific goals, beliefs, values, and attitudes. For example, some clients' religions may prohibit dancing or even listening to certain types of music. Finally, it is important that therapists monitor the proximity between couples when they dance, in light of the issues with which couples are dealing.

References

Csikszentmihalyi, M. (1990). *Flow: The psychology of optimal experience.* New York: HarperPerennial.

Doherty, W. (2002). Bad couples therapy. *Psychotherapy Networker,* November/December, 26–33.

Gorham, L. J. (1995). Dance therapy and self psychology. *Clinical Social Work Journal, 23*(3), 361–373.

Hawkes, L. (2003). The tango of therapy: A dancing group. *Transactional Analysis Journal, 33*(4), 288–301.

Hecker, L. L., & Sori, C. F. (2007). Creating a special place. In L. L. Hecker and C. F. Sori (Eds) *The therapist's notebook. Vol. 2: More homework, handouts, and activities for use in psychotherapy.* New York: Haworth.

Kopp, R. (1995). *Metaphor therapy: Using client-generated metaphors in psychotherapy.* Bristol, PA: Brunner/Mazel.

Lerner, H. G. (1985). *The dance of anger.* New York: Harper & Row.

Lerner, H. G. (1989). *The dance of intimacy.* New York: Harper & Row.

Maeda, G. (Performer and producer). (1995). *Dining by pianolight, Vol. III: Dessert, Anyone?* [CD]. Studio City, CA: Pianolight Music.

Middelberg, C. V. (2001). Projective identification in common couple dances. *Journal of Marital & Family Therapy, 27*(3), 341–352.

Mills, L. J., & Daniluk, J. C. (2002). Her body speaks: The experience of dance therapy for women survivors of child sexual abuse. *Journal of Counseling and Development, 80*(1), 77–85.

Minuchin, S. (1974). *Families and family therapy.* Cambridge, MA: Harvard University Press.

Minuchin, S., & Fishman, H. C. (1981). *Family therapy techniques.* Cambridge, MA: Harvard University Press.

Minuchin, S., Lee, W., & Simon, G. M. (1996). *Mastering family therapy.* New York: John Wiley & Sons.

Minuchin, S., & Nichols, M. P. (1993). *Family healing.* New York: The Free Press.
Minuchin, S., Nichols, M. P., & Lee, W. (2007). *Assessing families and couples: From symptom to system.* Boston: Pearson.
Murray, A. (1994). *Anne Murray: The best ... so far* [CD]. Hollywood, CA: Capitol Records.
Nichols, M. P., & Schwartz, R. C. (2004) *Family therapy: Concepts and methods* (6th ed.). Boston: Pearson Education.
Pistole, M. C. (2003). Dance as a metaphor: Complexities and extensions in psychotherapy. *Psychotherapy: Theory, Research, Practice, Training, 40*(3), 232–241.
Satir, V. (1988). *The new peoplemaking.* Mountain View, CA: Science and Behavior Books.
Watanabe-Hammond, S. (1990). Family dances and the rhythms of intimacy. *Contemporary Family Therapy: An International Journal, 12*(4), 327–338.
Weber, A. L. (1983). Memory [Recorded by G. Maeda]. On *Dining by pianolight, Vol. III: Dessert, anyone?* [CD]. Studio City, CA: Pianolight Music.
Whitaker, C. A., & Blumberry, W. (1988). *Dancing with the family: A symbolic-experiential approach.* New York: Brunner/Mazel.

Professional Readings and Resources

Bravo, L. (Producer). (1998). *Forever tango* [CD]. New York: RCA Victor.
Brooke, S. L. (2007). *The use of the creative therapies with sexual abuse survivors.* Springfield, IL: Charles C Thomas.
*Cole, N. K. (2000). *Unforgettable Nat King Cole* [CD]. Hollywood, CA: Capitol Records.
Espenak, L. (1981). *Dance therapy: Theory and application.* Springfield, IL: Charles C Thomas.
Feder, E., & Feder, B. (1981). *The expressive arts therapies.* Engelwood Cliffs, NJ: Prentice Hall.
*Fitzgerald, E. (2006). *Ella Fitzgerald: The very best of the song books* [CD]. New York: Verve Records.
Gottman, J. M. (1999). *The marriage clinic: A scientifically based marital therapy.* New York: Norton.
Halprin, A. (2000). *Dance as a healing art: Returning to health with movement and imagery.* Mendocino, CA: LifeRhythm Books.
Johnson, S. (2004). *The practice of emotionally focused couple therapy.* Florence, KY: Brunner/Mazel.
Levy, F. J., Fried, J. P., & Leventahl, F. (Eds.) (1995). *Dance and other expressive art therapies: When words are not enough.* New York: Routledge.
Ma, M. (Producer), & Mahers, M. (Director). (1993). *The wave: A revolutionary moving meditation* [videocassette recording]. New York: Raven Recording.
*Maeda, G. (Performer and producer). (1995). *Dining by pianolight, Vol. III: Dessert, Anyone?* [CD]. Studio City, CA: Pianolight Music.
Meekums, B. (2002). *Dance movement therapy: A creative psychotherapeutic approach.* Thousand Oaks, CA: Sage.
Murray, A. (1994). *Anne Murray: The best ... so far* [CD]. Hollywood, CA: Capitol Records.
Payne, H. (1992). *Dance movement therapy: Theory and practice.* New York: Routledge.
Satir, V. (1988). *The new peoplemaking.* Mountain View, CA: Science and Behavior Books.
*Stewart, R. (2002). *It had to be you ... The great American songbook.* [CD]. New York: J Records.
*Stewart, R. (2003). *As time goes by ... The great American songbook, Vol. II.* [CD]. New York: J Records.
*Stewart, R. (2004). *Stardust ... The great American songbook, Vol. III.* [CD]. New York: J Records.
Stewart, R. (2005). *Thanks for the memory ... The great American songbook, Vol. IV.* [CD]. New York: J Records.
Whitaker, C. A., & Blumberry, W. (1988). *Dancing with the family: A symbolic-experiential approach.* New York: Brunner/Mazel.

Wiener, D. (Ed.). (1999). *Beyond talk therapy: Using movement and expressive techniques in clinical practice.* Washington, DC: American Psychological Association.

Vaughan, S. (2000). *Dreamsville.* New York: Verve Records.

*Highly recommended for lyrics, variety, orchestration, and mood.

Bibliotherapy Sources for the Client

Bravo, L. (Producer). (1998). *Forever tango* [CD]. New York: RCA Victor.

Cole, N. K. (2000). *Unforgettable Nat King Cole* [CD]. Hollywood, CA: Capitol Records.

Fitzgerald, E. (2006). *Ella Fitzgerald: The very best of the song books* [CD]. New York: Verve Records.

Halprin, A. (2000). *Dance as a healing art: Returning to health with movement and imagery.* Mendocino, CA: LifeRhythm Books.

Ma, M. (Producer), & Mahers, M. (Director). (1993). *The wave: A revolutionary moving meditation* [videocassette recording]. New York: Raven Recording.

Maeda, G. (Performer and producer). (1995). *Dining by pianolight, Vol. III: Dessert, Anyone?* [CD]. Studio City, CA: Pianolight Music.

Murray, A. (1994). *Anne Murray: The best ... so far* [CD]. Hollywood, CA: Capitol Records.

Stewart, R. (2002). *It had to be you ... The great American songbook.* [CD]. New York: J Records.

Stewart, R. (2003). *As time goes by ... The great American songbook, Vol. II.* [CD]. New York: J Records.

Stewart, R. (2004). *Stardust ... The great American songbook, Vol. III.* [CD]. New York: J Records.

Stewart, R. (2005). *Thanks for the memory ... The great American songbook, Vol. IV.* [CD]. New York: J Records.

Vaughan, S. (2000). *Dreamsville.* New York: Verve Records.

Wright, J. P. (1992). *Social dance: Steps to success.* Champaign, IL: Leisure Press.

Handout 12.1: "May I Have This Dance?"

Suggested Music

The following is a carefully selected list of recommended songs for this activity, listed by categories. These are classics and most should appeal to all age groups. It is important to discuss a song with the couple before using it, as some music may have negative connotations for a client. Some couples may want to bring in their favorite music. CDs were selected that had numerous recommended songs, and a few songs are on multiple CDs by different artists. Lyrics are included in many of the CD inserts or online, and couples can be encouraged to share their reactions to them before or after they dance.

Goals and Titles	Artist	Title of CD; Label
Slow dance music to increase proximity and intimacy		
"The Nearness of You"[a]	Rod Stewart	"It Had to Be You;" J Records
"I'm in the Mood for Love"[a]	Rod Stewart	"As Time Goes By;" J Records
"Someone to Watch Over Me"[a]	Rod Stewart	"As Time Goes By;" J Records
"I Only Have Eyes for You"[a]	Rod Stewart	"As Time Goes By;" J Records
"Embraceable You"	Rod Stewart	"Stardust;" J Records
"Embraceable You"[a]	Ella Fitzgerald	"The Very Best...;" Verve Music
"Embraceable You"	Sarah Vaughan	"Dreamsville;" Verve Music
"Body and Soul"	Sarah Vaughan	"Dreamsville;" Verve Music
Slow dance music to recall fond memories		
"(I Love You) for Sentimental Reasons"[a]	Rod Stewart	"Stardust;" J Records
"(I Love You) for Sentimental Reasons"[a]	Nat King Cole	"Unforgettable;" Capitol Records
"Stardust"[a]	Rod Stewart	"Stardust;" J Records
"These Foolish Things"	Rod Stewart	"It Had to Be You;" J Records
"'Til There Was You"[a]	Rod Stewart	"As Time Goes By;" J Records
"Where or When"[a]	Rod Stewart	"As Time Goes By;" J Records
"Where or When"[a]	Ella Fitzgerald	"The Very Best...;" Verve Music
"My Heart Stood Still"	Rod Stewart	"As Time Goes By;" J Records
"A Nightingale Sang in Berkeley"[a]	Rod Stewart	"Stardust;" J Records
"I've Got a Crush on You"	Rod Stewart	"Thanks for the Memory;" J Records
"Polka Dots & Moonbeams"	Sarah Vaughan	"Dreamsville;" Verve Music
"That Sunday, That Summer"[a]	Nat King Cole	"Unforgettable;" Capitol Records
"Tenderly"[a]	Nat King Cole	"Unforgettable;" Capitol Records
Slow dance music to create a positive mood		
"Smile"	Rod Stewart	"As Time Goes By;" J Records
"What a Wonderful World"[a]	Rod Stewart	"Stardust;" J Records
"Blue Skies"	Rod Stewart	"Thanks for the Memory;" J Records
"'S Wonderful"[a]	Ella Fitzgerald	"The Very Best...;" Verve Music

(continued)

Handout 12.1 *(continued)*

Goals and Titles	Artist	Title of CD; Label
Slow dance music that expresses attraction		
"You Go to My Head"	Rod Stewart	"It Had to Be You;" J Records
"It Had to Be You"	Rod Stewart	"It Had to Be You;" J Records
"Bewitched, Bothered, Bewildered"[a]	Rod Stewart	"As Time Goes By;" J Records
"Night and Day"[a]	Rod Stewart	"Stardust;" J Records
"Bewitched"[a]	Sarah Vaughan	"Dreamsville;" Verve Music
"I'm in the Mood for Love"[a]	Sarah Vaughan	"Dreamsville;" Verve Music
Slow dance music that expresses love and romance		
"The Way You Look Tonight"	Rod Stewart	"It Had to Be You;" J Records
"The Very Thought of You"[a]	Rod Stewart	"It Had to Be You;" J Records
"The Very Thought of You"	Nat King Cole	"Unforgettable;" Capitol Records
"Isn't It Romantic?"	Rod Stewart	"Stardust;" J Records
"My One and Only Love"[a]	Rod Stewart	"Thanks for the Memory;" J Records
"The Man I Love"	Ella Fitzgerald	"The Very Best...;" Verve Music
"Misty"	Sarah Vaughan	"Dreamsville;" Verve Music
"Mona Lisa"	Nat King Cole	"Unforgettable;" Capitol Records
"Nature Boy"[a]	Nat King Cole	"Unforgettable;" Capitol Records
"Darling, Je Vous Aime Beaucoup"	Nat King Cole	"Unforgettable;" Capitol Records
"Non Dimenticar"	Nat King Cole	"Unforgettable;" Capitol Records
Slow dance music that expresses love everlasting and commitment		
"I'll Be Seeing You"[a]	Rod Stewart	"It Had to Be You;" J Records
"Every Time We Say Goodbye"	Rod Stewart	"It Had to Be You;" J Records
"That's All"[a]	Rod Stewart	"It Had to Be You;" J Records
"Time After Time"	Rod Stewart	"As Time Goes By;" J Records
"Until the Real Thing Comes Along"	Rod Stewart	"As Time Goes By;" J Records
"Long Ago and Far Away"	Rod Stewart	"Thanks for the Memory;" J Records
"My Funny Valentine"	Rod Stewart	"Thanks for the Memory;" J Records
"My Funny Valentine"[a]	Ella Fitzgerald	"The Very Best...;" Verve Music
"Unforgettable"[a]	Nat King Cole	"Unforgettable;;" Capitol Records
"Could I Have This Dance?"	Anne Murray	"The Best...So Far;" Capitol Records
Slow dance music that expresses the desire to live in the moment		
"For All We Know"	Rod Stewart	"It Had to Be You;" J Records
"The Nearness of You"[a]	Rod Stewart	"It Had to Be You;" J Records
Slow dance music to express a longing		
"Someone to Watch Over Me"[a]	Sarah Vaughan	"Dreamsville;" Verve Music
Slow dance music to identify pursuer–distancer pattern		
"Baby, It's Cold Outside"	Rod Stewart	"Stardust;" J Records
Slow dance music for reconciliation		
"I Can't Get Started"	Rod Stewart	"Stardust;" J Records
"A Kiss to Build a Dream On"	Rod Stewart	"Stardust;" J Records
"Taking a Chance on Love"	Rod Stewart	"Thanks for the Memory;" J Records

(continued)

Handout 12.1 *(continued)*

Goals and Titles	Artist	Title of CD; Label
Slow dance music that expresses commitment		
"Crazy She Calls Me"	Rod Stewart	"As Time Goes By;" J Records
"Our Love Is Here to Stay"[a]	Rod Stewart	"As Time Goes By;" J Records
"Our Love Is Here to Stay"	Nat King Cole	"Unforgettable;" Capitol Records
"Nevertheless"	Rod Stewart	"Thanks for the Memory;" J Records
Slow dance music to express regret		
"Thanks for the Memory"	Rod Stewart	"Thanks for the Memory;" J Records
"Don't Get Around Much Anymore"	Nat King Cole	"Unforgettable;" Capitol Records
"Smile"[a]	Nat King Cole	"Unforgettable;" Capitol Records
"Autumn Leaves"[a]	Nat King Cole	"Unforgettable;" Capitol Records
Slow dance music for termination		
"We'll Be Together Again"	Rod Stewart	"It Had to Be You;" J Records
"As Time Goes By"	Rod Stewart	"As Time Goes By;" J Records
"That's All"[a]	Rod Stewart	"It Had to Be You;" J Records
Fox trots		
"Manhattan"	Rod Stewart	"Stardust;" J Records
"Blue Skies"	Rod Stewart	"Thanks for the Memory;" J Records
"You Send Me"[a]	Rod Stewart	"Thanks for the Memory;" J Records
"I've Got My Love to Keep Warm"	Rod Stewart	"Thanks for the Memory;" J Records
"Let's Fall in Love"	Rod Stewart	"Thanks for the Memory;" J Records
"All the Things You Are"	Ella Fitzgerald	"The Very Best...;" Verve Music
"Too Marvelous for Words"	Ella Fitzgerald	"The Very Best...;" Verve Music
"Night and Day"[a]	Ella Fitzgerald	"The Very Best...;" Verve Music
"I Get a Kick Out of You"[a]	Ella Fitzgerald	"The Very Best...;" Verve Music
"Cheek to Cheek"[a]	Ella Fitzgerald	"The Very Best...;" Verve Music
"It's Only a Paper Moon"	Nat King Cole	"Unforgettable;" Capitol Records
"Orange Colored Sky"	Nat King Cole	"Unforgettable;" Capitol Records
"Almost Like Being in Love"	Nat King Cole	"Unforgettable;" Capitol Records
Swing		
"It Don't Mean a Thing"	Ella Fitzgerald	"The Very Best...;" Verve Music
"Blue Skies"	Ella Fitzgerald	"The Very Best...;" Verve Music
"I Got Rhythm"	Ella Fitzgerald	"The Very Best...;" Verve Music
"That Old Black Magic"	Ella Fitzgerald	"The Very Best...;" Verve Music
"Take the 'A' Train"[a]	Ella Fitzgerald	"The Very Best...;" Verve Music
"Avalon"	Nat King Cole	"Unforgettable;" Capitol Records
"Thou Swell"[a]	Nat King Cole	"Unforgettable;" Capitol Records
Tangos		
Select songs		*Luis Bravo's Forever Tango (1998); RCA*

[a] Highly recommended.

Handout 12.2: Process Questions to Be Used before and after a Couples Dance

Preliminary Questions to Use before Dancing

- When you hear the word "dance" what comes to your mind?
- What past experiences—positive or negative—have you had related to dance?
- When, where, and how often have you danced as a couple? Do you currently dance?
- Do you have a special song that you think of as "Our Song?" If so, why is it special?

Follow-up Questions

- What was it like to slow dance together? What were your reactions?
- What was it like to lead or follow?
- What was your comfort level, and did it change as the dance progressed?
- What did you notice about your partner? (physical self, looks, scents, etc.)
- What was your reaction to the music? To the lyrics?
- What thoughts and feelings came to you as you danced?
- What changed as you continued to dance?
- Who had the harder time with this?
- Did this bring back any memories? If so, what were they?
- What was it like not to talk during the dance? Or, if you talked, what did you talk about?
- How do you feel now after dancing, and how did you feel before the dance?
- If you could have changed anything about your dance, what would it be?
- Who or what might get in the way of your dancing together more often?
- What reaction might others (e.g., children) have to seeing you dance?

– 13 –

"Let Me Show You the Ropes!"

Catherine Ford Sori

Type of Contribution: Activity, Homework

Objective

This experiential activity utilizes ropes in therapy sessions with couples to address various therapeutic issues and to promote change. Ropes can be used to help couples understand problems related to issues such as closeness and distance, problems with intimacy, patterns of communication, roles, coalitions in families, loyalty issues, and triangles. This chapter will focus on the dyad of the couple within the context of the family system.

Rationale for Use

Family therapy was predicated on the notion that individuals in a family are part of an interlocking system and that movement or change in one member will have an impact on other family members. Some therapists may use visual representations to help families understand this concept, such as a mobile that shows how the movement of one element causes subsequent movement in the other elements that are attached to the mobile. This may be a helpful metaphor, but because of its abstract nature its use in therapy is somewhat limited. Yet clients often benefit from understanding the reciprocal nature of relationships and in becoming aware of the role each person plays in maintaining the problems. This can help families begin to see new possibilities in how they can relate to one another and solve their problems.

Virginia Satir (1972, 1988), one of the pioneers of the experiential school of family therapy, is known for her creative use of ropes to assist families in understanding the interconnectedness of family relationships. Satir stated,

> Used as a metaphor for relationships, ropes can serve to make the family network come alive for its members. This technique is an excellent way to demonstrate how one part of the family system affects the rest of the system. (Satir & Baldwin, 1983, p. 251)

In her books, *Peoplemaking* (1972), *The New Peoplemaking* (1988), and *Satir Step by Step* (Satir & Baldwin, 1983), Satir suggests giving each family member a piece of rope to tie around his or her waist, as well as a much longer piece for each person to connect from the "self" waist rope to each other family member's waist rope. Thus, all family members would be literally connected to each and every other family member by not one, but two ropes. Satir would then demonstrate how each person is affected by being tugged at when another person moves away, and what happens if family members try to move about independently, as if they were doing their daily tasks. Her use of ropes illustrates the many entanglements and tensions that can occur in family relationships, how impossible it is to attend to each family member simultaneously, and how family members require freedom to maneuver in relation to other family members (Satir & Baldwin). She explained:

> Ropes can also be used as a metaphor for illustrating other types of interaction, connections, or relationships when one wants to raise participants' awareness or demonstrate how to transform tension and stress into a more relaxed state. (Satir & Baldwin, 1983, p. 251)

Satir used ropes as well as other powerful activities, such as sculpts and family reconstruction (Satir & Baldwin, 1983), to advance the goals of experiential family therapy, which included promoting more open and honest communication among family members.

Experiential activities can be especially useful when therapists feel stuck or that therapy is not moving forward. Simply getting clients up and moving suggests new possibilities for changing patterns of interactions (see Dermer, Matson, & Sori, this volume). This chapter offers various ways for using ropes to bring about not only the preceding goals of experiential family therapy, but also those of structural family therapy and Bowen systems theory.

Ropes and triangulation. Ropes are useful when working with couples to illustrate the concepts of triangulation and triads. The idea of triangulation using ropes can be utilized from either a Bowenian or a structural family therapy perspective. Bowen believed that a triad is the smallest, most stable unit and that when a relationship between two people (such as a couple) becomes stressed, the inclination is for one of them to involve a third party (Bowen, 1978).

Minuchin discussed the concepts of triads in his classic book, *Families and Family Therapy* (1974, p. 102). He explained three types of rigid triangles where children become involved in their parents' relationship in ways that are not healthy. In this current chapter they are described as a (1) "tug-of-war," where both parents are pulling at the child to demand loyalty or attention; (2) detouring conflict, where disputes between a couple are stifled and submerged, and then projected onto a child who becomes the symptom bearer; and (3) cross-generational coalition, where a parent aligns with a child against the other parent. In all of these, the partners avoid dealing with their couple issues by focusing on issues related to children or parenting.

"Tug-of-war." The first type of rigid triangle Minuchin (1974, p. 102) discusses, which can happen when children are drawn into the relationship of their parents, occurs when

> Each parent demands that the child side with him against the other parent. Whenever the child sides with one, he is automatically defined as attacking the other. In this highly dysfunctional structure, the child is paralyzed. Every movement he makes is defined by one parent as an attack.

This "tug-of-war" type of rigid triangle is often seen in cases of high-conflict divorce, where each parent may blame the other and demand loyalty from the child, often asking children to report on what takes place at the ex-spouse's home or conveying to children that it is not okay to love the other parent or enjoy time spent with him or her. Children are often caught unarmed and unprotected in the middle of this conflict, which can seriously wound them. In these cases the partners need to deal with their own anger and hostility, instead of involving a child in the conflict.

Detouring conflict. This occurs when spouses appear to be living in harmony, but there is underlying conflict, and this stress is projected onto a child. Instead of dealing with issues related to the marital relationship, the couple focus their energy on child issues. According to Minuchin (1974, p. 102),

> The negotiation of spouse stresses through the child serves to maintain the spouse subsystem in an illusory harmony. The spouses reinforce any deviant behavior in the child because dealing with him allows them to detour or submerge their own spouse subsystem problems in problems of parenting.

This detouring takes different forms. In some families the parents appear to stand together to attack and blame a child as being "the problem" and the root of the family's difficulties. In other families the parents appear to be united in their definition of a child as being ill or weak, and they join forces to help or protect the child (Minuchin, 1974, p. 102). Minuchin, Rosman, and Baker (1978) found that this last type of detouring occurred often in families who had a child with a somatic illness.

Stable cross-generational coalition. According to Minuchin (1974), a cross-generational coalition occurs when one parent aligns with a child in a rigid coalition against the other parent. The over-closeness between parent and child is contrasted to the distance between the child and the other parent, as well as distance between the spouses. Any attempt the child makes to move closer to the parent who is the "outsider" is perceived by the close parent as being disloyal. This child loses the right to have a relationship with both parents and may have difficulty developing autonomy during adolescence. This type of coalition is often seen in stepfamilies, where a biological parent and child are aligned against the stepparent (Hecker & Sori, 2006); in families where a child has been triangled into a coalition with one parent following an extramarital affair (Sori, 2007); or in families where the relationship between an ill child and the caretaking parent becomes so intense that the spouse and other children feel left out (Sori & Biank, 2006).

Ropes and patterns of couple complementarity. Couples often develop complementary roles and ways of relating that, when they become rigid, can be unhealthy. One common rigid complementary pattern is the pursuer–distancer, which occurs when one partner attempts to get closer to the other, who then distances. Often the more the pursuer pursues, the more the distancer distances, and vice versa. Another example of complementarity is the blaming–attacking pattern, where couples are locked in a vicious pattern of blaming and attacking one another as a way of regulating their anxieties related to intimacy (see Middelberg, 2001). A frequent goal among structural family therapists who work with couples is to alter rigid complementary patterns in order to change the structure of the family and promote healthier family functioning (see Dermer et al., this volume; Middelberg, 2001; Minuchin, 1981; Minuchin, Nichols, & Lee, 2007). Ropes can be used to illustrate patterns of complementarity in couples such as the pursuer–distancer, as well as to physically depict the degree of closeness each partner experiences in the relationship.

These activities are meant to be used to illustrate and concretize concepts and patterns that are often the focus of a couple's therapy within the context of the family system. They often increase the intensity in sessions by "making the covert overt" and thus should be used with discretion, and only when therapists are well joined with clients.

Materials

Ropes of various lengths (e.g., 20–24 feet; 15 feet; 10 feet) are needed for *Let Me Show You the Ropes.* The ropes should be lightweight but thick enough to allow them to be easily tied and untied for the various activities described next.

Instructions

Therapists can introduce this activity to illustrate a topic that has been the focus of discussion by asking if the couple will stand so that the therapist can "show them the ropes." Chairs, tables, and other furniture should be pushed to the corners of the room to allow as much space to be utilized for the rope activities as possible. The couple should be instructed to hold the rope loosely in only one hand, adjusting the distance between them so that the rope is taut at all times and making sure never to let the rope go slack. Therapists can tell couples that the ropes will be used to demonstrate characteristics of their relationships, or patterns of interactions, and that many clients find these activities helpful in exploring new ways to relate to one another.

Using ropes to represent the couple's degree of intimacy. The therapist can give each partner one end of a long piece of untied rope, approximately 20–24 feet, or as long as the room will allow. Each partner is then asked to demonstrate how close he or she feels they were as a couple at various points in their relationship. These points might include significant times or events such as (1) when they were first dating, (2) when they got engaged, (3) when they were on their honeymoon, (4) during the first year of their marriage, (5) after the birth of their first child, (5) when the first child entered adolescence, (6) after the deaths of close family members such as grandparents, (7) when the first and last children left home, and (8) any other significant life event, such as a serious illness, loss of a job, financial stressors, etc. Finally, each partner is asked to use the rope to demonstrate how close the couple is currently and what each one's ideal degree of closeness or intimacy would be.

These rope demonstrations can be useful to illustrate how intimacy and closeness in marital relationships often fluctuate over the years and how different partners desire different degrees of proximity. These differences and illustrations provide useful information in assessing complementarity in the couple, such as a pursuer–distancer patterns. The length of the rope that symbolizes their current degree of intimacy, as well as their ideal relationship, can be useful in goal setting and in exploring what or who may be preventing them from shortening the distance between them. For example, there might be a coalition between one of the spouses and a child, and this would lead naturally into the cross-generational rope demonstration described later.

Using ropes to illustrate a couple's complementary pattern of blame and attack. In conjoint therapy ropes can be used to illustrate rigid complementary patterns in couples that may no longer be functional. To demonstrate the complementary pattern of blaming and attacking in conflictual couples, the therapist can give each partner one end of a long, untied rope and ask each to adjust the length to represent the closeness each feels when the couple is locked in a battle of attack and blame. Keeping the rope taut, they can then take turns, with first one blaming or attacking spouse (#1) stepping forward and thrusting the rope toward the other spouse (#2), who must step back to keep the rope from slacking, but who then retaliates by lunging forward and thrusting the rope back at spouse #1, who then must step back, etc.

Back and forth their dance goes like a porch glider that goes nowhere, but whose squeaky noise attracts attention. Therapists might point out that this thrusting and sparring is much like a swordfight, which can lead to an exploration of where each partner learned to negotiate relationships in such a manner (see Minuchin et al., 2007); why they feel they need a sword to protect themselves from one another; what happens if one partner becomes wounded or if anyone else ever gets wounded by getting too close to the battle or by trying to stop it; if there is ever a winner; and what might happen if one partner were to put down his or her sword.

Using ropes to demonstrate a couple's complementary pattern of pursuer–distancer. After discovering that one partner often pursues the other, who, when pursued, usually distances, a couple may be given a length of untied rope and then each asked to position themselves to reflect the proximity or degree of closeness each one feels in their relationship. After telling the couple the rope cannot go slack but must be kept taught, the pursuing spouse is asked to move toward the partner, who must distance to keep the rope taut. The pursuer can be encouraged to keep trying to gain proximity, while the distancer continues to move away to maintain a stable distance. The couple can then be asked to switch roles. Because the rope must remain taut, the couple not only can see, but also physically experience their complementary "dance," which illustrates that no matter who is moving, the distance between them remains constant. As in the previous instance, this activity can lead into a discussion of where each partner learned his or her role (see Minuchin et al., 2007). It may also clarify the need for therapy for a resistant client and can provide an impetus to help partners relinquish their rigid complementary roles that are not working so that they can move toward a new "dance," or way of interacting. In addition, when used this way, ropes can be quite useful to begin to explore anxiety related to intimacy or sexual issues.

Using ropes with couples to demonstrate patterns of triangulation. A couple who has experienced problems from triangulation can be given a very long length of rope that is tied together, making a large loop. Each partner can be asked to hold the rope stretched out to show how close they were at different points in their relationship (e.g., dating, engaged, newlyweds, etc. up to the present), as described earlier. Then the therapist can also take hold of the rope to represent whatever or whoever has been triangled into the couple's relationship (i.e., an affair partner, work, Internet pornography, alcohol, gambling, etc.). As previously described, the rope should be held loosely in one hand and should be kept taut, and the couple and therapist should form a wide triangle. The therapist, still taking the role of whatever has been triangulated into the couple's relationship, then begins to walk forward. Since the rope must remain taut, the couple ends up backing away from each other. The therapist eventually stops, standing either right in the middle between the partners or closer to one partner (e.g., if there was an affair, closer to that partner), which means the other partner must back up and move even further away from the spouse. This illustrates how anything that becomes triangulated in the couple's relationship increases the distance between them; this can motivate clients to strengthen the boundaries around their relationship to block out that intrusion, allowing them to access more proximity to one another.

In a similar fashion, ropes can be used with families to illustrate numerous family therapy concepts, such as coalitions, detouring, and problems with life cycle transitions. The following sections include instructions on how to use ropes to show the three types of rigid triangles where children are involved in the couple conflict discussed earlier (see Minuchin, 1974). It is important to note that when using ropes to demonstrate the problems that occur when a child is involved in a rigid triangle with the parents, therapists should use care and professional discretion in deciding whether to actually include the child in the activity, or whether to have the therapist stand in to represent the child in the activity in conjoint sessions.

Using ropes with couples or families to illustrate cross-generational coalitions. One common problem seen in families is the cross-generational coalition, where a child is aligned with one parent against the other parent. This creates a loyalty conflict for the child, who is afraid to approach the distant parent for fear of losing the close relationship with the aligned parent (see Minuchin, 1974). Once a therapist has become aware of a coalition and feels ready to challenge the family, ropes are an excellent and somewhat playful method to make the invisible visible and to illustrate the unfairness and harmful effects to the child as well as the couple. This is done in a manner very similar to the previous one describing triangulation: The couple and a child (or therapist standing in for the child) are asked to loosely hold a circular rope in one hand, always keeping it taught.

First the therapist can illustrate how optimally families should be flexible and allow all family members to move toward and away from one another at different times. For example, the child might move closer to Mom to talk about friends or to go shopping, and then be able to move closer to Dad to go to a baseball game. When the couple move toward one another (i.e., to have private conversations or be intimate), the child must back away from them to keep the rope taut. Likewise, when a child moves away from parents toward the outside world, parents must draw closer together in order to allow the child enough rope to move away. All of these movements require families to be flexible and adaptable.

To illustrate a cross-generational coalition, the therapist can have the child (or therapist standing in for the child) and parent who are in a coalition face each other standing very close, with the proximal parent standing between the child and distant parent, thus blocking the child from seeing or moving toward the distant parent. The therapist can then explore what it is like when these positions become rigid: Everyone loses. The child who is cemented so close to one parent cannot move toward the other, distant parent. The distant parent is alone and far from both spouse and child, and the parent in a coalition loses the chance for any relationship with his or her partner. Once this picture becomes clear, therapists can elicit the natural love and concern most parents have for their children. The couple could be asked to enact a conversation, perhaps where the close parent is encouraged to challenge the distant parent to get more involved with parenting, and the distant parent clarifies how the close parent gets in the way of this happening.

Using ropes with couples or families to illustrate a "tug-of-war." Ropes can also visually depict what happens when both parents demand that the child side with them against the other. This "tug-of-war" can be especially virulent in situations of divorce or following the discovery of an affair. To illustrate this tug-of-war, the therapist can take the very long rope that is tied in a loop and have each parent and the child (or the therapist, who is representing the child) loosely hold the rope. The child stands in the middle, while the parents walk clockwise in a complete circle around the child until they resume their original places. The tug-of-war begins as each parent demands loyalty and attempts to pull the child closer. In turn, the other parent demands loyalty and tugs on the opposite side of the rope to try to move the child closer in that direction. However, the child is stuck in the middle, feeling literally "squeezed" and unable to be close to either parent. Then both parents are asked to pull gently on the child simultaneously. The child is trapped, like a fly in a Venus flytrap, and cannot leave.

If the therapist is role-playing the child, it can be useful to have each parent also role play the child to increase empathy for the son or daughter, as they experience mild physical discomfort from being tugged at from opposite sides of the rope. This activity concretizes how children are in a no-win situation when both parents are vying for their loyalty. Therapists should also emphasize that the presence of the child tied between them blocks them from dealing with their problems with one another; to do so, they would first have to free the child.

Instructions on using ropes to demonstrate couples who detour conflict onto their child. To demonstrate how couples can detour their conflict onto a child, the therapist should ask the couple to stand close together, with each one holding the rope as described before. Since they are close and the rope must remain taut, this means that the child must back away and be a distant third point in this triangle. From here, the therapist can follow the directions that follow to illustrate one of the two ways couples detour conflict from their relationship onto a child.

Scapegoated child. The parents should stand close together as described earlier, but turn back to back. Their heads should be turned so that each is looking at the child (or substituting therapist) in an angry manner; the child stares back at them. In this position, the couple is unable to look at each other. Their physical proximity represents pseudomutuality, but their focus on the child and their positions relative to one another prevent them from looking at each other or directly discussing any problems in their own relationship. To do so, they would have to turn around and focus their attention on one another, instead of on the child. Borrowing a metaphor from Minuchin to illustrate the reciprocal nature of this situation, the clinician might comment that the parents seem like jailers who are imprisoned, and the child is a prisoner who is also a jailer (Minuchin et al., 2007). The therapist might ask the couple what other problems might grab their attention if the problems with the child were to disappear, and what it would be like to face one another to discuss those issues. This can lead quite naturally into asking the couple to enact such a discussion.

Somatic child. To illustrate a rigid triangle involving a somatic child the activity should start as described before. However, this time the family is given a very short rope and the couple stands shoulder to shoulder facing the child (or therapist portraying the child), who is again the focus of all their attention. The parents are asked to stare intently at the child, who cannot look away, while they all freeze in this pose for several minutes. Each person can be asked to describe what he or she sees and what and who he or she cannot see or do by being frozen in this position. The parents are not able to turn toward one another to talk or to focus on each other, as all their attention is focused on the child. The child is frozen, closely attending to what is going on between the parents, like a barometer of their relationship, and is not free to turn around to engage in other relationships or activities. The therapist might comment that they are all like birds trapped in a golden cage (Minuchin et al., 2007), unable to be free to fly away, or like the animals turned to concrete statutes by the White Witch in Narnia (Lewis, 1950), frozen in place and waiting to be magically freed.

These rope activities can be quite useful to help couples better understand their relationships within the context of the family, and to increase the intensity in sessions to prepare clients for other follow-up interventions or discussions. They should be utilized as part of an overall treatment plan to bring about specific therapeutic goals in couples therapy.

Brief Clinical Vignette

Gregory and Jennifer had been married for 4 years when they sought couples counseling. Together they had a 2-year-old daughter, and Jennifer had a 14-year-old son from her previous marriage. This was Gregory's first marriage. He was a medical doctor in a large group practice, and Jennifer was their office manager. Their presenting problem was that Jennifer had discovered that Gregory had been viewing pornography on the Internet, and had also been chatting on e-mail with a former nurse from his office. Further assessment during the first few sessions revealed that this stepfamily appeared to have a cross-generational coalition: Jennifer was closely aligned with her biological son, George, against Gregory. While she complained that Gregory was not involved at all in parenting either child, she admitted to having often criticized his prior attempts to discipline, quickly jumping in, especially to protect her son from any criticism.

Gregory had distanced from both his stepson and his wife prior to becoming involved with pornography. At times Jennifer would try to approach Gregory for more connection, but as soon as any issues arose with the children, she would react and he would quickly retreat to the Internet. At other times, Gregory would try to move closer to Jennifer, but, if she thought he was being critical of George, she immediately became defensive and protective and distanced from her husband. Gregory would then give up and once again retreat to the Internet. After several attempts at goal setting and discussing boundaries and their patterns of interacting, the therapist felt frustrated at this very bright and articulate couple who just did not seem to "get it." They were stuck in a cross-generational coalition common to stepfamilies, and their attempts to occasionally pursue one another only led to distancing from each other.

At the beginning of the third session the clinician asked the clients if they would be willing to let her "show them the ropes." The couple agreed, and together they all pushed back the furniture to make space for the activities.

First, the therapist handed Gregory and Jennifer a long length of untied rope and asked each in turn to use it to illustrate the degree of closeness they felt at different points throughout their relationship. Gregory demonstrated that he had felt closest to Jennifer right before they were married, because she seemed to need him to be a husband and a father to her son. But the distance slowly increased over the years of their relationship, and now he felt they were at opposite ends of the 20-foot rope. Surprisingly, Jennifer's demonstration was very similar to Gregory's. However, she said that currently she needed a much longer rope because, since his involvement on the Internet and her discovery of his e-mails to the nurse, she had a difficult time trusting Gregory. Both were in agreement as to what their ideal relationship would look like: There would be only a short rope separating them. This activity led to the first of several discussions about what would have to happen to shorten the rope, what Jennifer needed from Gregory to begin to restore trust, and what Gregory needed from her to become more involved with the family as a husband and father.

The clinician then used the rope to illustrate the pursuer–distancer pattern the couple had described in their relationship. They were instructed to keep the rope taught at all times. Jennifer was asked to try to move closer to Gregory, but he was told to retreat because he sensed she was critical of his parenting. Next the therapist explained that when distance leads to loneliness, the distant spouse may then try to seek proximity from the other partner. So Gregory was asked to begin to move closer toward Jennifer. However, now Jennifer would react to something Gregory said about George, so she would retreat, keeping the rope taught. They were encouraged to enact this "dance" several times, while the clinician emphasized that despite all this movement that resembled a "cha-cha," they never got any closer together. This can leave both partners feeling isolated and lonely and can leave a couple vulnerable.

Next the therapist demonstrated what can happen when something or someone comes between partners. Taking a 24-foot length of rope and tying the ends together, the therapist invited Gregory and Jennifer each to hold the rope loosely in one hand, while she also held the rope, making an equal triangle. She emphasized that they must keep the rope stretched tight. The therapist explained that she would serve as the third point in the triangle, representing the Internet pornography and e-mails that had come between them. Gradually, the therapist began walking toward them, reminding the couple that they had to move apart to keep the rope from becoming slack. As she stood between them blocking their access to one another, they discussed how important boundaries are around a couple's relationship, which must be carefully guarded from intruders.

At the end of the session each partner was asked to move the therapist (representing Internet pornography and e-mails) to a spot that depicted how much distance they thought they had already established from the problem, as well as ideally how far away they would like those problems to be. Gregory moved the therapist several feet away from the middle of their relationship, which naturally shortened the distance of the rope between Jennifer and him. Jennifer was not ready to accept that this distance had yet been achieved. But, ideally, both agreed that there was not a rope long enough to separate them from those problems; they wanted scissors to cut that part of the rope completely off, leaving them closer. This session ended much differently; both seemed softer toward one another and much more hopeful.

In the next session the couple could hardly wait to tell the therapist their exciting news. They had purchased their own rope (without prompting from the clinician!) and each night had "measured" how close they felt and had discussed what would help increase trust and strengthen the "rope between them" so that nothing could get in the middle of their relationship again. After highlighting this breakthrough with some discussion, the therapist asked the couple if they would try yet another rope activity. They enthusiastically agreed.

This time, the clinician used the long, tied rope to illustrate the cross-generational coalition in the family. She took the role of George and stood close behind and facing Jennifer, who was then between her and Gregory. Gregory had to be reminded that he must move back in order to keep the rope from becoming slack. Holding these positions, each person talked about what it felt like to be in this rigid triangle. Representing George, the therapist described feeling unsure of why Mom always felt he needed protection from Gregory and that he also felt somewhat resentful because he was a guy and did not need "protecting" and because Mom's interference prevented him from having the kind of relationship he had always wanted with a father. Jennifer's face registered first surprise and then comprehension as she listened to the therapist's explanation of what she thought it felt like to be George.

Gregory's voice broke as he described what it was like to feel like an outsider "looking in" on the close relationship between Jennifer and her son. The therapist asked where he had learned to be satisfied with the role of an outsider. Gregory briefly described that, when he was a child, his father worked two jobs, and his mother had been so involved in caring for his sister, who had cystic fibrosis, that he sometimes felt invisible to both parents. He threw himself into his studies, hoping to gain attention and win parental approval that never came. After his sister died, both parents retreated behind a wall of silence. At times, in fact, he felt that he was watching a silent movie. Gregory became a doctor and continued to focus most of his energy on his work until he met Jennifer. For the first time, he felt loved and like he could be part of a family. But gradually he retreated, as more and more he felt once again like an outsider, looking in at Jennifer's close relationship with the children. Jennifer was clearly deeply moved by this story.

When Jennifer was asked where she learned that she must protect her children from having a relationship with their father, she told her own story. Jennifer's parents divorced when she was 5 and her sisters were 3 and 2. Afterward, her father disappeared from their lives. Shortly thereafter her mother remarried a man who was a good provider, but who would become verbally abusive when he drank. This abuse became increasingly violent, and Jennifer's mother was unable to protect herself or her children from his drunken slaps and beatings. Jennifer took on the role of the protector, trying to shield her younger siblings, running to the neighbors for help, or calling the police. She determined that no one would ever treat her or her children in an abusive manner when she grew up.

In that session, while still standing in the pose holding the rope, Jennifer softened when she reflected on Gregory's story and admitted that he had never been violent or abusive toward her or her children. Gregory responded that he now realized why Jennifer was "such a mother bear," and his voice was thick as he purposed in his heart never to hurt her or cause her to doubt him again.

As they began a natural enactment discussing these issues, the therapist (representing the problems with Internet porn and e-mails) silently and slowly began backing away. This gentle tug on the ropes nudged the couple closer to one another, and they ended the discussion holding each other's hands (which still held onto a very short length of rope), with tears in their eyes.

While there was still much work to be done, this was clearly a turning point in this couple's therapy. Each week they reported back to the therapist the results of their self-imposed nightly "rope homework," where they used a rope to measure how close they felt and to indicate the degree of success they had in setting more appropriate boundaries around their relationship. At termination they reported they had met all their goals, and they eagerly brought in a camera and asked the therapist to take their picture showing them with their ropes. They planned to put the photograph on the refrigerator to remind them of how they had "learned the ropes" together.

Suggestions for Follow-Up

Following the lead of the couple in the vignette, therapists can suggest couples use ropes at home between sessions. They can use a rope several times a week to measure how close they feel and can keep a record measuring the length of the rope to discuss in sessions. Solution-focused questions can be integrated with rope activities. For example, the therapist can ask couples to demonstrate exceptions to the problem to show when they were closer and can explore what was happening during those times when their rope was shorter or when nothing was triangled into their relationship.

From a transgenerational perspective, couples can be asked to use ropes to depict closeness and any rigid triangles in each partner's parents' relationship. Additional ropes can be added to illustrate Bowen's concept of interlocking triangles. For example, in a case of a cross-generational coalition where a mother is closely aligned with an ill child, leaving the father largely uninvolved except for being the wage earner, additional ropes can be used to demonstrate the triangles formed with the mother, father, and well siblings (who often feel they cannot intrude on the intense relationship between the ill child and caretaking mother); another rope can illustrate the triangle formed by the ill child, caregiving parent, and well child (who often resents all the attention the ill child receives, and who may feel abandoned); and the distant parent, well sibling, and ill child (who may feel guilty for all the attention and resources he or she receives, and miss the prior close relationships with siblings and the noncaretaking parent) (see Sori & Biank, 2006).

Therapists can also discuss how parents need different lengths of ropes for different stages of their children's development. When children are infants and toddlers, parents need to keep the ropes short to keep their children closely tethered, to nurture and protect them. As children grow parents need increasingly longer ropes to allow them more freedom to interact with the world. Children who are triangled into their parents' conflict will have a difficult time forging their own adult interpersonal relationships, as those ropes can be binding for a lifetime. And couples who have remained rigidly at opposite sides of a long length of rope for many years will struggle to navigate the space between them when they need to pull together to face difficult times such as death and loss, and when the children are gone and they are alone.

There are undoubtedly countless other possible ways to utilize ropes in couples or family therapy. With a little creativity and a bit of rope, clinicians can help free clients from the rigid patterns that bind them and bring them to therapy "all tied up in knots." We are only limited by the size (and number) of our ropes!

Contraindications for Use

While very skilled and seasoned therapists may utilize rope activities in early sessions, they are recommended only when a strong therapeutic alliance has been established. It is always prudent to avoid such interventions before taking adequate time to first hear everyone's view of the problem and to assess the sequence of interactions that maintains the problem. Before attempting any rope interventions, it is wise to experiment with colleagues or a supervisor to practice how to adapt the activity to best fit specific clients' needs and circumstances. Ropes can be used even with clients who are not ambulatory, but should be avoided with clients who have suffered any abuse, especially if it involved being tied, restrained, or bound.

References

Bowen, M. (1978). *Family therapy in clinical practice.* Northvale, NJ: Jason Aronson.

Dermer, S., Matson, J., & Sori, C. F. (this volume).

Hecker, L. L., & Sori, C. F. (2006). Divorce and stepfamily issues. In C. F. Sori (Ed.), *Engaging children in family therapy: Creative approaches to integrating theory and research in clinical practice* (pp. 177–204). New York: Routledge.

Lewis, C. S. (1950). *The lion, the witch, and the wardrobe.* London: Geoffrey Bles.

Middelberg, C. V. (2001). Projective identification in common couple dances. *Journal of Marital & Family Therapy, 27*(3), 341–352.

Minuchin, S. (1974). *Families and family therapy.* Cambridge, MA: Harvard University Press.

Minuchin, S., & Fishman, H. C. (1981). *Family therapy techniques.* Cambridge, MA: Harvard University Press.

Minuchin, S., Nichols, M. P., & Lee, W. (2007). *Assessing families and couples: From symptom to system.* Boston, MA: Pearson.

Minuchin, S., Rosman, B., & Baker, L. (1978). *Psychosomatic families: Anorexia nervosa in context.* Cambridge, MA: Harvard University Press.

Satir, V. (1972). *Peoplemaking.* Palo Alto, CA: Science and Behavior Books.

Satir, V. (1988). *The new peoplemaking.* Mountain View, CA: Science and Behavior Books.

Satir, V., & Baldwin, M. (1983). *Satir step by step: A guide to creating change in families.* Palo Alto: CA: Science and Behavior Books.

Sori, C. F. (2007). "An affair to remember": Infidelity and its impact on children. In P. Peluso (Ed.), *Infidelity: A practitioner's guide to working with couples in crisis.* New York: Routledge.

Sori, C. F., & Biank, N. M. (2006). Counseling children and families experiencing serious illness. In C. F. Sori (Ed.), *Engaging children in family therapy: Creative approaches to integrating theory and research in clinical practice* (pp. 223–244). New York: Routledge.

Professional Readings and Resources

Lerner, H. G. (1985). *The dance of anger.* New York: Harper & Row.

Lerner, H. G. (1989). *The dance of intimacy.* New York: Harper & Row.

Minuchin, S., Lee, W., & Simon, G. M. (1996). *Mastering family therapy.* New York: John Wiley & Sons.

Minuchin, S., & Nichols, M. P. (1993). *Family healing.* New York: The Free Press.

Whitaker, C. A., & Blumberry, W. (1988). *Dancing with the family: A symbolic-experiential approach.* New York: Brunner/Mazel.

Bibliotherapy Sources for the Client

Gottman, J. M. (2000). *The seven principles for making marriage work.* New York: Three Rivers Press.

Gottman, J. M. (2002). *The relationship cure: A 5-step guide to strengthening your marriage, family, and friendships.* New York: Three Rivers Press.

Lerner, H. G. (1985). *The dance of anger.* New York: Harper & Row.

Lerner, H. G. (1989). *The dance of intimacy.* New York: Harper & Row.

– 14 –

Assessing Trust in Action
The Couples Leaning Exercise

Daniel J. Wiener

Type of Contribution: Activity

Objective

The purpose of this activity is to provide both therapists and clients who are in couples therapy with an experiential demonstration of how interpersonal trust operates and can improve in the relationship. The activity offers couples a visual representation of the trust they have in one another and can offer a way for the therapist to assess and process important relational information.

Rationale for Use

Trust between partners is an important dimension in couples therapy. In Bowenian family systems therapy, trust is a marker or criterion that distinguishes stages of marital conflict (Guerin, Fay, Burden, & Koutto, 1987), with consequences for the types of interventions attempted by the therapist. However, verbal descriptions of trust elicited during therapy sessions are conceptual summaries that often do not correspond well with the experiences and behaviors of couples in their lives outside therapy. In some cases, the in-the-moment social demand characteristics of the session may lead clients to minimize or exaggerate the trust they experience; in others, their descriptions are less than reliable because the respondents may have drawn overgeneralized conclusions or be implicitly comparing the felt degree of trust to unstated expectations. For these reasons, in-session enactments serve to overcome the deficiencies of talk-only therapy (Minuchin, 1974).

The couples leaning exercise (CLE) is an action demonstration that offers the general advantages characteristic of action methods when used in psychotherapy, notably providing clients "with alternative frameworks for their experiences that engage the senses, often in novel ways" (Wiener & Oxford, 2003, pp. 5–6). Unlike verbal–conceptual formulations, which purport to describe then-and-there experience, such action demonstrations are here-and-now concrete experiences that demonstrate truth in experience (Wiener, 1999). As an example, the therapist Bunny Duhl wrote of a previously verbally manipulative client: "She enacted her real feelings and experience in typical fashion; the body in action did not lie" (Duhl, 1999, p. 88). In therapeutic work using action techniques, clients' verbal descriptions of their relationship functioning are frequently at variance with their in vivo performances. The advantages of assessment via such action techniques are not limited to the information the therapist gains; additionally, clients become aware of new possibilities for how their relationship may function differently.

The CLE assesses the degree of comfort partners experience in entrusting and being entrusted with their own and their partner's physical safety. The CLE has considerable sensory and emotive impact, allowing clients to experience a number of aspects of trust and perceptions of trustworthiness both in themselves and in their partners.

Instructions

The CLE, similar in form to the "trust-lean" exercise used in adventure-based training (Neill, 2004), is usually introduced once couples therapy is under way, following an orientation to couples therapy and therapist's joining, and following a discussion of the degree of trust that each partner asserts is extended to and received from the other. This discussion is often accompanied by further exploration of the degree to which each partner expected and/or agreed with the verbal formulations of the other.

At this point the therapist asks, "Would you be willing to try an experiment about trust?" Telling them that they will each have a turn, the therapist asks both partners to remove their shoes. The therapist explains that there are two roles in this activity—one being the "leaner" and one being the "supporter"—and that the partners will have a chance to be in both roles. The therapist then asks for a volunteer for the leaner role. One partner then leans against a wall or closed door, with shoulders only touching the vertical surface and feet on the floor, shoulder-width apart, about 15 inches from the edge where the wall or door meets the floor. This partner is called the leaner. The therapist invites the leaner to experiment with moving his feet closer to and farther away from that edge and to see at what distance he is committing his balance to the leaning and how comfortable he is once his feet are placed. The therapist then invites him to close his eyes and rate the leaning on a 10-point comfort scale, from "1" (highly uncomfortable; basically cannot stand it) to "10" (perfectly comfortable, even enjoyable). The therapist may suggest that the leaner experiment with changing the distance of his feet from the edge to increase the comfort level and rerate this optional distance.

The partner, who up until now was a bystander, becomes the supporter. At this point, the therapist asks the supporter whether she believes she can support her partner's weight while he leans backward against her hands. Often there is some hesitation or doubt expressed, partially based on the partners' disparity in size or weight. The therapist usually does not ask the supporter to scale for confidence but assures her that the leaning will be gradual and that she can safely call out for the leaner to stop or reverse the transfer of his weight at any point.

Next, the leaner moves away from the wall. The therapist demonstrates a stance for the supporter to take, standing behind the leaner, palms on his upper back about 2 inches in and below the corners of his shoulders, elbows slightly bent, torso leaning slightly toward the leaner, legs apart, one in front of the other, the front foot pointing forward toward the leaner, the rear foot planted at a right angle to the front foot (a "T" stance).

Now the leaner is asked to stand with his back to the supporter, and the supporter takes the "T" stance, placing her hands on the leaner's back under his shoulders. The therapist instructs him to begin to lean backwards on his heels, keeping the length of his own body straight. After asking the supporter whether she is securely balanced, the therapist supervises her to absorb the leaner's weight, telling the partners that they can call out to stop the leaning should either feel unsafe. Usually, the therapist stops the progression of the leaning at around a 30° angle, then asks the leaner to rate his comfort on the same 10-point scale used when leaning against the wall or door earlier. The therapist then asks for a qualitative verbal comparison of the experience of leaning on the partner to the earlier leaning against the door. While they are still leaning, the supporter is asked how comfortable she is with her supporting role, using the same 10-point scale. The therapist then ends the exercise and invites the couple to return to their pre-enactment seating to further process their experiences.

Brief Clinical Vignette

Mike and Fern, married 6 years and now in their late 30s, entered couples therapy, dismayed by a recent upward spike in the frequency and intensity of their quarreling. Their mutual unhappiness had recently uncovered apparent limits to their marital adjustment. The way that Fern described it was that "too much is changing too fast and we're not handling it well." These recent changes included Mike's recent job change, necessitating his longer commute; the entry of their only child,

4 years old, into a private preschool program; the worrisome illness of Fern's mother, living 4 hours' drive away; and financial pressure stemming from all of these issues. Each partner appeared highly critical of the solutions proposed by the other and was shaken by the intensity with which his or her own suggestions were rejected. What made this pattern still more problematic was their demoralization at now failing to reach an agreement, which they had regularly done in the past.

During the initial three sessions the therapist established that their goals for their family remained highly similar and that their reactivity did not result from their inability to hear one another; in fact, the congruence of their communication was distinctly superior to that of most spouses entering couples therapy. The therapist next gave them a number of action tasks (Wiener, 1994) designed to assess their capacity to attend to one another, to cooperate, and to validate each other's reality. Mike's and Fern's performance on these earlier action tasks showed that they were mutually attentive and capable of validating one another's reality but had difficulty in yielding to the other's ideas. It was decided to explore this dynamic further by offering them the CLE.

The therapist had Mike lean first against the door; he gave the comfort rating as "9.5." When leaning against Fern's hands, Mike became visually tense, pulling his head forward as his body slowly leaned back. As Fern drew her arms back, Mike took a step back, ending his leaning on Fern. Mike quickly explained, without any coaxing, that he was not sure that Fern could hold him; Fern reported irritation that he would not give her the chance.

Deciding not to allow Fern to have a turn leaning until they had processed what had already happened, therapist and clients returned to their pre-enactment seating. Fern spoke first, quietly but with intensity: "Mike, you can't stand letting me be in charge, can you?" She then cited an example of Mike's micromanaging their navigation to a recent party when Fern drove. Mike countered that he was just ensuring that they would arrive on time. The therapist took the opportunity to bring the couple back to the CLE. "Mike, you said you doubted that Fern *could* hold you, right?" Mike nodded. "Fern, would you be willing to hold me? I'm about your size, Mike." Fern assented and the therapist leaned on her hands at about a 30° angle; Fern had no difficulty. At this, Mike shook his head. "I guess I'm just not comfortable with falling backwards," he stated.

"Okay," the therapist said. "Would you be willing to lie on the floor where you can't fall, and let Fern hold your head?" Mike agreed, and he was instructed to lie on the floor on his back while Fern, sitting on the floor, cradled his head in her lap. "Now, let go completely," the therapist told Mike. "Let Fern move your head gently up, down, and sideways a little distance." This was done for 20 seconds. Mike appeared to allow this, but rated the experiences a "4" on the comfort scale. When Fern was asked how completely Mike had given up control to her, she said he had only briefly relaxed his neck muscles, allowing her to move his head.

When all had gotten back to their seating, Mike spoke first. "I guess I really don't like losing control," he said slowly. "I trust you, honey, but..." he trailed off. Fern gave his hand a short squeeze and looked inquiringly at the therapist. "Let's try the leaning the other way around," the therapist suggested. After Fern had rated her leaning on the wall a "10," Mike positioned himself behind her, placing his hands on her shoulders. "Ready?" he asked. Fern nodded and Mike slowly moved his hands back. Fern said, "Hold me more in the middle," and straightened up. Mike moved his hands toward her spine and began to lower her. "Okay, I can go further," Fern answered when he had stopped at about 20°. Fern coached Mike to keep lowering her until her body was at a 45° angle, at which point the therapist asked them to return to standing. Fern reported she was at an "8" with leaning on Mike; Mike said he had been fine with holding her but a bit "put out" by her bossing him. All returned to their seats.

"Fern, how much did you feel in control when leaning on Mike?" the therapist asked. Fern allowed that she had kept herself comfortable by instructing Mike. The therapist told her that it appeared that she had leaned so far back to make a point; Fern owned that her actions now seemed competitive, somehow. Mike brought up how he was reminded of Fern's "rubbing his nose in it" when he had returned from a grocery shopping errand without bringing home some items she had requested. "Both of you are capable people," the therapist observed, "but you get anxious and don't credit one another with being responsible. What's lacking here is validating each other's competence and creating a team effort." Both agreed that they wanted the other's trust and felt deprived by the other's criticism of the opportunity to be acknowledged for making a positive contribution.

Over the next 3 weeks, the therapist gave the couple two homework assignments. First, twice during the week, each was to come up with and request three things each wanted help with from the other; second, each was to take 5 minutes before bedtime every night to express appreciation for what the other had done to make life easier or better that day. During the sessions, the therapist again coached them through the CLE, having the couple report on their ongoing experience and inviting them to take the chance to see what full trust felt like. While not always needed, both the homework and repeated use of the CLE appeared to heighten the issue of interpersonal trust as core to the improvement of their relationship.

After two further sessions, therapy tapered off to twice monthly and ended after a total of 11 sessions. In the terminal session, Mike and Fern each reported that they had "found their groove again" and that they were confident they could handle things from here on. Laughingly, the therapist reminded them that asking for help, should it again be needed, was not a sign of weakness. At a follow-up phone call 5 months later, all was well.

Suggestions for Follow-Up

While it occasionally can be helpful to have the couple practice the CLE at home, it is preferable to coach them toward an in-office "success experience" as was done with Mike and Fern. When the CLE is used primarily to assess trust constraints in the relationship, the exercise will have served its purpose in heightening awareness of the issue and therapy can proceed without attempting it again. Sometimes, the CLE brings up traumatic or at least painful recollections of an earlier betrayal of trust, which then becomes the focus of further therapy. And, as in the case of Mike and Fern, working on barriers to trust is greatly facilitated by a concrete demonstration of trust's operation in action.

Contraindications for Use

Contraindications fall into four categories: (1) when there are physical disparities or disabilities that make the CLE physically unfeasible or unsafe; (2) when the couple presents in crisis and the enactment of this exercise would heighten already manifest anxiety; (3) when the issue of trust is, itself, toxic (e.g., following the recent revelation of an affair); or (4) when one or both partners are too shy, embarrassed, or self-conscious to perform this enactment in the presence of a therapist.

References

Duhl, B. S. (1999). A personal view of action metaphor: Bringing what's inside outside. In D. J. Wiener (Ed.) *Beyond talk therapy: Using movement and expressive techniques in clinical practice.* Washington, DC: APA Books.

Guerin, P. J., Jr., Fay, L. F., Burden, S. L., & Kautto, J. G. (1987). *Evaluation and treatment of marital conflict: A family-stage approach.* New York: Basic Books.

Minuchin, S. (1974). *Families and family therapy.* Cambridge, MA: Harvard University Press.

Neill, J. (2004, November 13). Trust lean: A description of a trust-building activity. Retrieved June 25, 2007, from http://www.wilderdom.com/games/descriptions/TrustLean.html.

Wiener, D. J. (1994). *Rehearsals for growth: Theater improvisation for psychotherapists.* New York: Norton.

Wiener, D. J. (Ed.). (1999). *Beyond talk therapy: Using movement and expressive techniques in clinical practice.* Washington, DC: APA Books.

Wiener, D. J., & Oxford, L. K. (Eds.). (2003). *Action therapy with families and groups: Using creative arts improvisation in clinical practice.* Washington, DC: APA Books.

Professional Readings and Resources

Fisher, R. (2002). *Experiential therapy with couples: A guide for the creative pragmatist.* Phoenix, AZ: Zeig, Tucker & Theisen.

Wiener, D. J. (1994). *Rehearsals for growth: Theater improvisation for psychotherapists.* New York: Norton.

Wiener, D. J. (Ed.). (1999). *Beyond talk therapy: Using movement and expressive techniques in clinical practice.* Washington, DC: APA Books.

Wiener, D. J., & Oxford, L. K. (Eds.). (2003). *Action therapy with families and groups: Using creative arts improvisation in clinical practice.* Washington, DC: APA Books.

Bibliotherapy Sources for Clients

Goldsmith, B. (2005). *Emotional fitness for couples.* Oakland, CA: New Harbinger.

Gottman, J., & Silver, N. (1999). *The seven principles for making marriage work.* New York: Three Rivers/Random House.

McKay, M., Fanning, P., & Paleg, K. (2006). *Couple skills: Making your marriage work* (2nd ed.). Oakland, CA: New Harbinger.

– 15 –

Me-You-Us
A Model for Understanding and Intervening with Couples

Charles A. Waehler

Type of Contribution: Activity, Homework

Objective

The objective of this exercise is to help couples understand their interactions and connections with one another, identify their current struggles and challenges in relation to one another, and set, articulate, negotiate, and work toward goals for what a successful relationship would look like for each person. This model can assist in the therapeutic process with couples presenting with a variety of different problems.

Rationale for Use

The "Me-You-Us" model involves asking people to consider their relationship in terms of three overlapping circles. The three circles involve one entitled "me," one entitled "you," and one entitled "us." Several relational aspects can be represented with this model. For one, the relative size of each of the three circles can represent the general emphasis or energy that is experienced by each person. Similarly, the amount of overlap or distinction among the circles can convey the closeness and distance that the individual who is creating the model experiences.

The general intent of having people create a model for themselves is to have them consider their relationship in terms of themselves and what they are creating together as a couple. Depending on therapeutic goals or stage of therapy in which the model is introduced, therapists may direct clients to draw a model that represents themselves in terms of their typical interaction, their worst moments, or ideal situations toward which the couple might be striving. Also, depending on the approach being undertaken by the therapist, this visual representation can help convey sometimes complex theoretical concepts (e.g., differentiation of self in Bowenian family therapy and boundary awareness and management in structural family therapy). Additionally, such visual representations can serve to help clients convey relational styles more fully by offering an alternative expressive medium for the emotionally or verbally constricted individual.

Conceptualizing the "me" and "you" portion of the model might be the most obvious for most individuals to identify. The relative size of these circles can depict the degree to which a person feels emotionally content or depleted, or a sense of being ignored or attended to. Their positions relative to each other can represent a sense of being dominant or submissive, promoted or minimized. The "us" portion may represent an opportunity for increased new understanding. This is because so many couples are not used to thinking in terms of what they are creating together and also because this representation of "us" is not well conceived within our larger culture: People with Eurocentric backgrounds tend to conceptualize their worlds in individualistic terms. Additionally, the "us" that couples are trying to create can be highly idiosyncratic. For some couples, the "us" portion of their representation might include solely their interactions with one another, while a different couple might choose this portion of their model to include immediate family members. A third couple might choose to include even more extended family members within this portion of their representation. Therefore, having each person in the couple consider who might best represent the "us" portion of the model will illuminate similarities and differences in personal priorities and help facilitate discussions about familial identities, activities, and interactions.

This appreciation that couples are made up not only of "me" and "you" but also of a shared "us" can diffuse the competitiveness that sometimes becomes manifest when people feel that every time they give something to their partner, they are entitled to request something in return as if all give and take has to be balanced perfectly. In this way, therapists can use the model to get past this "you win/I lose" mentality and instead consider interactions in terms of "you gain; therefore 'us' gains; therefore 'I' gain as well."

Five key ways and reasons for using this activity with couples can be to have the "Me-You-Us" model:

1. Serve as a visual aid for each member of a couple to conceptualize and express his or her perceptions about the member's current roles within the dyad and in relation to his or her partner;
2. Serve as a visual aid and communication aid for each member of a couple to conceptualize and express his or her perspective for the optimal partnership scenario he or she would like to achieve;
3. Serve as a mechanism for the couple to negotiate what might be a shared vision with which they could each have enough of their personal perceptions and roles satisfied to become more sustaining;
4. Serve as a visual aid with which to assess progress from an initial starting point toward a more desirable functional outcome; and
5. Facilitate a discussion about how couples give of themselves to their partners in such a way that facilitates both the growth and satisfaction of the partner and also the growth and expansion of what the couple is attempting to achieve together.

Instructions

With a simple piece of paper and a pencil, a therapist can introduce the concept of the "Me-You-Us" model by drawing a circle on a page. Therapists can introduce this activity in any manner that they believe might facilitate engaging the couple in the activity. For instance, the therapist might take an educative stance in the midst of what feels like a moment of competition within the couple to talk about the possibility of seeing exchanges as win–win opportunities. Conversely, clinicians might use self-disclosure as a way to introduce the model in ways that are pertinent to one's own life. Alternatively, the therapist can start by talking about the familiar entity of "me" by picking one member of the couple (perhaps putting the person's name on it) and talking about her or his likes and dislikes, interests and activities. Then the therapist can draw another circle (in whatever relation is deemed to be therapeutically useful at that moment) and, in addition to talking about some of the individual aspects of this person's life, begin to explain this circle in relation to the other.

After some discussion, the therapist can introduce the idea of the third aspect of the relationship: the "us"—those aspects of the couple that they are creating and blending together in the ways that they have sought to share together, give to each other, and grow together. One concept to talk about at this point could center on how one person giving of herself or himself to the other person can be seen as promoting the other person, *as well as* enhancing the "us" portion of the model. Thus, constructive giving can also result in high personal return (in terms of inflating the shared "us" portion of the model).

A therapist might also illustrate the utility of this model by talking about some typical couple interactional styles represented within certain "Me-You-Us" models, such as a constrained, group-focused couple in which neither member tended to engage in any activities separate from the larger family/community (see Figure 15.1); an independent, self-focused, couple in which there was very little interaction between them, but many solitary activities undertaken by each (see Figure 15.2);

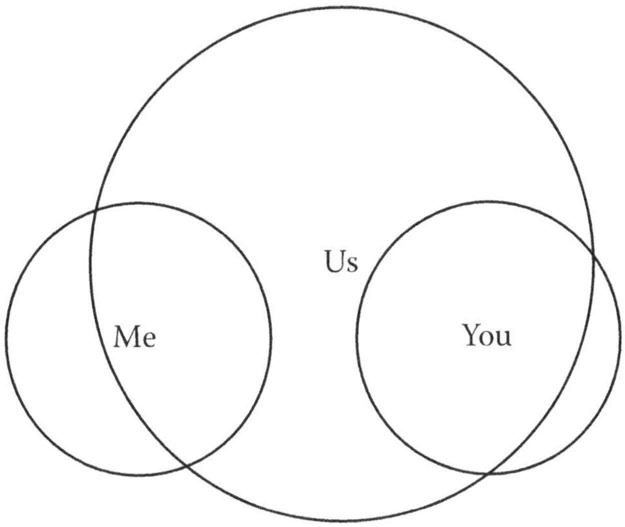

FIGURE 15.1

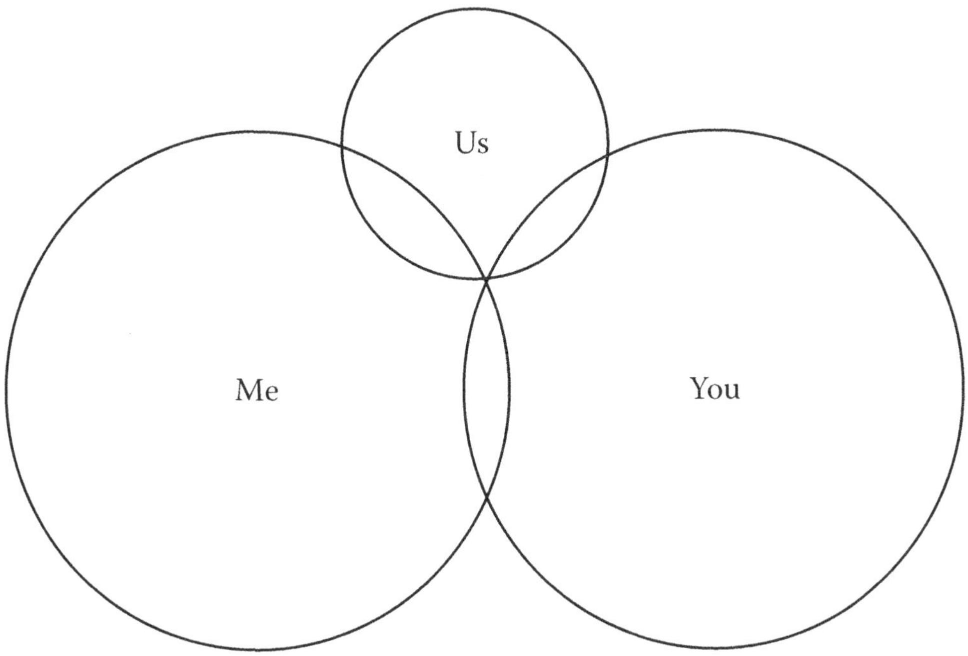

FIGURE 15.2

an unequal, domineering relationship where the man who drew this figure saw the woman ("you") as being the center of all attention and decisions with little consideration given to other people's consideration, least of all himself (see Figure 15.3); the balanced, differentiated, and engaged couple configured as the ideal situation to which a gay couple was stri ving as opposed to their current situation in which the "me" and "you" figures were distinct from one another (much like Figure 15.1) and their high community involvement ("us" activities) dominated their lives (see Figure 15.4). (See Fincham, Fernandes, & Humphreys, 1993; Mason, Hannah, Luquet, & Hendrix, 2005).

Therapists can then invite clients to spend time thinking independently about (a) how each of them would represent their relationship as it now exists, and (b) what their ideal configuration might look like. Spending time reflecting on these patterns, as well as how they are similar and different

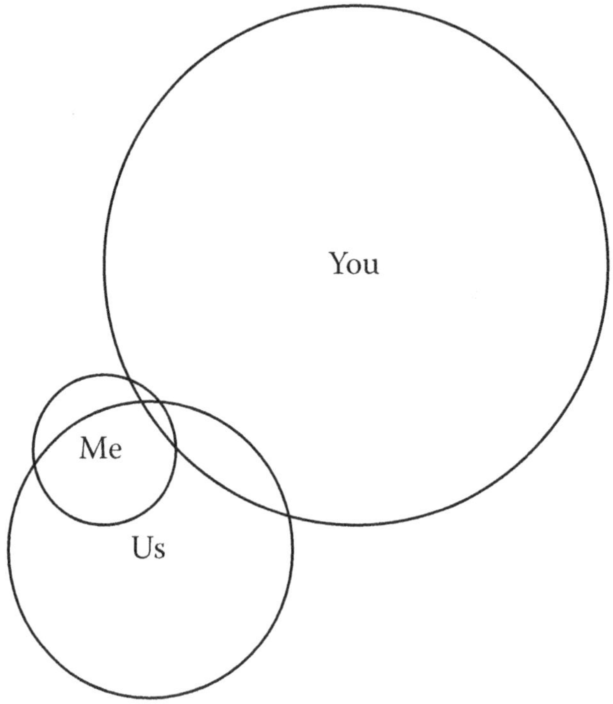

FIGURE 15.3

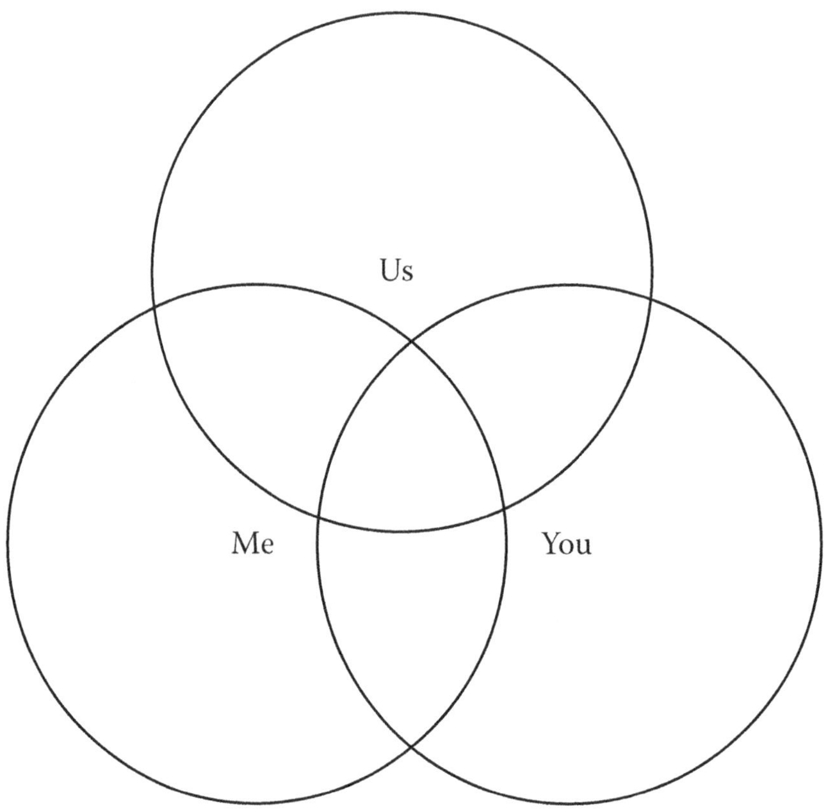

FIGURE 15.4

from the partner's, can help bring insight for each individual and serve to provide constructive talking points about which each may be less defensive than if he or she was sharing spontaneously at the moment. Another option is for the therapist to draw her or his own conception of the couple (either for personal understanding, to better understand which client she or he might be most aligned with, and/or to share with the couple for educational purposes). Depending on the point of therapy during which this exercise is applied the model might be used as an educational activity for the couple, an assessment device for the therapist, a reflective exercise to view relationship progress, or an instructive guide to talk about a specific transaction being discussed at that moment. Regardless of the specific intent, the "Me-You-Us" model can be a powerful intervention within psychotherapy by visually representing the couple's typical or exceptional interactional style in a way that they are unable to experience within themselves, due to psychological naiveté or some blockage due to their proximity to the issues at hand.

Some therapeutic encounters might also necessitate introducing a fourth factor into this model: the "other." Such a modification of the model would introduce an influential characteristic that puts a great deal of gravitational pull on the "Me-You-Us" system. This might be an ongoing or past affair, a special-needs child, a stressful job, an illness, an upcoming military service or other exceptional vocational demands, or a substance-abuse problem or pornographic obsession. In short, this "other" domain would represent any characteristic that is siphoning off energy from the couple in such a way that it is unequally influencing one or the other partner so that each of the other entities is impacted. Though these might represent horrific notions for the couple or altruistic endeavors by one partner, including them in the model may help the couple understand their current activities with this important issue in the mix.

Benefits of using this model with couples can be manifold. Perhaps most importantly this model gives a visual representation of concepts that are often quite esoteric and therefore not so available to many couples entering therapy. Educational studies have demonstrated that people learn best when they are taught through methods that make use of multiple sensory inputs (e.g., Waehler & Sivec, 1998). By having such a concrete representation at hand, the therapist is given a specific tool with which to promote understanding and change within the system.

Brief Clinical Vignette

Although Phil and Kathy were entering counseling at her insistence, they both reported being dissatisfied for the last several years of their 8-year marriage. During their intake session, the couple voiced accusations and vague statements of discontent toward one another, along with a strong love and commitment for their 6- and 4-year-old daughters, who made them hope that their marriage would continue and be stronger. At the end of the session, the therapist introduced the "Me-You-Us" model as a homework assignment for each of them to work on independently.

The next session began with a review of the models each had produced. Kathy went first, continuing with her major theme from the first session that Phil was distant from her. She tearfully relayed that she had made the "us" circle larger in her model (see Figure 15.5) because she had turned to the time she spent with her extended family as a way to maintain her well-being in the face of her "uninvolved" husband. Phil smiled during much of Kathy's presentation. When asked about that, he produced his drawing and announced, "I am surprised about how similarly we have constructed these, but I also see a big difference in how we got there." He went on to relate that he also saw Kathy spending a lot of time with her family, but his explanation for being distant from her was because he felt "squeezed out" due to the closeness (and the "closedness") that he experienced with her family (see Figure 15.6). Phil said that he had not thought too much about it until he had to work on his model, but he came to realize that his well-being was maintained by trying to remain independent from her family (and consequently from Kathy as well).

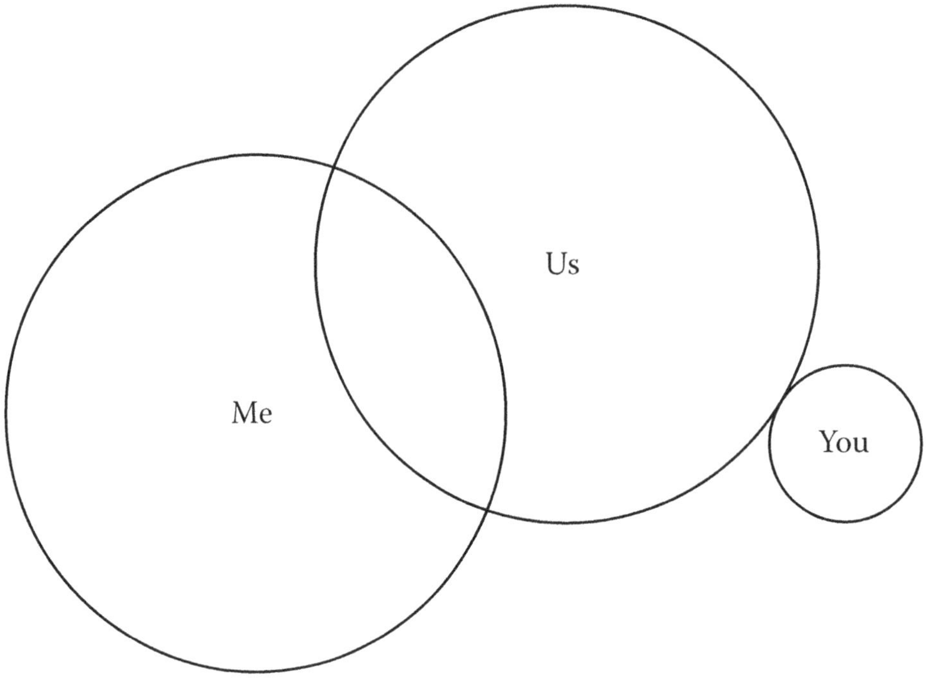

FIGURE 15.5

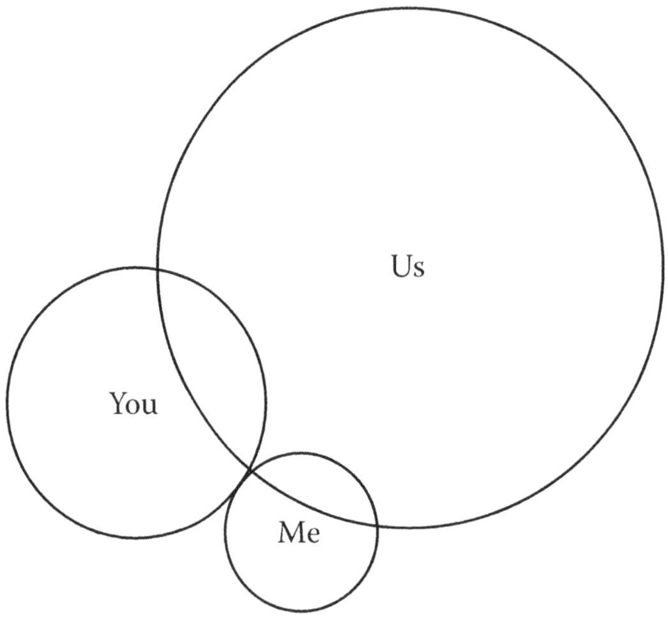

FIGURE 15.6

Because of the similarity with which Kathy and Phil constructed their visual models, the couple was able to relate to one another cooperatively and engaged in a positive dialogue about how each of them was experiencing Kathy's family. Because their models had helped this couple see commonality in their viewpoints, further discussion about what each person wanted to change became a constructive exercise. They immediately went into a discussion about Kathy's family, but instead of their usual pattern of addressing traits (i.e., shortcomings) of particular family members (with therapist assistance), they stayed focused on their own personal feelings and experiences in this regard and how these were impacting the relationship they wanted to create with each other. With this in mind, the therapist had them work together to construct a new consensus model for their marriage (see Figure 15.7) that each person could endorse as a desirable goal. With this new vision in mind, Kathy said that she would be happy to spend less time with her family, while Phil came through on his commitment to be more engaged with activities involving Kathy and their daughters. At the end of a successful, brief therapy relationship, Phil and Kathy reported that they would reflect on the model they developed together and contrast it to the one each of them had originally derived, to assess their family plans and personal initiatives.

Suggestions for Follow-Up

There are several ways to use the "Me-You-Us" model over time, including as a method by which to "check in" with client progress and thereby assess and measure any change. Additionally, with a client who presents with a set of goals that vacillate with time or in interaction with her or his partner, this model can be used to help a client remain consistently committed to personal constructive goals set for therapy.

Contraindications for Use

This activity is contraindicated for couples who are currently experiencing abuse.

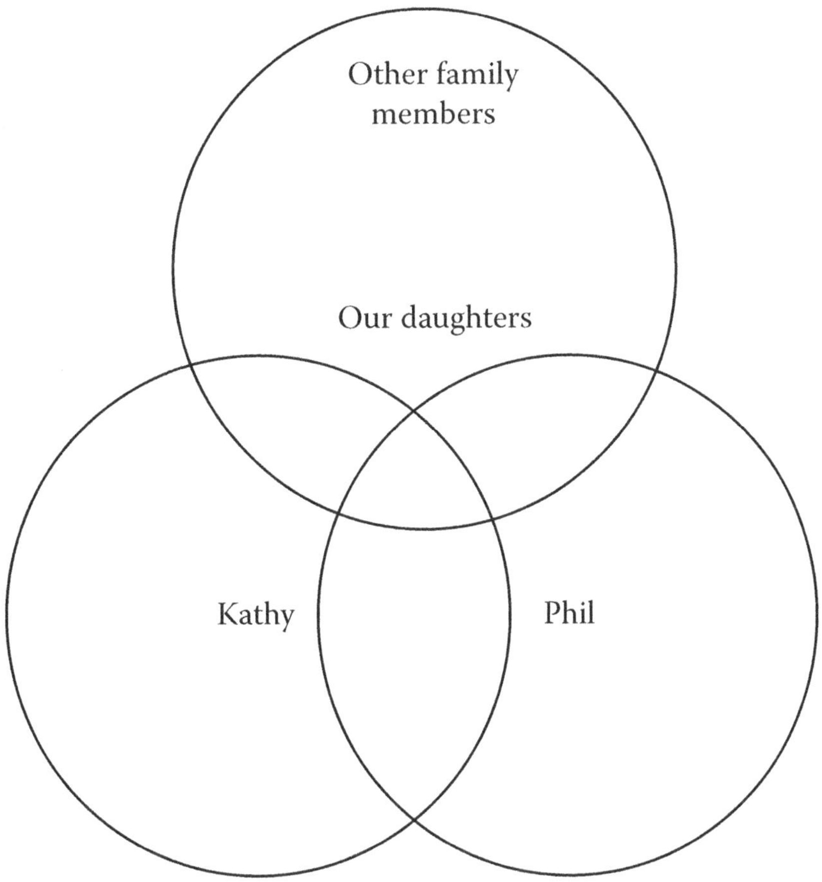

FIGURE 15.7

References

Fincham, F., Fernandes, L., & Humphreys, K. (1993). *Communicating in relationships: A guide for couples and professionals.* Chicago: Research Press.

Mason, R. C., Hannah, M. T., Luquet, W., & Hendrix, H. (Eds.). (2005). *Imago relationship therapy: Perspectives on theory (Imago).* San Francisco: Jossey–Bass.

Waehler, C. A., & Sivec, H. J. (1998). Critical thinking applications in personality assessment. In L. Handler, & M. Hilsenroth (Eds.), *Teaching and learning personality assessment* (pp. 83–106.). Hillsdale, NJ: Lawrence Erlbaum Associates.

Professional Readings and Resources

McKay, M., Fanning, P., & Paleg, K. (2006). *Couple skills.* Oakland, CA: New Harbinger.

Weiss, R. S. (1977). *Marital separation.* New York: Free Press.

Bibliotherapy Sources for the Client

Goldsmith, B. (2003). *Emotional fitness for couples.* Oakland, CA: New Harbinger.

Gottman, J. (1994). *Why marriages succeed or fail: And how you can make yours last.* New York: Fireside.

Hendrix, H. (1992). *Keeping the love you find.* New York: Simon & Schuster.

Hendrix, H., & Hunt, H. (2003). *Getting the love you want workbook: The new couples' study guide.* New York: Simon & Schuster.

– 16 –

"Are We There Yet?" *A Method for Quantifying Progress in Couples Treatment*

Israela Meyerstein

Type of Contribution: Activity

Objective

The purpose of this activity is to offer a quantifiable evaluation method for measuring clients' differing or similar perceptions of longitudinal progress in couples treatment. Information from the activity is also utilized to further guide sessions on the journey through couples treatment.

Rationale for Use

A familiar experience for those who have driven a car on a long trip, especially with passengers of the younger variety in the back seat, is the plaintive call: "Are we there yet?" Like a road trip, therapy is a guided journey from a starting point to a destination—a mutually shared experience in which the therapist uses client input to elicit new ideas and behaviors, and the clients take responsibility for their growth. Clients are asked at the outset, "What would you like to accomplish as a result of coming in together?" By soliciting information about client goals and dreams, the therapist offers hope to make the future better. As in a journey, treatment is a longitudinal process, with beginning, middle, and end points. Our contemporary therapy culture mandates clear objectives, underscoring the importance of setting goals, observing, and measuring behaviors. Periodic review and evaluation of progress are important components of such treatment.

This author, an integrative systemic couples therapist, uses an evaluative exercise referred to as "the percentages." While based on solution-focused scaling techniques (Berg & deShazer, 1993; Kowalski & Kral, 1989; Lipchik & deShazer, 1988; Shilts & Duncan, 2003), this exercise can be used with any couples treatment approach that focuses on behavior, cognition, emotions, and interactional patterns, and it works with all kinds of clients, regardless of emotional aptitude. Like scaling techniques, it transforms abstract concepts of emotional experience into tangible observations (Berg & de Shazer), and it privileges clients' ongoing subjective perceptions (deShazer, 1994).

The percentages exercise is more than a scaling measure to elicit a more positive perceptual reality for the individual client, as it is generally employed by solution-focused therapists. Rather, it is used interactionally, both as a bona fide self-assessment tool as well as a tool to compare and contrast perceptions of each partner, solidify points of consensus, and explore differences via dialogue. Often the therapist is surprised by what the clients report and benefits from learning the clients' perceptions. Client feedback helps the therapist assess progress and give reinforcement, recalibrate pace, rejoin the more discouraged partner, honor the difficulty of making changes, or examine unvisited issues. Optimally, the therapist initiates the exercise when he or she feels treatment is at least at the halfway mark. The middle phase of treatment can be a "wilderness" time when both therapist and family members are seeking signposts to determine accomplishment as well as the remaining work ahead. The percentages exercise is also a useful tool when therapy is drifting, if the therapist is feeling stuck, or if the couple questions, "Where are we going?" or "How much longer till we get there?" The therapist can preempt resistance by responding in a nondefensive manner through proposing the percentages exercise, which actively solicits client feedback and evaluation and collaboratively seeks greater clarity.

Instructions

The therapist suggests that the couple should "take stock of where you've come in treatment, where you are now, and where you still need to go." The therapist asks each member of the couple to freely associate and to privately think of three numbers from 0 to 100%. These three numbers are to represent

> how you feel in the relationship or about the relationship. The first number should describe how you felt at the outset of treatment, the second number is for how you see or feel things are right now, and the third number is where it will be when you feel satisfied, or at your goal. Remember that 100% is not an option, since no people or relationships are perfect, and 0 is also unlikely.

The therapist then sits quietly, waiting for the partners to privately reflect. The therapist anticipates that the couple's numbers may differ because they are two different people. The therapist advises that one partner not change his or her numbers upon hearing the partner's response. Sometimes partners may wish to write down each of their numbers.

The therapist's stance is one of curiosity, attentive listening, and acceptance. Partners are encouraged not to overreact to their partner's percentages, but to listen with respectful interest. The therapist asks for one partner's three numbers all at once, and then asks for the other partner's responses. This is followed by a request for an explanation for the numbers given in terms of observed behaviors. Responses about the first set of numbers (outset) are generally just accepted. If one partner reacts strongly to hearing a much lower number, the therapist might seek clarification or acknowledge the problem-laden beginnings. The second set of numbers (present moment) usually reflects a significant improvement. The therapist asks the partners to describe what behaviors they have observed that account for the improvement. The constructed focus on acknowledging positive behaviors and noticing synchronicity between partners helps create a mood of accomplishment, optimism, and hope.

The last numbers (end goal) represent where each partner would like the relationship to be. The therapist then asks, "What do you think will be happening, and what will each of you be doing or noticing between now and when you reach your goal percentage? What will you need to keep doing, do more of, or start doing in your relationship to get to your goal?" This last question provides an opportunity for each partner to state his or her expectations, which can be charted in the next phase of treatment, and it also identifies what each will take responsibility to do on his or her part for continued progress.

The exercise is intended for use in session, but if time runs out, it can also be assigned to be completed as homework for the next session. It can also be repeated later in treatment or as part of approaching termination. Once a couple is around 85–90% of the way to their goal, they often feel the main ingredients remaining are time, consistency of practice leading to greater trust, and confidence in the new ways they are relating. Occasionally, this exercise may identify a significant relationship issue that hitherto had not been broached.

Brief Clinical Vignette

Sandy and Dave, a couple in their mid-40s with a teenage son and daughter, sought marriage counseling with the author. Dave, a successful workaholic businessman, was chronically depressed and prone to outbursts of rage at Sandy and his oldest son, who underachieved and got into trouble. Sandy, a part-time nurse, was protective of her son and rarely enforced consequences, partly to compensate for Dave's harshness. Dave felt undermined in his attempts to discipline, and both felt uncared for by the other. Sandy felt burnt out as Dave's emotional cheerleader and seemed chronically frustrated with him. To complicate matters, Dave had dabbled in a brief affair with an employee, complaining that his marriage lacked intimacy and that he was not attracted to Sandy.

It took quite a while to wind down the extramarital liaison, begin making emotional repair, and begin to restore trust in the couple's relationship. But soon the focus turned to parenting issues, and a goal was to foster more collaboration between Sandy and Dave as parents. Family sessions were held to improve Dave's relationship with his son. While Dave remained depressed despite medications, he decided to recommit to working on the marriage. Both Dave and Sandy acknowledged that the other had been trying to make improvements, and they wanted to improve their relationship since they had invested so many years in the marriage and family.

The therapist felt some progress had been made, and suggested the percentages exercise to measure "how each of you sees the relationship, where we've come from, and what we most need to attend to now and in the future." When asked for his three numbers, Dave indicated 30, 50, and 75%. He expected little of marriage due to his depressive slant and an unhappy upbringing. He wanted credit for ending the affair and he voiced his commitment to Sandy, although he felt very lonely in the relationship. He stated he felt currently at 50% because he noticed Sandy had been trying to support him in parenting.

Sandy's numbers were 15, 55, and 85%. Her first numbers were depressed due to the affair. She did recognize that Dave had been yelling less at his son, and Sandy and Dave were developing into a more effective team as parents. Sandy stated the relationship was currently at 55% because, although Dave was coming home earlier, he still spent time isolating at home. Despite the affair, Sandy very much wanted the relationship to succeed and hoped for 85% because she felt they had experienced a much fuller and happier connection in the past. When asked what each of them needed or would anticipate seeing in the relationship to steer it toward the range of 70–85%, Sandy explained that she wanted Dave to make her feel like number one; perhaps if Dave romanced her, she might begin to feel more hopeful and friendlier. Sandy also planned to start an exercise program to feel better about herself physically.

Dave missed the adoration he used to get when Sandy was his cheerleader, feeling that Sandy was generally disinterested in him, and he felt lonely. He recognized that he was drawn to the other woman because she put him on a pedestal and made him feel special. When asked what each could do in the direction of more "interested adoration" and "expressed romance," they identified steps that could be taken, and they explored what was difficult for each of them to take these steps. Sandy and Dave were able to identify the next lap of their journey and commit to that challenge. The midtreatment evaluation exercise acknowledged some progress and projected future steps that were needed in their treatment.

Later in treatment, when the therapist felt more positive work had been done, she suggested doing the exercise again. While their percentages continued to climb, Sandy mentioned that she still harbored some old resentment towards Dave. This was from the time when they had lost a baby through miscarriage several years before and she had felt unsupported by Dave. It is not uncommon that some early experience of buried loss reemerges years later. Treatment then focused on processing Sandy's feelings, with the therapist helping Dave listen and respond in a more empathic way, resulting in continued improvement. At termination they reported their percentages were near their goals, and both were confident that their scores would continue to climb.

Suggestions for Follow-Up

Because the percentages exercise identifies desired future behaviors, perceptions, and experiences, it has a built-in natural follow-up for the therapist to inquire in future sessions what each has been doing or noticing relative to the stated objectives, and what ingredients need to be built in. When clients are asked to notice and credit each other's efforts, there is opportunity for mutual positive reinforcement. If clients report little change since the last session exercise, the therapist can explore each person's ideas of why he or she could not take the steps requested. The therapist can also search for any obstacles that may be operating (beliefs, loyalties, resistances, fears) that prevent moving toward the goals.

At times deeper issues may surface requiring attention, but more often clients tend to follow their prescribed intentions for behavior, since it is their idea and in the interest of improving their relationship. Sometimes just identifying the steps, focusing on solutions, and taking personal responsibility for actions creates enough energy and momentum to set the process in motion.

The percentages exercise can be repeated towards the end of treatment, when the therapist and/or the couple are spacing out sessions and considering termination. The exercise can identify the progress accomplished, as well as indicate what is still left to do (i.e., put in more time, more consistency, tweak things a bit, etc.). It can be used to focus on winding down and on what the couple can continue accomplishing on their own.

Contraindications for Use

This exercise is part of a larger context of treatment and should not be viewed as the heart of the therapy. It is a most useful addition to the therapist's repertoire in the area of evaluation. The "percentages exercise" should not be used too early in treatment before some progress has occurred, and a useful distinction between treatment outset and present time can be made. Also, in a crisis-ridden situation, one should wait until some stability has been achieved. The exercise presumes a working relationship in which members are sufficiently engaged; otherwise, the value of the activity will be questionable. The therapist should not be discouraged if low numbers are given initially. However, if clients have been coming for a while and not experiencing progress, the exercise also could lead to a discussion of why things are stuck.

The therapist may have to repeat the instructions and acknowledge that it is hard to give a specific number to relationship experience. Care should be taken not to judge the percentage numbers given, and not to allow partners to judge each other's numbers; rather, couples should be encouraged to view all feedback as useful information. ("Let's see what we can learn from this.") If partners are wary about the other changing his or her numbers, the therapist can request that clients write their numbers down.

The therapist should help calm anxieties if numbers are very different, since the goal is not to synchronize, but for each to give input and learn about the other. The use of percentages will hopefully not remind clients of school performance and evaluation, particularly because this self-assessment puts the clients in charge. The goals of the exercise are, in part, to turn over more responsibility for evaluation and continued progress to the couple. The therapist needs to be vigilant to steer the discussion of percentages into observed behavior and steps for continued growth.

References

Berg, I. K., & de Shazer, S. (1993). Making numbers talk: Language in therapy. In S. Friedman (Ed.), *The new language of change: Constructive collaboration in psychotherapy* (pp. 5–24). New York: Guilford.

de Shazer, S. (1994). *Words were originally magic.* New York: W. W. Norton.

Kowalski, K., & Kral, R. (1989). The geometry of solution: Using the scaling technique. *Family Therapy Case Studies, 4,* 59–66.

Lipchik, E., & deShazer, S. (1988). Purposeful sequences for beginning the solution-focused interview. In E. Lipchik (Ed.), *Interviewing* (pp. 105–117). Rockville, MD: Aspen.

Shilts, L., & Duncan, B. L. (2003). Integrating externalization and scaling questions: Using visual scaling to amplify children's voices. In C. F. Sori, L. L. Hecker et al., *The therapist's notebook for children and adolescents: Homework, handouts, and activities for use in psychotherapy* (pp. 230–236). New York: Haworth.

Professional Readings and Resources

Berg, I. K., & deShazer, S. (1993). Making numbers talk: Language in therapy. In S. Friedman (Ed.), *The new language of change: Constructive collaboration in psychotherapy* (pp. 5–24). New York: Guilford.

Hoyt, M. F., & Berg, I. K. (1998). Solution-focused couple therapy: Helping clients construct self-fulfilling realities. In F. M. Dattilio (Ed.), *Case studies in couple and family therapy: Systemic and cognitive perspectives* (pp. 203–232). New York: Guilford.

Kowalski, K., & Kral, R. (1989). The geometry of solution: Using the scaling technique. *Family Therapy Case Studies, 4,* 59–66.

Bibliotherapy for Clients

Gottman, J. (1994). *Why marriages succeed or fail: What you can learn from the breakthrough research to make your marriage last.* New York: Simon & Schuster.

O'Hanlon, B. (1999). *Do one thing different: Ten simple ways to change your life.* New York: HarperCollins.

Schultheis, G. M., O'Hanlon, B., & O'Hanlon, S. (1998). *Brief couples therapy homework planner.* New York: Wiley.

SECTION IV: FAMILIES AND GROUPS

– 17 –

The Family Boundaries Game

Kimberly Laninga, Rita L. Sanders, and Dreena E. Greenwood

Type of Contribution: Activity

Objective

The *Family Boundaries Game* is a life-size board game that the therapist constructs to familiarize family members with the idea of the family as a system. Several objectives may be accomplished through the use of this game.

The first objective is for family members to recognize both their own uniqueness and their special role within the family. The second objective involves an introduction to the subject of boundaries, facilitating a discussion of rules and roles within the family (Minuchin, 1974). This occurs as a family participates in an activity that requires them to follow rules and guidelines, take turns, and answer questions that are designed to elicit candid and subjective responses from family members. A third objective of this activity is to promote movement in the family in two ways. As family members act as game pieces, they must physically move from one space to the next, thereby promoting literal movement. Additionally, many families who enter therapy are "stuck." For example, a family may have a maladaptive style of communication due to boundaries between the subsystems that are too rigid. Participation in the *Family Boundaries Game* enables them to break a pattern such as this by allowing family members to speak freely. In this way, there is figurative movement within the family from a place of little communication or continual arguing to allowing family members to express themselves without fear of recrimination, which is one component of appropriate boundaries.

Rationale for Use

Information and insight alone may or may not be enough to facilitate change within a family system. According to Gil (1994), the aim of play therapy is to provide an avenue for children to connect with and articulate their emotions in a more adaptive way. Additionally, more difficult emotions may be processed and harmful behaviors replaced with healthier ones. Gil contends that family play aids the therapist in assessing and gathering additional information regarding the family. Family play therapy also helps bypass the normal defenses that many adults, as well as children, have in place, since it is often safer and easier to talk about difficult issues through the metaphors represented in play. This encourages more open communication and meaningful understanding among all family members.

Many adults tend to lose their playfulness as they grow older, and in relationships choose to limit their exchanges to reasonable discussions. In general, it is more difficult for children to engage in that type of interaction since their primary means of communicating is not through language, but through play. In fact, young children's level of cognitive development can limit their ability to understand and actively participate in talk therapy. Many therapists are unsure of just how to engage both children and adults in sessions in ways that are meaningful to all family members (Sori, 2006). For families to find a common ground, it may be more beneficial for parents to enter the world of their children through the use of play (Gil, 1994). This game provides the family with a safe activity in which change can take place, and it incorporates elements of both play and discussion, thereby bridging the gap between the adult and child worlds.

The use of the life-size game board with the family members functioning as game pieces introduces boundaries to the family in a fun, nonthreatening, metaphoric way. Permeable boundaries within a family are a vital, necessary part of successful family and individual functioning (Hecker, Mims, & Boughner, 2003). Rigid or enmeshed boundaries may be in place for a variety of reasons, including but not limited to a lack of understanding, inappropriate hierarchies, or parents' lack of differentiation from their families of origin.

Having family members physically move from one space to the next will help them consider the importance of personal space, as well as encourage a connection to one's physical body, while facilitating a deeper, more honest, and personal response when answering the questions. In families where hyperactivity or impulse control are issues, this game can be beneficial in teaching self-control by compelling members to wait to take a turn. The questions in the *Family Boundaries Game* (see Handout 17.2) help family members gain insight into themselves and others in the family. The therapist can then use members' responses to facilitate discussion of appropriate versus inappropriate boundaries. In addition, the therapist can comment on observations of family members' verbal and nonverbal communication and interaction while the game is in progress.

This game provides a fun and safe outlet for family members to move around and interact with each other in a new way, therefore lowering the natural tendencies to resist change in a well-established system and opening up new possibilities for change. For instance, in a family system with rigid boundaries, this activity may provide access to other family members that typically may not be available. In family systems with diffuse boundaries, this activity provides structure with rules and physical boundaries that may be lacking within the system.

The *Family Boundaries Game* may also assist families who may be adjusting to a new family structure. Changes in family structure have increased within the past few decades (Carter & McGoldrick, 1999), and the traditional family structure is no longer the norm. Today's family households may take many forms, including single divorced parents, single unmarried parents, remarried families, unmarried partners, grandparents raising grandchildren, foster families, gay or lesbian partners, and widows or widowers. Within these family structures, family members may live in the household all or part of the time, such as in the case of parents with joint custody of children (Carter & McGoldrick).

Although structures have changed considerably over time, many families may expect the family system to work the same as the traditional family structure, due to lack of role models and information on forming functional nontraditional families (see Hecker & Sori, 2006). This activity provides families with a method to experiment and adjust to different ways of operating. Therapists can tailor the questions in Handout 17.2 to meet the unique needs of the families with whom they are working, whether families whose boundaries are rigid or enmeshed or families who need help in adjusting to a new structure.

Another benefit of this game is the building of stronger bonds among family members. As with any achievement, developing good relationships requires effort. By encouraging honest responses, without judgment, appreciation for each other may be further enhanced.

Materials Needed

See Handout 17.1.

Instructions

The game board is set up by attaching poster boards end to end in the chosen configuration by using string or yarn. The game may be set up in any configuration by the therapist. Examples of various configurations may include a square, a zigzag, or an "L." The number of family members and available space may determine the layout and quantity of squares. Handout 17.2 contains questions that can be photocopied on card stock and then cut out. These question cards are placed upside down in a pile within reach of the board. Players take turns selecting a card, answering the question, and then rolling a die. All players are given two *pass cards* at the start of the game, which can be used to "pass" on questions they do not want to answer. Determination of who goes first is at the therapist's discretion or can be established with a roll of the die.

If parents need to be empowered in an effort to establish an appropriate hierarchy within the family, the therapist may ask a parent to go first. If a child does not understand the rules of the game or a particular question within the game, he or she should be directed to ask the parents (not the therapist) for help in order to help establish parental authority.

The player selects a question from the pile of cards and answers it accordingly or uses one of his or her two *passes* to skip answering. The questions are designed to encourage members to explore various aspects of themselves, such as likes and dislikes, what sets them apart from others in the family, and what they think and feel about their family. See Handout 17.2 for a list of possible questions. Ideally, therapists should tailor questions specifically for the family with whom they are working.

After answering or passing, the question is returned to the bottom of the pile. Questions may be answered multiple times by different family members. If necessary, questions can be shuffled. After answering, the player then rolls the die and moves ahead the appropriate number of spaces. If a player lands on directive space, he or she follows the instruction and his or her turn ends. If a player lands on a blank space, his or her turn ends. This process is repeated for each player until all family members have reached the end.

The therapist can also be selective in choosing questions already included in the play therapy that are best suited for the situations of that particular family. Not all of the questions included must be utilized. Therapists can always enhance the *Family Boundaries Game* with additional questions that reflect the many different situations that families may encounter.

If a player lands on an occupied space, he or she must move back to the last available unoccupied space. This is an important concept when discussing boundaries because, within families, *each member must be allowed to have his or her own space.* However, if the two family members are willing to negotiate the boundaries and occupy the same space, sharing is permitted. The following rules apply:

- Players roll to see who goes first (unless otherwise indicated).
- Each player, in turn, selects a card, answers the question, and then rolls the die.
- Each player has two *passes.*
- Two players may not share the same space without agreement and negotiation of the space.
- Game is complete when all players have reached the finish line.

Therapists may introduce the *Family Boundaries Game* by inviting the family to play a game together that may help them get to know both themselves and each other better and that will help facilitate an examination of how they relate to one another. As they play the game, they should be honest in their answers and really listen to how others answer their questions. They may also want to think about how they would answer others' questions. The object of the game is not winning or losing. Instead, the object is for everyone to cross the finish line feeling as if he or she has not only gained a voice within the family, but also has heard the others. The clinician can give token prizes (e.g., stickers or suckers) to everyone at the end of the game.

Clinical Vignette

Fourteen-year-old Marcia and her family came to counseling because she had become sullen, was caught smoking, consistently broke curfew, and was hanging out with older teenagers who had little supervision. Her parents, Kenny and Susie, were in their late 30s. Susie admitted to searching her daughter's room on numerous occasions, reading her journal, and going through her purse, while Kenny was covertly monitoring her instant messaging and e-mails. Fueling their behavior was the fear that Marcia might become pregnant or addicted to drugs. This fear was leading to enmeshed boundaries. In addition, Marcia's 12-year-old sister Maria habitually barged into Marcia's bedroom without knocking and "borrowed" her clothes without asking. This infuriated Marcia, but neither Kenny nor Susie saw a problem with Maria's behavior, and in every way considered Maria an obedient child.

Marcia had little autonomy or space to herself, and communication with her parents had broken down. Maria's failure to respect her sister's space and belongings was ignored as the parents focused all their energy and attention on monitoring Marcia's behavior. Maria's apparent bids for attention were being overlooked.

When talking to the therapist, Marcia indicated that she felt as if she had no privacy, that her parents wanted her to be just like them, and that they did not trust her. Marcia stated that Maria could "do no wrong" in their parents' eyes. She wondered aloud why she should have to share her clothes with Maria.

It was important for the family to begin recognizing the need to allow Marcia a certain amount of freedom and privacy, while maintaining appropriate limits. Marcia, in turn, needed help to see how her actions were contributing to her parents' controlling and invasive behavior. Maria also needed suitable and age-appropriate limits, while being encouraged to discover her personal strengths, likes, and dislikes.

Since communication between Marcia and her parents consisted mainly of arguing, the therapist suggested playing the *Family Boundaries Game*. She introduced the game in the following way:

> Since there seems to be a lot of arguing, I think it would be good to find a way to minimize that. I have a game that the family can play together, yet each person will be able to maintain his or her individuality. There are no winners or losers in this game since everyone will cross the finish line before the game is over, so in that way, it's not really competitive. The idea is to be as honest as possible in answering the questions and to listen to what the others have to say without judging their answers. When others are taking their turns, no one else gets to respond to what they say. It would be a good idea to think about how *you* would answer the questions that they pick; however, you cannot comment when it is someone else's turn. Afterward, everyone will have an opportunity to talk about what they thought of the game, and about their own answers and those of other family members.

Although Marcia was initially skeptical about playing a game with her family, after some coaxing by her younger sister she relented and joined in with the rest of the family, all of whom were willing to participate. The therapist went on to explain the actual rules of the game, and then they began playing.

Each member rolled the die to see who would go first. Susie rolled the highest number, so she started. Her first question was, "Name something that bugs you about another family member." Without hesitating, she replied that she hated that Kenny did not enforce the rules, thereby forcing her to do all of the disciplining. Because that seemed to be her role, the kids failed to see her as anything but "the heavy." Kenny's face registered surprise. This was apparently the first time Susie had voiced her frustration. As he started to retort, Marcia reminded him that no one was allowed to respond during someone else's turn.

The game progressed without incident after that. One of Kenny's questions was, "If you had one wish, what would it be and how would it change things?" His normally tough exterior softened considerably and he said, "That we could spend more time together as a family. I miss seeing Marcia's smile, especially. If we did things together, we might not fight so much." In processing his answer later, Kenny came to understand his difficulty in allowing his older daughter to grow independently of him, while remaining a stable person for her to come back to as needed. He realized how much he missed the silliness that he and Marcia had shared when she was younger.

On one of Marcia's turns, the number she rolled would have placed her on the same space as Maria. Marcia hesitated, not wanting to negotiate sharing the space. Maria saw Marcia's consternation and invited her to come up and join her there. On another turn, Marcia's question read, "Name something positive about another family member." She thought for a moment and said, "My mom sometimes breaks the rules, like taking me out of school for a half day so we could go shopping."

A question that Maria drew was, "What makes you feel sad?" Right away she said that she and Marcia did not share a room anymore and that made her sad. Maria confided that she really wanted to be like her big sister and enjoyed spending time with her. After the game was over, Marcia decided to set aside certain clothes that Maria could borrow without asking, but asked that she knock before coming into her room. Marcia also said that she would try to spend a little more time just hanging out with Maria playing video games.

After the game was completed, the therapist asked the family members for their reactions to playing the game, the rules of the game, and the questions and responses brought out while playing. Kenny voiced that it was difficult to keep from responding to others' answers during the game, especially when he did not agree with something that was said. He felt as if he should be able to defend himself. Marcia said that it was hard to be honest sometimes because she was afraid of getting in trouble. Overall, however, their feedback was positive.

Susie was surprised to discover how much she focused on the weaknesses within the family, while overlooking the strengths exhibited by both the family as a whole and the individuals within the family. She found that when others were answering questions, she tried to think of how she might answer them. She found that it would have been difficult to answer the more positive questions as quickly as others had. She had been fixated for so long on what was *not* working that she would have had to take considerably more time to find something positive to say about some of the others. She also felt that when the family spent time together, they were always fighting.

To her credit, Marcia was able to explain to her parents her need for some space. She made compromises about whom she could hang out with and agreed to start obeying curfew. This came after Kenny talked about how he missed the time they used to spend together. Her parents agreed to start trusting her in small ways, and as she confirmed that their trust was well placed, they would lessen their intrusive behaviors.

Suggestions for Follow-Up

The therapist can use information gained from the game to help the family attain healthier boundaries as needed. The therapist may suggest to the family modifying the game for future use by creating their own questions. The game may be modified to meet the needs of those with physical disabilities by turning it into a table game.

Contraindications for Use

While the presence of abuse in a family is evidence of poor boundaries, there must be sufficient safety measures in place so that family members do not suffer repercussions for answering questions honestly.

With families whose boundaries are extremely rigid, other work may be necessary to provide them with enough flexibility before joining in an activity in which all are expected to contribute openly. As always, a multicultural perspective must be integrated into the activity. The therapist must keep in mind the cultural norms, values, and language of the family while preparing questions.

References

Carter, B., & McGoldrick, M. (1999). Overview: The expanded family life cycle. In B. Carter & M. McGoldrick (Eds.), *The expanded family life cycle: Individual, family, and social perspectives* (pp. 1–26). Needham Heights, MA: Pearson Education.

Gil, E. (1994). *Play in family therapy.* New York: Guilford.

Hecker, L. L., Mims, G., & Boughner, S. R. (2003). General systems theory, cybernetics, and family therapy. In L. L. Hecker & J. L Wetchler (Eds.), *An introduction to marriage and family therapy.* New York: Haworth.

Hecker, L. L., & Sori, C. F. (2006). Divorce and stepfamily issues. In C. F. Sori (Ed.), *Engaging children in family therapy: Creative approaches to integrating theory and research in clinical practice* (pp. 177–204). New York: Routledge.

Minuchin, S. (1974). *Families and family therapy.* Cambridge, MA: Harvard University Press.

Sori, C. F. (2006). On counseling children and families: Recommendations from the experts. In C. F. Sori (Ed.), *Engaging children in family therapy: Creative approaches to integrating theory and research in clinical practice* (pp. 3–20). New York: Routledge.

Professional Readings and Resources.

Bailey, E. C. (2005). *Children in therapy: Using the family as a resource.* New York: W. W. Norton.

Cloud, H., & Townsend, J. (1992). *Boundaries: When to say yes, when to say no.* Grand Rapids, MI: Zondervan.

Cloud, H., & Townsend, J. (1998). *Boundaries with kids.* Grand Rapids, MI: Zondervan.

Keim, J. P. (2000). Oppositional behavior in children. In C. E. Bailey (Ed.), *Children in therapy: Using the family as a resource* (pp. 278–307). New York: W. W. Norton.

Minuchin, S., Nichols, M. P., & Lee, W. (2007). *Assessing families and couples: From symptom to system.* New York: Pearson Education.

Sori, C.F., Hecker, L.L., & associates. (2003). *The therapist's notebook for children and adolescents: Homework, handouts, and activities for use in psychotherapy.* Binghamton, NY: Haworth.

Bibliotherapy Sources for the Client

Allen, R. (2007). *The complete guide to parallel parenting: Establishing appropriate boundaries for families of divorce.* Belvedere, CA: Nipomo.

Clapp, G. (2000). *Divorce and new beginnings.* New York: John Wiley & Sons.

Partow, C., & Partow, D. (1996). *Families that play together stay together!* Minneapolis, MN: Bethany House.

Visher, E. B., & Visher, J. S. (1991). *How to win as a stepfamily* (2nd ed.). New York: Brunner Routledge.

Handout 17.1: Materials Needed to Construct the Family Boundaries Game

The following materials, which are available at craft stores, are needed to create the game board:

- Several 28 × 22-in. poster boards. Twenty to thirty poster boards should provide an adequate size game board. However, this number may need to be adjusted or smaller poster boards used according to available space, configuration, or number of family members. As in traditional board games, spaces often vary by color. In this game, multicolored poster boards are visually appealing but not necessary. There is no significance to the colors. As a less expensive alternative, file folders may be substituted for the poster boards.

  The directives "move up one space," "lose a turn," and "move back one space" should be written on three separate boards. Additionally, the "start" and "finish" spaces should also be identified.
- Hole punch
- Yarn or string to attach boards together
- Cardstock for copying the questions (see Handout 17.2) or index cards (3 × 5 or 4 × 6). These may be laminated to increase durability.
- Styrofoam cube constructed to resemble a die and numbered one through six (two dice may be necessary depending on the size of the family)

Handout 17.2: Questions for Boundaries Game

These questions can be photocopied on card stock and cut out to make question cards for the game. Alternatively, they can be printed on copy paper or glued to 3 × 5 or 4 × 6 index cards, and then laminated to help them last longer.

Name something that bugs you about another family member.

Name one thing you would like to do better.

What do you like least about living in this family?

If you could change roles with another person in the family, who would it be and why?

If you have a personal space, how do others let you know they would like to share it?

What makes you feel happy?

If you have a personal space, are you able to share it with others? If not, why not?

What is your favorite activity to do with someone else?

How honest can you be when talking with other family members?

What makes you feel sad?

Say something positive about another family member.

What do you dislike about your family?

Do you have a space that you can call your own? If so, describe it.

What makes you feel mad?

How do you say no to others?

How do you react when others say no?

How do you help support other members of the family?

How do you handle negative emotions?

What happens when you like someone in your family that another family member dislikes?

How big a role have you played in the things that have happened in your family?

What role, if any, have you played in the things that have happened in your life?

How much say do you have in making your own decisions?

How do you feel about recent changes in your life or in your family?

How much control have your parents exhibited in your life?

What holidays does your family observe?

How or when do you receive encouragement from your family?

How do you get along with your siblings?

What traditions does your family practice?

What do you think are your family's weaknesses? How could they be improved?

Who soothes you when you are upset?

What do you like best about living in this family?

If your family had a title, what would it be?

Would you like more time and/or space for yourself? If so, how would you obtain it?

Name something you like about yourself.

What do you do to help out in your family?

Name one person you would like to spend more time with.

What do you like about your family?

If you were granted one wish, what would it be and how would it change things?

What are you most afraid of?

How do you communicate with your family?

Who makes the rules in the family?

Name something that makes you special and different from others in your family.

Who enforces the rules in the family?

What is your favorite activity to do alone?

What happens if you say no to someone else?

How do you work out your problems?

What do you do to help the parent–child relationship?

How safe is your environment?

What sports, activities, clubs, or special events do you participate in?

What types of pictures, souvenirs, and mementos of your family do you want to keep around?

What is it like to express negative and positive feelings within your family? How do you express these feelings?

Do you feel respected by your family? Why or why not?

Do you have a special friend you talk to? If so, describe that person.

How are warmth, kindness, respect, and love shown in your family?

Describe your family's religious beliefs, if any.

What kinds of chores do you do around the house?

How or when do you encourage others in your family?

What do you think are your family's biggest strengths?

What is your biggest gripe?

"Mother Says/Father Says..."

Miriam Claire Godwin and April M. Hames

Type of Contribution: Activity

Objective

This activity is designed for use with families who are working on realigning the hierarchy in their family system. It is an experiential activity in which family members practice placing the parents in the appropriate parental system or subsystem hierarchy in a game-like activity. Parents give directives and children respond.

This activity can be used with single-parent and two- parent families. In single heterosexual parent families, the parent should say "Mother says" or "Father says." In two-parent families, parents can confer for shared directives and say "Mother and Father say." Also, parents can work as a team and take turns giving their own directives by saying "Mother says" or "Father says." This language can be adapted for homosexual parents.

Rationale for Use

The definition of a normal family is not the absence of problems, but a functional structure for dealing with those problems (Nichols & Schwartz, 2004). Most families experience some level of disruption as their members undergo developments within the family life cycle. Such problems arise when there is not an established parental and child subsystem (Minuchin, 1974).

In their work relating to systems and families, Becvar and Becvar (1999) provide several theoretical approaches to facilitating change in family systems. Many of their pragmatic suggestions relate to this activity. They suggest that it is constructive to facilitate conditions within a family that foster and further individual self-esteem. Stable and consistent leadership by the parent or parents is a crucial step toward constructive behavior because good feelings and self-esteem come from productivity (Becvar & Becvar). In "Mother says/Father says ..." parents have an opportunity to lead effectively and children have a chance to experience listening and obeying in a friendly, safe setting. According to Becvar and Becvar, therapists should help families bring their expectations into focus. This experiential activity allows parents to practice feed-forward messages (learning to request the desired behavior) rather than criticizing undesirable behaviors. It can also teach participating family members that if you treat someone as he or she *could* be, there is an increased possibility for the desired behavior to occur.

This activity combines the structural and experiential family therapy models. In structural family therapy, the therapist joins the family in a position of leadership, maps their underlying structure, and intervenes to transform that structure (Minuchin & Fishman, 1981). The therapist's role is to disable defenses and ease anxiety, support proper parental authority, facilitate enactments, assist with structural mapping, shape competence within individuals and the system, and help establish healthy boundaries with families. Experiential theorists give emphasis to the idea that self-fulfillment depends on family cohesiveness (Whitaker, 1976). Unlike most systems approaches, the emphasis is on expanding experiences; the assumption is that opening individuals to their own experience is a requirement for facilitating change in the family. In this activity, these two theoretical approaches work synergistically to provide the experience of appropriate family hierarchy.

The purpose of this activity is to help families realign the hierarchy in their family system. The game allows family members to practice placing parents in their proper hierarchical positions. It models an important part of an appropriate parental subsystem: Parents give directives and children respond to them with fitting action. This activity is based on the old childhood game of "Simon Says"; however, it has been adapted to replace "Simon" with the parents of the family. This intervention allows the family to perform new skills in a playful activity. Playing "Mother says/Father says ..." requires leadership and good decision-making skills from parents and attentive listening and self-control from children.

In this setting, parents typically will not give an inappropriate directive and children will usually listen carefully. This activity provides families with a positive, unique framework for experiencing family functioning based on clear generational boundaries where the parents maintain control and authority. This is known as functional family hierarchy. Also, they will have a confidence-building, positive experience in which they may have fun. Families with a long history of problems may not have had many recent familial experiences that were enjoyable. By removing inhibitors that may prevent improvement or resolution, this activity can potentially unlock resources and provide renewed energy for coping with problems and future efforts to change.

Instructions

In this activity, parents can give any appropriate directive they choose (e.g., "touch your toes," "shake your leg"). A directive is an order or instruction typically issued by a central authority in an effort to direct or guide behavior. This game is very similar to "Simon Says." If the parent precedes the directive with "Mother says," "Father says," or "Mother and Father say," children should follow the direction. However, if the parent or parents do not precede the directive with "Mother says," "Father says," or "Mother and Father say," children should not respond. If the children do respond to a directive without the critical "... says," the children are to be eliminated from that round. The therapist and parents may use this opportunity to discuss what happens in "real life" when they do something they are not supposed to do. This can be an opportunity to use the game to learn things that are applicable in families' everyday lives.

The following directions explain how to use this activity in family sessions:

1. Discuss with the family how the traditional game of "Simon Says ..." is played (i.e., tell the family, "Only perform the action if it begins with 'Simon' says ..."). Explain the change in the leader from "Simon" to "Mother" or "Father." The leader (traditionally "Simon," but for this activity "Mother" or "Father") calls out instructions and the participants follow the instructions until told to stop.
2. Inform the family that instead of "Simon Says," they will be playing "Mother Says ...," "Father Says ...," or "Mother and Father Say ..." and they are required to follow the instructions of the leader at all times during the game or they will be "out" and removed from the game until the next round.
3. Explain to the children that they will be "out" of that round of the game if they follow an instruction given by the leader that does not begin with "Mother says/Father says...." When children are "out" for the remainder of a round, they should be encouraged by the therapist to cheer their siblings on and offer support.
4. Ask the leader (Mother and/or Father) to stand on a chair or stand on a porch (if outdoors) and have the children stand below on the floor or in the yard. If the parent is unable to stand, have the children sit on the floor beside the parent. However this takes place, make sure the leader is physically higher than the children so that the family can experience the leader being "higher" than them in the hierarchical structure of their family system.
5. Begin the game and allow the leader to take charge of the activity until it is complete.

6. After the game is over, process the activity with the following questions:
   a. What was it like to give directions and have them followed by the children?
   b. What was it like to work as a team (if both parents participated)?
   c. What was it like to follow all the directions given by the parents?
   d. Why is it important to follow parental directions and what could happen if they fail to do so in real-life situations?
   e. Where were the family's ongoing disagreements during the activity and how were they able or unable to leave them out of the game?
   f. What would have been different if the leaders had given the directions under the assumption that one or more of the children would not follow them?
   g. How were the children able to choose their behaviors in response to the directives instead of simply reacting? Do not neglect the fact that it is difficult and requires diligence and attentiveness from the children.

Brief Clinical Vignette

The therapist used this activity with a family with a single mother, Katie (35), and her three young children, Angie (10), Beverly (7), and Charles (5). The mother had been the victim of domestic violence for most of the children's lives. The children had witnessed numerous violent incidences between their mother and father, Donnie (33), as well as daily substance abuse by their father that provoked the violent acts.

The father had been removed from the home and, in therapy, the oldest child, Angie, was working toward lessening her parentified role. Angie had often been the caretaker of her mother following the violence. She was also the caretaker of her younger siblings during the violence and when her mother was recovering from the violence inflicted upon her. Angie was having a difficult time adjusting to the role of a typical child now that the violence had been removed from her home and continually overstepped her mother's parenting role.

The therapist engaged the family in this activity outdoors. During their in-home therapy, the therapist had Katie stand on the cement front porch of their home and placed the children in the yard, below her, facing Katie and waiting for directives. The therapist explained the rules to the family and helped facilitate the first round of the game.

At first, the children were resistant to their mother's directives, but were eventually able to play the game according to the rules. They jumped when their mother said to jump, walked when their mother instructed them to walk, and were "out" of the game if they did something their mother did not prompt with "Mother says . . . ."

After the family had an opportunity to play several rounds of the game, the therapist stopped the activity and gathered the family into a circle to process their experience. Katie reported that it was enjoyable for her to be able to regain her role of parent and have her children listen to her directives, even if for a short time period and in a playful manner. The children reported that it was enjoyable to listen to their mother and try to stay in the game by doing so. Angie, who had the most difficulty following her mother's directives during the initial rounds of the game, reported she realized this is the way it should be in her family, but her history often made it difficult in "real life." The family reported this was a fun way to readjust to the "way things should be" in their family functioning.

Suggestions for Follow-Up

Following this game the therapist can inquire of the children whether they could play this game nonverbally (e.g., gestures, body language, and facial expressions). This will naturally lead into a discussion of how nonverbal communication is very important in a family. This is a fun variation of the game.

The therapist can also inquire of the parents whether the game helped them have the confidence to give directives to their children and/or stepchildren once they were back in the typical home environment.

Finally, therapists can discuss if or how family interactions have changed since the last session when the family participated in "Mother says/Father says . . . ." Families may also be encouraged to play this game as a homework assignment to continue to reinforce positive changes.

Contraindications for Use

Do not use this activity if any abuse (sexual, physical, or emotional) is currently suspected in the presenting family. There may be situations in these families where obeying a parental directive would be harmful to children. Do not use this activity with a family that is in crisis or is actively grieving. This activity also may not be appropriate for families with rigid internal boundaries. In these families, this activity may further legitimize the extreme separateness between parents and children. If only one parent is having difficulty establishing appropriate parental hierarchy in the family, only that person should lead in an effort to balance the parental subsystem's hierarchy. Another option would be for the effective leader to help support the less effective leader while he or she is leading the family during the activity. This would include those learning to live in blended families. However, this activity is not recommended for recently married blended families until the stepparent has spent time building a relationship with the stepchildren (see Hecker & Sori, 2006).

References

Becvar, D. S., & Becvar, R. J. (1999). *Systems theory and family therapy: A primer* (2nd ed.). New York: University Press of America.

Hecker, L. L., & Sori, C. F. (2006). Divorce and stepfamily issues. In C. F. Sori (Ed.), *Engaging children in family therapy: Creative approaches to integrating theory and research in clinical practice* (pp. 177–204). New York: Routledge.

Minuchin, S. (1974). *Families and family therapy.* Cambridge, MA: Harvard University Press.

Minuchin, S., & Fishman, H. C. (1981). *Family therapy techniques.* Cambridge, MA: Harvard University Press.

Nichols, M. P., & Schwartz, R. C. (2004). *Family therapy: Context and methods* (6th ed.). New York: Allyn and Bacon.

Whitaker, C. A. (1976). The hindrance of theory in clinical work. In P. J. Guerin (Ed.), *Family therapy: Theory and practice* (pp. 154–164). New York: Gardner Press.

Professional Readings and Resources

Haley, J. (1988). *Problem-solving therapy* (2nd ed). San Francisco: Jossey–Bass.

Patterson, J., Williams, L, Grauf-Grounds, C., & Chamow, L. (1998). *Essential skills in family therapy: From the first interview to termination.* New York: The Guilford Press.

Satir, V. M. (1972). *Peoplemaking.* Palo Alto, CA: Science and Behavior Books.

Bibliotherapy Sources for the Client

Dinkmeyer, D. C. (1983). *The parent's guide: STEP/teen systematic training for effective parenting of teens.* Lebanon, IN: American Guidance Service.

Levy, R., O'Hanlon, B., & Goode, T. N. (2002). *Try and make me! Simple strategies that turn off the tantrums and create cooperation.* Emmaus, PA: Rodale Books.

Phelan, L. (1995). *Parenting 101.* Woodridge, IL: Great Quotations.

Smith, C. A. (1999). *Encyclopedia of parenting.* London: Routledge.

– 19 –

The "Out of Control" Balloon
Using Spirituality as a Coping Resource

April Michele Hames and Miriam Claire Godwin

Type of Contribution: Handout, Activity

Objective

This activity is designed to assist family members in separating stressors that they are able to control from stressors that they are unable to control. There is a spiritual element to this activity, so be sure to use it with families that have expressed a desire to incorporate spirituality into their treatment. It can be used with people of faith who believe in a higher power.

Rationale for Use

Sense of control is a widely utilized construct in social psychology (Wolinsky et al., 2004). A strong sense of control is thought to buffer psychosocial pathologies and minimize social, psychological, and medical consequences. People need and want to perceive that they have control over events, even those controlled by chance. It is easier to accept self-blame than to believe adverse events can happen by chance. By accepting self-blame, individuals are able to perceive some control over events.

According to Rotter's (1954) social learning theory, people's actions are predictable on the basis of their values, expectations, and the situations in which they find themselves. The locus of control (LOC) construct within social learning theory is the belief that goal attainment is either within the control of a person (internal control) or is controlled by outside factors (external control). Perceived control can be defined as a generalized expectancy for internal control as opposed to external control of reinforcements (Lefcourt, 1982) or the belief that one can determine one's own internal state and behavior, influence one's environment, and/or bring about desired outcomes (Pallant, 2000).

Family is a social antecedent of LOC. An attentive, responsive, and reliant family environment is a precursor of the development of internal LOC (Lefcourt, 1982). According to Lefcourt, a less responsive and less opportune family environment creates a climate of fatalism and helplessness that is reflected in the subsequent development of an external LOC. This is the result of chance instead of external LOC based on the belief in powerful others. These individuals often realize that there is minimal reciprocity between the quality of their efforts and quality of their rewards. Access to opportunity for appropriate responses, especially in the home, seems to be crucial in the development of an internal LOC. The contingent responsiveness intrinsic to a nurturing yet autonomous home seems to be the necessary component for the development of internal control.

A family's perception of whether they can resolve and/or manage a crisis situation can determine how they react to it (Ingoldsby, Smith, & Miller, 2004). Life satisfaction for family members is positively associated with social support and perceived control (Lucke, Coccia, Goode, & Lucke, 2004). Family beliefs related to perceived ability to control outcomes can facilitate adaptation to stressful circumstances (Kazak et al., 2004). Identifying and changing these beliefs has been shown to decrease emotional distress in a range of situations. Spiritual and religious beliefs are examples that may foster adaptation by helping families cope with a perceived lack of control.

Everyone struggles with stressors in daily life. Some stressors are completely out of the client's control (e.g., a disability or illness of a family member) and some stressors are in the client's control (e.g., how they cope with the disability or illness, complying with medical advice). Families are challenged by many things that are out of their control, yet they may take responsibility for those things and feel guilt, anger, and/or anxiety. They often blame themselves for the things that are out of their control and feel negatively about themselves because they cannot gain control of the uncontrollable. This activity aims to empower the family to focus on the controllable elements in their lives and give the uncontrollable aspects to a "Higher Power" (or whatever spiritual practice to which they may belong) by highlighting what stressors in their family life they can control. By "giving" or "casting" the uncontrollable things away to a "Higher Power," the family will hopefully feel a sense of peace and understanding that they are a part of something greater than themselves, and that they are not alone in their struggle with the stressors that challenge their family, yet are out of their control. They will also be able to maximize perceptions of both internal and external LOC related to powerful others by recognizing and utilizing both perceptions of control.

The purpose of this activity is to symbolically give away the uncontrollable problems via external LOC to a higher power. Giving or casting away the uncontrollable increases individuals' external LOC. This facilitates building an external LOC in powerful others. When an individual or family has a high internal LOC, as most do, establishing a higher external LOC is an effective way to maintain some level of control in situations that may otherwise be considered uncontrollable.

Supplies

The following is a list of the inexpensive supplies needed to conduct this activity:

Plain paper
3 × 5 cards
Permanent marker
Pen or pencil
Polaroid or digital camera
Helium filled balloons (any shape and size will do, but no Mylar balloons)

There should be either one balloon per family member, or they can share and write all stressors on a shared balloon, based on the therapist's discretion.

You may be able to obtain these in the floral department of a local grocery store. They often have balloons with their company logo that they are willing to donate or sell for a small fee.

Instructions

Following is a list of steps to take to prepare the family for this activity, as well as instructions on how to conduct and then process the *Out of Control Balloon* intervention. Therapists should:

1. Instruct each family member to make a list of all the stressors in their lives on the handout entitled "Current Stressors."
2. Encourage them to share their lists aloud with their family.
3. Discuss with the family what it means to them to be able to "control" something and what it means not to be able to "control" something.

4. Instruct family members to revisit their "Current Stressors" handout and cross off each stressor over which they have some control.
5. Encourage them to share how they exert influence over each stressor for which they do have some control. Ask each family member how it feels to be able to control those stressors in their lives.
6. Process with the family what stressors they could not mark through on their handout and why they feel those stressors are "out of their control" (i.e., something they have no ability to change), as well as how they feel about not being able to control them.
7. Explore what makes the uncontrollable so difficult.
8. Instruct family members to write the names of stressors that are out of their control on their helium-filled balloons, using a permanent marker. Each family member should have his or her own balloon, or the family can choose to share one balloon for a more collective experience.
9. Process with the family what it would be like to "give" the stressors that are out of their control to a "Higher Power" (or God, or whatever term fits their religious or spiritual belief system) in which they believe. Discuss with them how this could occur and how they would feel about relinquishing the uncontrollable.
10. Process how it would feel to stop blaming themselves for the things that are out of their control and focus their attention on things that they are able to control. Discuss what, if anything, each person would like to say as he or she releases the balloons. On 3 × 5 cards have each person write down the name of the stressors and, below that, what they want to say as they release the balloons to symbolize letting go of trying to control things they cannot change.
11. If possible, take the family outdoors and instruct them to release their "out of control" balloons and allow their stressors to be taken over by a "Higher Power." For those who cannot go outdoors (e.g., due to incarceration, hospitalization, physical disability), other family members may be asked to release balloons, or the therapist can agree to do it. If possible, take photographs as each family member is in the act of letting go of his or her "out of control" balloons.
12. Process with the family what it was like to release their "out of control" stressors and how their lives will be different now that they can focus on things they can control.

Brief Clinical Vignette

The therapist used this activity with a single-parent family that was coping with the autism spectrum disorder (ASD) diagnosis of the youngest of the three children. The siblings, Lisa (10 years old) and Mel (8 years old), often expressed anger about the behavior of 5-year-old Greg. They reported frequent worry about their mother, Jill (45 years old), her ability to manage Greg, and anxiety about going out in public with their brother. He experienced frequent "meltdowns" and generally undesirable behavior when in the community.

In a session that included Jill, Lisa, and Mel, the therapist gave each family member the handout and instructed them to list all the things they were worried about: the stressors in their lives. Lisa and Mel initially had difficulty listing their concerns, but the therapist encouraged them to list as many things as they could so that the activity would be as helpful as possible.

With the help of the therapist, Jill, Lisa, and Mel reviewed their lists and marked through all the stressors that were in their control (e.g., how they react to a "meltdown" in public). The therapist processed with the family how they were able to control all of the items they marked and encouraged them to list how they could continue to control such things in the future.

Then the therapist had the family process all the things that were out of their control (e.g., how others react to "meltdowns" when in the grocery store). The therapist had the family discuss their feelings about not having control over these particular things. The family also discussed how they could support each other when dealing with these concerns in their lives.

The therapist had Jill, Lisa, and Mel complete the activity by writing their uncontrollable stressors on a balloon with a permanent marker. Each family member had a balloon for the writing activity. Before releasing each balloon, the family processed what it would feel like to give these items over to a "Higher Power" and trust that their faith in that "Higher Power" would help them cope with the stress evoked by the uncontrollable things in their lives. The therapist asked them what they wanted to say when they released the balloon, and Jill decided on a prayer, which she wrote down on a 3 × 5 card below the list of the stressors that were out of their control. The family released the balloons and Jill prayed aloud that God would take away the stressors and help them cope with what they could not control. The therapist took a few pictures that showed the family holding the balloon string together and then releasing the balloon, all looking up at the sky with hopeful and happy expressions on their faces.

Lisa and Mel expressed feelings of joy and relief after they passed on their stressors to God. Jill shared that it was helpful for her to hear what was concerning her children so that she could relate to and further address their concerns. The family expressed that it was very helpful to focus on what they had the ability to control and change in their lives and leave the rest up to their "Higher Power."

Suggestions for Follow-Up

The therapist should use subsequent sessions to revisit the activity. It is helpful to process with the family whether they were truly able to "let go" of the things in their life that are out of their control and concentrate on what they do have the ability to control. The handout can be kept to remind both the family and therapist what stressors the family was dealing with at the last visit. The photographs and 3 × 5 cards are also visual reminders of their commitment to letting go, and can be used in follow-up sessions. Clients could make a collage out of the pictures and the cards, or they could construct a family book, which could be added to with additional materials throughout the course of therapy. The therapist should encourage the family to revisit the activity on their own when "uncontrollable" things arise in order to discuss what they are unable to control and want to "release." Lastly, the therapist may process with the family the importance of feeling as if they control certain aspects of their life.

Contraindications for Use

Do not use this activity if clients are functionally impaired in a way that would make this activity difficult to comprehend. The therapist should use his or her clinical judgment to decide whether or not suggesting this activity is appropriate based on the family's outlook, reality of their future, spiritual orientation, and possible employment venues.

References

Ingoldsby, B. B., Smith, S. R., & Miller, J. E. (2004). *Exploring family theories.* Los Angeles: Roxbury Publishing.

Kazak, A. E., McClure, K. S., Alderfer, M. A., Hwang, W., Crump, T. A., Le, L. T., et al. (2004). Cancer-related parental beliefs: The Family Illness Beliefs Inventory (FIBI). *Journal of Pediatric Psychology, 29,* 531–542.

Lefcourt, H. M. (1982). *Locus of control: Current trends in theory and research* (2nd ed.). Hillsdale, NJ: Lawrence Erlbaum Associates.

Lucke, K. T., Coccia, H., Goode, J. S., & Lucke, J. F. (2004). Quality of life in spinal cord injured individuals and their caregivers during the initial 6 months following rehabilitation. *Quality of Life Research, 13,* 97–110.

Pallant, J. F. (2000). Development and validation of a scale measuring perceive control of internal states. *Journal of Personality Assessment, 75,* 308–337.

Rotter, J. B. (1954). *Social learning and clinical psychology.* Englewood Cliffs, NJ: Prentice Hall.

Wolinsky, F. D., Metz, S. M., Tierney, W. M., Wyrwich, K. W., Babu, A. N., & Kroenke, K. (2004). Test–retest reliability of the Mirowsky–Ross 2 × 2 index of the sense of control. *Psychological Reports, 94,* 725–732.

Professional Readings and Resources

Bandura, A. (2004). Health promotion by social cognitive means. *Health Education & Behavior, 31*(2), 143–164.

Clements, S., & Cummings, S. (1991). Helplessness and powerlessness: Caring for clients in pain. *Holistic Nursing Practice, 6*(1), 76–85.

Levenson, H. (1974). Activism and powerful others: Distinctions within the concept of internal–external control. *Journal of Personality Assessment, 38,* 377–383.

Navon, S. (1999). The non-illness intervention model: Psychotherapy for physically ill patients and their families. *The American Journal of Family Therapy, 27,* 251–270.

Wolinsky, F. D., Wyrwich, K. W., Babu, A. N., Kroenke, K., & Tierney, W. M. (2003). Age, aging, and the sense of control among older adults: A longitudinal reconsideration. *Journal of Gerontology, 58B*(4), S212–S220.

Bibliotherapy Sources for the Client

Glasser, W. (1999). *Choice theory: A new psychology of personal freedom.* New York: Harper.

Hammond, M. M. (2004). *Get over it and get on with it: How to get up when life knocks you down.* Colorado Springs: WaterBrook Press.

Maziarek, J. (2003). *Spirituality simplified.* Villa Park, IL: Spirit Simple Enterprises.

Schwartz, B. (2004). *The paradox of choice: Why more is less.* New York: HarperCollins.

Siegel, D. J. (2007). *The mindful brain: Reflections and attunement in the cultivation of well-being.* New York: W. W. Norton.

Wicks, R. J. (2007). *Crossing the desert: Learning to let go, see clearly, and live simply.* Notre Dame: Sorin Books.

Handout 19.1: "Out of Control" Balloon

Client Name________________________ Date_______________

Current Stressors

Please list all the current stressors in your life. Once you have finished, review the list and mark through all of the stressors you are somewhat able to control.

I get stressed about...

____

____

____

____

____

____

____

____

____

____

Touchstones
Connecting to Memories of a Loved One[*]

Catherine Ford Sori

Type of Contribution: Activity, Handout

Objectives

This activity is designed to help children and families who have experienced the death of a close family member. The activity has several purposes: First, it is designed to open family communication and help clients elicit and share positive memories of their deceased loved one. Second, clients select and/or create tangible objects to help them retain their memories, as well as a sense of connection to the deceased and to one another. Finally, therapists who integrate spirituality can use stones to provide inspiration for clients who are struggling with religious or spiritual issues. This activity may be adapted for use with children or adults in individual sessions, family treatment, couples therapy, or in child or adult bereavement group sessions. While this chapter focuses on using stones in grief counseling, *Touchstones* is not limited to this population, but can be used with child or adult clients who present many other presenting problems, such as anxiety, depression, behavior problems, etc.

Rationale for Use

Both child and adult clients often benefit from activities that are experiential and that can be integrated into family play therapy (see Dermer, Olund, & Sori, 2006; Gil, in Sori, 2006). This activity introduces a playful element to counseling and offers clients the possibility of seeing things in a new way, due to the sometimes magical "as if" quality of make-believe play (see Ariel, Carel, & Tyano, 1985; Sori, 1998). Using objects such as stones or shells to metaphorically and concretely represent a goal, a memory, or a story can promote more open sharing because a metaphoric representation often sidesteps client resistance to talking about difficult subjects. Working with objects that are metaphors can also allow unconscious material to emerge. According to Dermer and colleagues, "In short, play provides a metaphorical channel whereby children can communicate their thoughts and feelings, beliefs and ideas, including their perception of themselves—often by projecting them onto an object" (2006, p. 38). Gil and Sobol (2000) point out how valuable the language of play can be, as it can reveal the inner experiences and reactions of children as well as their desires and needs. This is all especially important with working with grieving children and families.

This activity can promote some of the goals of experiential family therapy, which include promoting more open and honest communication and family connections and uncovering and sharing emotions (Satir, 1988; Satir & Baldwin, 1983), as well as discovering individual and family strengths and

---

[*] Note: The author has long used stones in therapy, and the idea was borne out of her personal experience of connecting memories of her grandfather to see shells he had given her as a child. Sea shells are now symbolic in her family as a way to connect the generations.

opportunities to promote resiliency (see Klimes-Dougan & Kendziora, 2000; Walsh, 2006). These are often important goals when counseling bereaved families.

Touchstones fits especially well with the premises of narrative therapy. Narrative therapists help clients re-story their lives by first hearing clients' dominant stories of a problem or of their lives, and then uncovering more positive but subjugated stories. These preferred stories can be useful to help clients view themselves and their problems in a new way and to uncover hidden strengths and resources that clients had overlooked. Clients' subjugated stories often tell a different story—perhaps of forgotten strengths or positive characteristics, unique outcomes, or times of resiliency that have been overshadowed by the dominant story. Once uncovered, these subjugated stories can be highlighted and heralded as alternative ways of thinking about oneself and how one approaches a problem (see Dermer et al., 2006; Freedman & Combs, 1996; Freeman, Epston, & Lobovits, 1997; Simons & Freedman, 2000; White & Epston, 1990). This re-storying can be useful in helping clients make meaning of a death, or of the deceased's life, or of the client's ability to cope and carry on.

Working with grieving clients. Too often, when a family experiences the death of a close relative, people draw apart as they attempt to make sense of and cope with the loss. This may be due to individual differences in how people process grief and express their emotions (Biank & Sori, 2006a). For example, some may want to talk about the deceased and share feelings of shock and sadness, while others may seek solitude and not be comfortable sharing their deep emotions. Parents often fear overwhelming their children with their grief and may subsequently downplay their reactions and even elect not to talk about the deceased or what happened that led up to the death. These parents may also not feel emotionally equipped or prepared to talk with their children. This can leave children feeling alone or even emotionally abandoned, with no one to turn to for comfort or for answers to the myriad of questions that they may have about illness, death, dying, or an afterlife (Biank & Sori, 2006a; 2006b; Sori & Biank, 2006). Adults and children may need individual or group grief counseling as a precursor to or concurrent with family therapy sessions.

Opening family communication is often a goal in family therapy, and this is especially essential when families are grieving. It is important for families to share their memories of a deceased parent or child, as this promotes intimacy and connection among survivors. Sharing special stories of the deceased and what that person meant to them allows family members to begin to share their grief, strengthening attachment among family members. It also helps keep the memory of the deceased alive, which is important for children who have lost a parent, want to remember that parent, and believe that he or she is watching over them (Biank & Sori, 2006b). Parents who can cry with their children (without decompensating or burdening the children), as well as share happy and funny memories of a deceased family member, model healthy grieving for their children.

Using stones with grieving clients. Touchstones offers therapists a different approach to encouraging bereaved clients to begin to share their memories of the deceased. Clients are offered an array of plain or inscribed stones, seashells, or differently sized and colored rocks or marbles, and asked to select one that somehow reminds them of a special memory, characteristic, or story of the deceased. They are then invited to share why they selected that particular stone. Some clients may wish to write special words, phrases, or quotes that are meaningful to them on the stones. The words might remind them of a characteristic of their loved one or offer the client a word of hope or encouragement to help them cope with their devastating loss. Clients can take turns selecting stones and sharing memories or stories with one another in this manner.

Use of stones to address spiritual or religious issues with clients. Clients who may be struggling with faith issues may select or create stones that have words to encourage them. Examples of such words include "faith," "trust," "believe," "hope," and "love." Some clients may identify a religious saying or a quote from the Bible or another religious book and may write that quote or the citation on a stone.

Touchstones has special benefits for children. These touchstones can represent a connection to memories of their lost loved one. The benefit of repeating this exercise periodically is that children develop a collection of touchstones that are meaningful and tied to positive memories. The collection is portable and can accompany children wherever they go. This activity also gives children and adults permission to talk and ask questions about issues related to death, dying, and an afterlife. Touching the stones can be a way for children to soothe themselves whenever they need to. For example, one 8-year-old boy carried a special stone in his pocket wherever he went. He touched it whenever he felt lonely or sad to remind him of a special memory of his mother and that she would always be with him in his heart.

Touchstones can be used to help clients set goals in the early stages of therapy, and in the middle stages to open family communication about issues that may be difficult for some clients to discuss (i.e., death of a close family member, struggles with faith issues, etc.). In the final stages of therapy *Touchstones* can be used to consolidate change and can serve as a concrete reminder of sources of strength, resiliency, and hope for continuing growth after therapy ends.

Materials

The materials that are needed can be purchased inexpensively at a craft store, ordered online, or gathered in nature. These include colored stones, marbles, seashells, or rocks of different sizes, colors, and textures. Care should be taken to get a variety of stones that are all different, if possible. Therapists may purchase both blank stones and stones with words already inscribed on them (e.g., an inexpensive selection is available at www.terrysvillage.com) to serve as prompts for clients. Clients may choose to paint or write words (see Handout 20.1 at the end of this chapter for a list of suggested words) on the blank stones, using permanent markers or craft paint. Some clients and therapists prefer to use blank stones. Each client will also need a small drawstring marble or favor bag or materials to create his or her own bag.

Instructions

This activity may be done in one session, or spread out over 2 or more weeks. The therapist may introduce this activity with a story:

> In many cultures, some ancient and some still alive (like Native Americans), when something important would happen in their lives that people wanted to remember, they would save some small thing (like a stone or feather). They would place it in a small pouch or bag, and they would carry that on their body. Those things inside were used to help them remember that special event. In a similar manner, Jewish priests would attach scriptures to their prayer shawls to remind them of God's word. So today, I am inviting each of you to select (or create) a bag that will carry a "touchstone." You will choose a touchstone to remind you of a memory, a special moment, or time you spent with the person you loved who has died. It could be a memory of an important day, a story, something that happened that meant a lot to you, or you can simply choose a stone that somehow helps you remember your loved one. You could also select a stone that has a word that has special meaning to you. Just like all people are unique and your loved one was special, notice that all of these stones are also different and can have unique meanings.

Children and adults each select one stone to represent a special memory of their loved one. Taking turns, they may continue to select different stones that correspond to a specific memory or that have special meaning for them. For example, one child selected a translucent blue stone to represent the memory of her mother taking her to the beach for her birthday, shortly before she died. Her father selected a large, hard rock because he remembered how strong his wife was in fighting cancer. Clients are then encouraged to take turns showing the stones they selected and sharing the associated memories with their family (or group). However, some may elect to keep the memory private.

Clients can also be asked to select stones with words inscribed on them that remind them of a characteristic or strength that the deceased had or that offer them strength or hope to carry on. The handout at the end of the chapter offers suggestions of words that could be inscribed on the stones. Clinicians can write the words on stones ahead of time, or clients can select words from the handout and use markers or paint to write the words on the blank stones that they select. Clients can also come up with their own unique inscriptions. For example, one woman wrote "La Rosa Blanca" on the inside of a large white seashell. This was her late husband's favorite poem, which he had often recited, and the seashell reminded her of all their wonderful trips to the ocean.

After selecting the stones and discussing their meaning, clients are given a bag or materials to create their own pouch for their touchstones. The bag should be large enough to contain all the stones that were selected. The bags and the stones can be used in the manner of a transitional object: Whenever children are missing the deceased or feeling sad, they can open the bag, touch one of the stones, and connect to the particular memory of their loved one that corresponds to the stone. Children may even find it helpful to carry a stone with them on special occasions. For example, one 9-year-old boy whose mother had died over the summer carried a reddish stone in his pocket on his first day back to school. The red reminded him of his mother's heart and how much she loved him, and helped him feel that she was watching over him.

If used as a group activity, a stone and memory can be selected and shared each week. This activity can be used at any point in treatment with individuals who have experienced a loss.

Brief Clinical Vignette

Marge and her two young children sought bereavement counseling one year after her husband Victor had been shot while riding his motorcycle. He had not been the intended target, but was caught in the crossfire of a gang shooting. This tragic loss was compounded by the fact that not quite a year before her husband's death, Marge's younger brother, Charles, had also been killed in a senseless drive-by shooting. Shortly after her husband's death, Marge and her two girls, Tania (age 7) and Temeshia (age 5), moved in with her mother and sister so that the girls could live in a safer neighborhood. Marge was a teacher's assistant, and she had been forced to take a second job working evenings and weekends at a neighborhood store to make ends meet following her husband's death. Her mother and sister were able to watch the girls when she had to work late.

Marge told the therapist that Tania was reluctant to talk about her father's or uncle's deaths, while Temeshia would burst into loud, uncontrollable sobbing whenever their names were mentioned. The therapist learned that Marge and the other adults in the house now avoided ever mentioning Victor or Charles, so as not to upset Temeshia. Consequently, several individual sessions were held with Marge to allow her to begin to express her grief and explore what these losses meant to her, without her need to shield Tania and Temeshia. Both of these deaths were more difficult to grieve due to the sudden and traumatic ways Victor and Charles had died (see Biank & Sori, 2006a; Webb, 1993).

As Marge began to share her experiences, the therapist learned that Marge had been sitting on the porch and had witnessed her brother's accidental shooting as he was bounding up the steps. She had been hysterical and cried for days, turning to her husband and children for support. One year later, when she saw two police officers come up those same porch steps, she experienced flashbacks and was near hysteria even before the officers told her that this time it was her husband who had been senselessly killed. This time she was even more bereft, and her mother had to care for the children for several weeks until she could face the world again. After that, she had tried to be stoic around the children, not wanting to burden them with her grief, which was so overwhelming.

Marge worked hard in therapy, and as she felt better she wanted to include her children in therapy. In family sessions the therapist encouraged Marge to use puppets, art, play therapy techniques, and bibliotherapy to educate the children about death and grief, and to give them permission to talk about their feelings (see Biank & Sori, 2006a). Tania's favorite books were *When Dinosaurs Die* (Brown &

Brown, 1996) and *Sad Isn't Bad* (Mundy, 1998). Temeshia wanted to hear *What's Happened to Auntie Jean?* (White, 1976) over and over again. This book was from a Christian perspective, and it helped the children to begin asking their mother questions, such as where heaven is and how people get there, and why God let daddies die when kids need their daddies. These were hard questions for Marge to tackle, but she did so in a quiet and calm manner. With coaching from the therapist, she first explained what happens to the physical body when someone dies, before then discussing her personal religious beliefs about death, God, and an afterlife in heaven (Biank & Sori, 2006b).

The family engaged in other family play activities, such as doing a family play genogram (Gil, 2003) and later a spiritual family play genogram (Sori, 2007). They also did several individual and family sandtrays, drew pictures of their family doing something, created a family puppet interview (see Biank & Sori, 2006a; Dermer et al., 2006; Gil, 1994; Gil & Sobol, 2000; Irwin & Malloy, 1994), and listened to and even danced to selected songs from *The Lion King* (Biank & Sori, 2006b). All of these activities helped the children begin to talk about their father and uncle and the changes in their lives. Other play activities were especially useful in helping them identify and discuss their emotions (Biank & Sori, 2003b) and to explore and expand on their coping skills (Biank & Sori, 2003a). The therapist also integrated relaxation and guided imagery into family sessions (Sori & Biank, 2003) and, at the children's encouragement, Marge began doing this activity every night when she put the children to bed, using a tape recording provided by the therapist. As Marge became less anxious and more comfortable talking with the children about their father and uncle, the children also relaxed, asked questions, and shared their feelings. If Marge allowed herself to cry she did not decompensate, but was able to comfort her children. At that point the therapist determined it was appropriate to invite the family to do the *Touchstones* activity.

With *The Lion King* music, which the children loved, playing softly in the background, the therapist took out numerous plain rocks, stones, seashells, and marbles of various shapes, sizes, and colors, and placed them on the table. She explained that each person could pick a stone that reminded her of either Victor or Charles in some way; perhaps it brought up a memory or reminded her of a story. Quietly and carefully they looked over the stones and made their selections. When they had finished, the therapist asked if anyone would like to talk about the stones they had picked for Victor's memory. Marge held up a piece of river rock, saying that it reminded her of Victor, who was her rock. She then held up a square-cut stone, saying this made her think of the Bible verse where Christ was the cornerstone of the church, and her faith in Christ had sustained her through 2 grief-stricken years. She had also selected a cats-eye marble, which reminded her that God's eye is on the sparrow, and He is always watching over her and the children.

Tania asked to go next, and with excitement she shared that she had also picked a cat's-eye marble. To her it meant that even though her father was in heaven, she knew he was always watching over her, and that one day she would see him again. Temeshia, who by this time was bouncing in her seat, held up a bluish stone. She said it reminded her of her daddy because blue was his favorite color and because he had taken her to swim in the blue water at a pool on the Fourth of July.

Next the therapist asked them to share the stones they had selected for Uncle Charles. This time Temeshia got to go first, and she held up a black stone with white specks on it. She said it reminded her of the stars in the sky, and that Uncle Charles was up there in heaven with her daddy. Tania then showed a rust-colored stone that reminded her of her uncle's red motorcycle, and how he had taken her for short rides down the block, and how much she had loved the feel of hanging onto her uncle while the wind whipped her hair and the engine roared. This led to some laughter and discussion, as Marge recalled how her brother had overcome her objections by "sweet talkin'" her, which he apparently did quite often! As Marge told more stories about Charles's ability to charm her, Tania quietly picked up a brown-colored stone. When her mother finished, she asked if she could take this stone as well, since it looked like chocolate and would remind her of her "sweet talkin'" Uncle Charles. The therapist then gave everyone a bag in which to keep their touchstones, and explained how they could all touch them or take them out and share their memories whenever they wanted.

In the next session the therapist followed up on some of the issues that had come up during the *Touchstones* activity. For example, they had a deeper discussion about Marge's faith, how it had helped her cope, and what dreams she and Victor had for their daughters. Marge showed the therapist that she had her pouch of touchstones in her purse, and that she used them to remind her of those memories of Victor and Charles and that God was watching over her and the girls. Tania reported that she had slept with her pouch under her pillow each night and was sleeping better because she felt safer and closer to her dad. Temeshia said that when she felt sad she touched her blue stone, and this helped her remember her daddy at the pool and she felt better.

In their final session the therapist spread out numerous stones on the table, but this time they all had words inscribed on them. After talking about their individual and family strengths, and how they had all changed and grown during the course of therapy, the therapist invited them to select stones to remind them of this experience. Marge quickly selected stones that said "trust," "strength," and "hope." She explained that these words reminded her to trust God for her future, that she had strengths she had not realized before, and that now she felt hopeful for the future. Tania's stones said "joy," "love," and "create," and she said that she had selected these to remind her of her father and uncle's love, as well as God's love. Tania said that she could feel joyful and happy again, that she loved all the play activities they had done (especially the art and sandtray), and that she wanted to continue being creative. Temeshia, who needed some help reading the words on the stones, selected ones that said "dance," "sing," and "laugh" because they had done all these things in counseling, and they had helped her to feel better.

Tania asked if they could use their stones in one last sandtray. In this sandtray they placed miniatures on the left side of the tray to represent their family before the deaths and many people, animals, houses, and religious symbols on the right side of the tray. In the middle was a bridge, and they lined all their stones over the bridge, linking the past to the present, and on to the future. At the girls' request, the therapist took pictures of the sandtray and of the family with their stones, which they took home to remind them of their experience in therapy.

Suggestions for Follow-Up

As mentioned in the preceding vignette, clients may wish to incorporate their stones into a sandtray following this activity. Clients can also draw a picture of the memory that is associated with the stone. Plain or construction paper can be used for drawing or writing the memories associated with each stone selected, and each client could have a folder or materials to make a cover to store his or her written or drawn memories. The stories or pictures can be put in a folder or bound with string, and children may decorate the cover as they choose, perhaps with a picture of their loved one. Miscellaneous art materials, such as glitter, stickers, sequins, or feathers, are often popular with children to use to decorate their folders or memory books. A Polaroid or digital camera can be used to photograph the stones, and these pictures can be given to clients to take home or can be added to the memory book.

At the end of therapy, clients can select or label stones with words that describe their strengths, what they have learned in therapy, or how they have achieved their therapeutic goals. Thus, stones can serve as markers for the progress clients have made and as tangible reminders of their attributes, all of which can be "touched" when they face difficulties after termination.

Contraindications for Use

Touchstones is not recommended for families who are in a crisis, or in the early stages of grief. Before beginning this activity clinicians should assess clients' ability to discuss the deceased without decompensating. It would not be advised to do this activity in a family session until parents are able to take care of their children's emotional needs. If done too soon, role reversal could occur and children could attempt to take care of a grieving parent.

This activity should be introduced only after the therapist has established a solid therapeutic relationship with child and adult clients and has created a climate of safety. Prerequisite activities should include a discussion of feelings, and children should be fairly comfortable talking about their loss. The therapist must be sensitive to never push children to talk or share a story of a special memory, but should consider their resistance as a sign that they are not yet ready to openly discuss the deep emotions tied to their memories. In a group, children who do not wish to share can still benefit from choosing touchstones by writing their associated memories, storing them in a special box, and listening to others share their stories. Later in therapy, they might be more open to sharing the stories associated with their touchstones.

References

Ariel, S., Carel, C. A., & Tyano, S. (1985). Uses of children's make-believe play in family therapy: Theory and clinical examples. *Journal of Marital and Family Therapy, 11,* 47–60.

Biank, N., & Sori, C. F. (2003a). A child's impossible and scariest task. In C. F. Sori, L. L. Hecker, & associates, *The therapist's notebook for children and adolescents: Homework, handouts, and activities for use in psychotherapy* (pp. 18–24). Binghamton, NY: Haworth.

Biank, N., & Sori, C. F. (2003b). Feeling faces prevent scary places. In C. Sori, L. Hecker, & associates, *The therapist's notebook for children and adolescents: Homework, handouts, and activities for use in psychotherapy* (pp. 3–8). Binghamton, NY: Haworth.

Biank, N. M., & Sori, C. F. (2006a). Helping children cope with the death of a family member. In C. F. Sori (Ed.), *Engaging children in family therapy: Creative approaches to integrating theory and research in clinical practice* (pp. 245–262). New York: Routledge.

Biank, N., & Sori, C. F. (2006b). Integrating spirituality when working with children and families experiencing loss of a parent. In K. B. Helmeke & C. F. Sori (Eds.), *The therapist's notebook for integrating spirituality in counseling, vol. II: More homework, handouts, and activities for use in psychotherapy.* Binghamton, NY: Haworth.

Brown, L. K., & Brown, M. (1996). *When dinosaurs die: A guide to understanding death.* Boston: Little, Brown and Co.

Dermer, S., Olund, D., & Sori, C. F. (2006). Integrating play in family therapy theories. In C. F. Sori (Ed.), *Engaging children in family therapy: Creative approaches to integrating theory and research in clinical practice* (pp. 37–65). New York: Routledge.

Freedman, J., & Combs, G. (1996). *Narrative therapy: The social construction of preferred realities.* New York: W. W. Norton.

Freeman, J., Epston, D., & Lobovits, D. (1997). *Playful approaches to serious problems: Narrative therapy with children and their families.* New York: W. W. Norton.

Gil, E. (1994). *Play in family therapy.* New York: Guilford.

Gil, E. (2003). Play genograms. In C. F. Sori, L. L. Hecker, & associates, *The therapist's notebook for children and adolescents: Homework, handouts, and activities for use in psychotherapy* (pp. 49–56). Binghamton, NY: Haworth.

Gil, E., & Sobol, B. (2000). Engaging families in therapeutic play. In C. E. Bailey (Ed.), *Children in therapy: Using the family as a resource* (pp. 341–382). New York: W. W. Norton.

Irwin, E. C., & Malloy, E. S. (1994). Family puppet interview. In C. Schaefer & L. Carey (Eds.), *Family play therapy* (pp. 21–34). Northvale, NJ: Aronson.

Klimes-Dougan, B., & Kendziora, K. T. (2000). Resilience in children. In C. E. Bailey (Ed.), *Children in therapy: Using the family as a resource* (pp. 407–427). New York: W. W. Norton.

Mundy, M. (1998). *Sad isn't bad: A good-grief guidebook for kids dealing with loss.* St. Meinrad, IN: Abbey Press.

Satir, V. (1988). *The new peoplemaking.* Mountain View, CA: Science and Behavior Books.

Satir, V., & Baldwin, M. (1983). *Satir step by step: A guide to creating change in families.* Palo Alto: CA: Science and Behavior Books.

Simons, V. A., & Freedman, J. (2000). Witnessing bravery: Narrative ideas for working with children and families. In C. E. Bailey (Ed.), *Children in therapy: Using the family as a resource* (pp. 20–45). New York: W. W. Norton.

Sori, C. F. (1998). Involving children in family therapy: Making family movies. In L. Hecker and S. Deacon (Eds.), *The therapist's notebook: Homework, handouts, and activities for use in psychotherapy* (pp. 281–284). Binghamton, NY: Haworth.

Sori, C. F. (2006). Family play therapy: An interview with Eliana Gil. In C. F. Sori (Ed.), *Engaging children in family therapy: Creative approaches to integrating theory and research in clinical practice* (pp. 69–90). Binghamton, NY: Routledge.

Sori, C. F. (2007). Spiritual play genogram. In L. L. Hecker, C. F. Sori, & associates, *The therapist's notebook II: More homework, handouts, and activities for use in psychotherapy.* Binghamton, NY: Haworth.

Sori, C. F., & Biank, N. M. (2003). Soaring above stress: Using relaxation and visualization with anxious children. In C. F. Sori, L. L. Hecker, & associates, *The therapist's notebook for children and adolescents: Homework, handouts, and activities for use in psychotherapy* (pp. 24–39). Binghamton, NY: Haworth.

Sori, C. F., & Biank, N. M. (2006). Counseling children and families experiencing serious illness. In C. F. Sori (Ed.), *Engaging children in family therapy: Creative approaches to integrating theory and research in clinical practice* (pp. 223–244). Binghamton, NY: Routledge.

Terry's Village. Resin inspirational rocks, item IN-91/2036; phone 1-800-862-2295 http://www.terrysvillage.com/tvweb/application?namespace=browse&origin=searchMain.jsp&event=link.itemDetails&demandPrefix=12&sku=91/2036&mode=Searching&searchDestinationJSP=/search/searchMain.jsp&erec=1&D=inspirational%2Brocks&Ntt=inspirational%2Brocks&Ntk=all&Dx=mode%252bmatchallpartial&Ntx=mode%252bmatchallpartial&N=0.

Walsh, F. (2006). *Strengthening family resilience* (2nd ed.). New York: Guilford.

Webb, N. B. (1993). Assessment of the bereaved child. In N. B. Webb (Ed.), *Helping bereaved children: A handbook for practitioners* (pp. 19–42). New York: Guilford.

White, M., & Epston, D. (1990). *Narrative means to therapeutic ends.* New York: W. W. Norton.

White, P. (1976). *What's happened to Auntie Jean?* Glendale, CA: Regal Books Division, G.L. Publications.

Professional Readings and Resources

Christ, G. H. (2000). *Healing children's grief: Surviving a parent's death from cancer.* New York: Oxford University Press.

Doka, K. J. (1995). *Children mourning: Mourning children.* Washington, DC: Hospice Foundation of America.

Fogarty, J. A. (2000). *The magical thoughts of grieving children: Treating children with complicated mourning and advice for parents.* Bursville, NC: Compassion Books.

Gil, E. (1994). *Play in family therapy.* New York: Guilford.

Grollman, E. A. (1991). Explaining death to children and to ourselves. In D. Papadatou & C. Papadatos (Eds.), *Children and death* (pp. 3–8). New York: Hemisphere.

Karns, J. T. (2003). Children's understanding of death. In C. Sori & L. Hecker (Eds.), *The therapist's notebook for children and adolescents: Homework, handouts, and activities for use in psychotherapy* (pp. 143–149). Binghamton, NY: Haworth.

McAdams, C., & Sweeney, D. S. (2006). Exploring spirituality with children in counseling. In K. B. Helmeke & C. F. Sori (Eds.), *The therapist's notebook for integrating spirituality in counseling, vol. II: More homework, handouts, and activities for use in psychotherapy* (pp. 83–91). Binghamton, NY: Haworth.

McGoldrick, M., & Walsh, F. (1991). A time to mourn: Death and the family life cycle. In F. Walsh (Ed.), *Living beyond loss: Death in the family* (pp. 30–49). New York: W. W. Norton.

Rando, T. (1988). *How to go on living when someone you love dies.* New York: Bantam Books.

Shapiro E. R. (1994). *Grief as a family process: A developmental approach to clinical practice.* New York: Guilford.

Smith, S. C., & Pennells, M., Sr. (1995). *Interventions with bereaved children.* Bristol, PA: Jessica Kingsley.

Sori, C. F. (2006). *Engaging children in family therapy: Creative approaches to integrating theory and research in clinical practice.* New York: Routledge.

Sori, C. F., & Hecker, L. L. (2003). *The therapist's notebook for children and adolescents: Homework, handouts, and activities for use in psychotherapy.* New York: Haworth.

Webb, N. B. (1003). *Helping bereaved children: A handbook for practitioners.* New York: Guilford.

Bibliotherapy Sources for the Client

Brown, L. K., & Brown, M. (1996). *When dinosaurs die: A guide to understanding death.* Boston: Little, Brown and Co.

Buscaglia, L. (1982). *The fall of Freddie the leaf: A story of life for all ages.* New York: Henry Holt & Company.

Grollman, E. A. (1991). *Talking about death: A dialogue between parent and child* (3rd ed.). Boston: Beacon Press.

Lewis, P. G., & Lippman, J. G. (2004). *Helping children cope with the death of a parent: A guide for the first year.* Westport, CT: Praeger.

Mundy, M. (1998). *Sad isn't bad: A good-grief guidebook for kids dealing with loss.* St. Meinrad, IN: Abbey Press.

Roels, E. D. (1983). *God understands.* South Holland, IL: The Bible League.

Rosenbltatt, P. C. (2000). *Parent grief: Narratives of loss and relationship.* Philadelphia: Brunner/Mazel.

Schaefer, D., & Lyons, C. (2001). *How do we tell the children? A step-by-step guide for helping children two to ten cope when someone dies* (3rd ed.). New York: Newmarket Press.

Vigna, J. (1991). *Saying goodbye to Daddy.* Morton Grove, IL: Albert Whitman.

White, P. (1976). *What's happened to Auntie Jean?* Glendale, CA: Regal Books Division, G.L. Publications.

Handout 20.1: Touchstones

The following is a list of possible words of inspiration, comfort, or encouragement that can be used on the touchstones.

Hope	Believe
Love	Faith
Endure	Trust
Inspire	Soar
Courage	Strength
Peace	Joy
Laugh	Sing
Dance	Rejoice
Wonder	Serenity
Power	Victory
Create	Smile
Blessed	Inspire
Friends	Family
Harmony	Dream
Overcome	Accept
Breathe	Relax
Rest	Sacrifice
Purpose	Play

– 21 –

The Toolbox
Using a Collage to Access Client Strengths

Susan N. Perkins and Megan L. Dolbin-MacNab

Type of Contribution: Activity, Handout

Objective

The objective of this experiential activity is to highlight client strengths and create hope by helping clients recognize and remember strategies and resources that they can use to reach a specified goal or overcome a presenting problem. In this activity, clients make a collage in order to create a visual representation of their strengths, resources, and skills. This activity can be adapted for use with individuals, including adults and children; couples; families; and groups. Although this activity is grounded in narrative therapy (Freedman & Combs, 1996), it can also be used by therapists of many theoretical backgrounds. Furthermore, therapists can adapt this activity to serve several purposes, including assessment, tracking progress, solidifying changes, and facilitating termination.

Rationale for Use

When clients come to therapy, they bring with them unique personal and relational strengths, ideas, experiences, and cultural contexts. Accessing clients' strengths and highlighting past successes are central to many therapy approaches and can enhance the effectiveness of therapy (Asay & Lambert, 1999; Freedman & Combs, 1996; Sharry, Madden, & Darmody, 2001; Walter & Peller, 1992). Congruent with the idea that accessing client strengths can be a powerful means for overcoming a presenting problem, the toolbox activity emphasizes solutions that have worked in the past (Freedman & Combs) and ideas for the future, which can foster a sense of competence and hope.

The toolbox activity is a strength-based intervention that highlights the abilities, strengths, and successes of a wide range of clients. By focusing on problem-solving strategies that have worked in the past (Freedman & Combs, 1996) or could work in the future, the goal of the activity is to emphasize clients' strengths and resources for resolving and managing their personal or relational difficulties. An underlying assumption of this activity is that clients have successfully implemented some strategies for solving their presenting problems that have at least partially worked in the past (Freedman & Combs; Freeman & Couchonnal, 2006; Freeman, Epston, & Lobovits, 1997; Payne, 2006). However, when their life circumstances or the presenting problem becomes more difficult, clients may forget to use those strategies. The toolbox activity is also based on the assumption that if clients have several strategies from which to choose for resolving or managing their presenting problem, they are more likely to use at least one successfully.

The toolbox activity is based on narrative therapy (Freedman & Combs, 1996). Narrative therapists focus on unique outcomes—times when the problem started but things turned out well regardless—to plot action for this to happen more often in the future (Freedman & Combs; Freeman & Couchonnal, 2006; Freeman et al., 1997; Payne, 2006). The toolbox activity supports the process of addressing unique outcomes by focusing on what clients did to succeed in overcoming the problem.

Then, when clients plan to use the strategies they identified through this activity in the future, they are beginning to extend their story so that it is not as problem saturated and a new, more helpful story can emerge (Freedman & Combs). For example, if a client uses meditation as a strategy for managing social anxiety, he might be asked to explain how meditation helped him get through his mother's birthday party. Then, he could be asked to brainstorm how he might apply this strategy to other anxiety provoking situations such as work meetings.

Although this intervention is grounded in narrative therapy, the toolbox activity is also based on the assumption that "doing" will have more impact for lasting change than will "telling." This experiential view is congruent with many theories of therapy, but forms the basis for experiential theory (Korb, Gorrell, & Van De Riet, 1989). Because of its experiential focus, this activity is particularly effective in situations when it is important for clients to remember a list of successful strategies for managing or resolving a problem, but when writing out that list would lack the impact desired. Moreover, by creating a visual representation of their resources and skills for managing and resolving problems, this activity provides clients with a visual reminder that they can refer to later.

Instructions

To conduct this activity, the therapist will need a variety of magazines, coloring books, scissors, markers, and glue sticks. Also needed is a large piece of poster board that will serve as the base of the toolbox collage. Local libraries often have outdated magazines that are free to the public. If this activity is being used with children, coloring books and children's magazines may be useful sources of images that include themes for children.

1. Before the client arrives, draw the toolbox design (see Handout 21.1) on the poster board. Although the toolbox design could also be copied onto large paper by printing it out at 140%, the poster board provides the necessary space for the collage and is sturdier than copy paper. Cut the toolbox design out of the poster board. Based on your theoretical orientation and the intended purpose of using the toolbox activity, you may prepare one toolbox for each person, one toolbox for the parents and one for the children in a family, or one toolbox for the whole family to work on together.
2. After beginning the session, introduce this activity as a way to help the client remember and, in the future, use the strategies that worked in the past to help him or her resolve or manage problems. Although there may be many problems that could be addressed with this activity, it is recommended that the therapist focus on a particular problem the client has been working on resolving.
3. Begin the activity by discussing with the client the things that he or she has done in the past that have helped to resolve or manage the problem. Then, brainstorm several strategies that have not been tried (but could be tried) for resolving or managing the problem. Allow the client to brainstorm unrealistic ideas, but focus the discussion on strategies that could be used in the future. As clients continue with the toolbox collage, this discussion will help prepare them to remember additional strategies that have worked, sometimes even realizing for the first time a strategy they used without thinking about it deliberately.
4. Give the client the cutout of the toolbox. Explain that, on one side of the toolbox, he or she will be placing images that illustrate strategies that have already been used and that have worked in helping to resolve or manage the problem. Explain that, on the other side of the toolbox cutout, he or she will be placing images to illustrate strategies that have not yet been tried but could, or images illustrating strategies that have worked for other people.
5. Spread out the magazines, scissors, pens, markers, and glue sticks where they can easily be seen and accessed by the client.

6. Ask the client to look through the magazines and cut out images that remind him or her of strategies that have been used to resolve or manage the presenting problem in the past. Also have the client search for images that represent strategies that he or she could use in the future. If the client is not able to find an image to illustrate any of the strategies, have the client use the markers to draw pictures or write a phrase to describe those particular strategies.
7. Because arranging the images on the toolbox cutout may provide an opportunity to gather more information, request that clients wait until they are satisfied with the number of images they have found before having them glue the images onto their toolboxes. Depending on the therapy goals and the theoretical orientation of the therapist, the therapist could ask the client to group individual, family, and couple strategies. Or, the client could be asked to group the images according to difficulty of implementation, frequency of use, or the time of day that the strategy would be implemented. Additionally, some therapists may choose to be very nondirective and reflective during this process, while other therapists might choose to be more directive and make suggestions.
8. After the images are glued onto the toolbox cutout, ask the client to describe the specific items on the collage. Then ask the client to reflect on the process of completing the activity. Some example questions might include:
   - When you looked at the number of strategies you came up with, how did you feel?
   - What new ideas did you think of that you have not tried yet?
   - What surprised you as you did this activity?
   - What was it like working together to remember and find strategies to solve this problem?
   - What unique piece did each person add to this collection of strategies?
   - What does it say about you as a person that you were able to think of and use these strategies?
   - How do the strategies on the toolbox collage compare to the strategies you expected you would think of?
   - When you started thinking of what caused different outcomes from the usual ones, was it easier to keep thinking about things that work? What does this mean to you?
   - How did the way you thought and felt about the problem change as you came up with more strategies?
   - What is the same or different between the two sides of the toolbox (strategies you have used and strategies you have not used but could)? How does this relate to how you might resolve or manage the problem in the future?
   - How might you implement these strategies for the purpose of managing or resolving your problem?
   - What would happen if these kinds of things occurred more often?
   - Who notices when you do the things in this toolbox?
   - Who in your life believes you can use these strategies more often and would cheer you on in that?
   - What things happen around you to help you use these strategies?
   - Throughout the activity or the discussion of the activity, the therapist should ask clarifying questions and make reflections.
9. Conclude the session by engaging the client in a discussion of how he or she will implement the strategies from the toolbox collage into daily life. Also discuss how the client could continue to add to the toolbox collage and refer to it whenever he or she feels the need.

Variations

Because of its flexible nature, there are many possible variations in the use of the toolbox activity. The toolbox activity could be adapted according to the setting, the needs of the client, the therapeutic goals, the presenting problem, the timing in the process of therapy, or even the theory of therapy being used. Possible variations in the use of the toolbox activity include the following.

1. This activity would work well in a variety of clinical settings, such as educational programs for couples, parents, or families; group therapy; play therapy; individual therapy; and classes.
2. The activity could be used to address a variety of presenting problems such as parenting skills for single parents or couples, stress management, depression, anxiety, grief, self-esteem, school achievement, managing ADHD symptoms, and relational problems.
3. There are a variety of times in the process of therapy when this activity can be used effectively. In the beginning stages of therapy, this activity could be used to understand what clients have tried. At a transition point, the toolbox activity could be useful in summarizing the progress of therapy. When transferring a client, this activity could be a way to summarize what the client has already accomplished. Finally, at the end of therapy, the toolbox activity could be a helpful way to summarize gains and to solidify changes for the future.
4. The toolbox collage, although grounded in narrative therapy (Freedman & Combs, 1996), can be adapted for use by therapists operating from other theoretical perspectives. In fact, a major strength of this activity is that it is very flexible and can be easily adapted. For example, a solution-focused therapist could use this activity to emphasize that the client is the expert on the strategies that work, and that the client, on one level, already has the solutions to his or her problems. Within a solution-focused framework, this activity can also be used to highlight exceptions to the problem (de Shazer & Molnar, 1984). In contrast, transgenerational family therapists could use this activity to illuminate triangles, alliances, and patterns of interaction in the family through attending both to process and to content. This could be done by using the toolbox activity with a family and observing their interactions. The toolbox activity could then be used to increase the adaptive capabilities of the individuals and family, which would work to relieve the presenting problem by providing clients with a range of ideas for dealing with the problem (Kerr & Bowen, 1988). Similarly, structural therapists could use the toolbox activity to identify boundaries, hierarchies, and coalitions between subsystems or within the larger family system (Minuchin, 1974). For structural therapists who use this activity, information about the process of interaction is just as valuable, if not more so, than the content of what the clients chose to put on the toolbox. Once these issues are identified, the toolbox activity can provide the therapist with an experiential opportunity to intervene in these areas.

Brief Clinical Vignette

Robert Lopez and his 7-year-old granddaughter, Nellie, came for therapy soon after Robert got custody of her. Nellie had been in trouble at school for hitting, kicking teachers, throwing tantrums, and refusing to cooperate. Robert was concerned about Nellie's behavior and was also worried about how Nellie was adjusting to living with him. Robert explained that as an infant, Nellie had been hospitalized for failure to thrive due to neglect. Robert blamed Nellie's social deficits, immaturity, and angry outbursts on this neglect and the unpredictable way in which Nellie had been shuffled from one person to another her whole life.

Therapy with Robert and Nellie progressed steadily overall, with a few wonderful victories, such as the first time Nellie hugged Robert without prompting and her first week at school with no bad reports from teachers. There were also rough moments, including sending Nellie home at the beginning of one session because she insisted on lifting up the blinds between therapy rooms, and when she made violent, threatening comments to the therapist. Nellie improved at school and home, and Robert became more comfortable and confident in his role as caretaker.

After 6 months of therapy, Nellie and Robert had achieved their initial goals. Robert handled setbacks well, and they were developing a secure, caring relationship. During the course of therapy, Robert and Nellie both learned many skills for dealing with the pressures of life and their relationship. Many times, though, they would forget these skills and their relationship problems would reemerge.

As part of the process of wrapping up therapy, the therapist decided to use the toolbox collage activity to help Robert and Nellie remember what had worked for them. The goal of this activity was to solidify the changes and to create a plan for remembering what worked when their problems reemerged. Fostering a sense of competence and confidence was the therapist's secondary goal.

In the last session, the therapist set up the toolbox activity by asking Robert and Nellie if they remembered what was going on in their lives when they first came for therapy. The therapist asked how things were different now and if they remembered what they did to make and keep those changes. They listed several things. Everyone agreed that it is easy to get out of the habit of using new strategies and that a reminder would be important in helping them maintain the changes they made. The therapist put the toolbox, poster board, magazines, coloring books, crayons, scissors, and glue on a small table and explained that they could create a toolbox of strategies to remind them of what worked in helping Nellie do well at home and school.

During the toolbox activity, Robert and Nellie brainstormed things that had helped them make positive changes in Nellie's behavior. Nellie found a picture of a computer and said that video games helped her do better. Robert mentioned that preparing for Thanksgiving together was a bonding experience and that Nellie followed directions well in decorating the table. He used a picture of a construction paper turkey cookie to represent Thanksgiving. Robert found a picture of a jar of peanut butter and said that after-school snacks helped Nellie settle into the evening. Robert even remembered strategies he had not used in a while. They also added strategies they had used but had not told the therapist.

When they declared themselves finished, the therapist asked them to pick their favorite pictures and say what they liked about those strategies and how they helped make their relationship better. The therapist asked Robert and Nellie when they could use these strategies in the future and how they would know they needed to look at their toolbox again. Robert said he would remember the strategies because, when he worked on projects at his house, he would have his tools out, and this would remind him of the "solutions" toolbox. He also said that, when Nellie got bad reports from school or when he was losing patience with her, he would get out the toolbox to remind himself of strategies he used in the past. Through creating these plans, the clients developed their own follow-up procedures and strategies for maintaining the changes they had made.

Suggestions for Follow-Up

Depending on when and how the toolbox collage is used, follow-up could be short term or long term. Suggestions for short-term follow-up include:

- Having clients look over the toolbox for 2 minutes every morning and glancing at it once during the evening;
- Assigning the couple or family to refer to the toolbox throughout the week when they feel overwhelmed; and
- Asking clients to add to the toolbox both at home and in sessions; when this happens, have clients report on the new ideas they have had and how they have worked.

Possibilities for long-term follow-up include:

- After doing the toolbox activity in an earlier stage of therapy, referring to it in later sessions;
- Using the toolbox to reflect on therapy by having the clients bring it back to session when the goals of therapy have been reached; and
- Discussing with clients how they know they need to refer to their toolbox even after therapy is terminated.

Contraindications for Use

While the toolbox collage activity can be widely applied and adapted, it would not work well with some clients. First, in cases where safety is of concern (e.g., domestic violence or abuse or neglect), carefully assess anxiety and tension in the room before beginning and also throughout the activity. In situations where there is a possibility of violence toward oneself or others, these issues should be addressed first. Certainly, the toolbox could be part of addressing how these problems are handled, but ensuring safety is always the first priority. If the toolbox activity is used in these cases, also carefully debrief afterward, assessing safety again.

Clients who are not able to recognize strategies that have worked or who have not tried several different strategies for addressing their problems might find that their toolbox would be discouragingly empty. Moreover, clients need to be able to think abstractly so that the images for their collage can represent strategies for resolving or managing a problem. If their thinking is too concrete, they may not find pictures that would work and may have a difficult time making the connection between this activity and their day-to-day lives.

Finally, when clients are feeling overwhelmed by their problems, they may see the toolbox activity as too playful or as not focused enough on the problem. To assess this, notice the tone of therapy and ask questions about strategies they have used that worked or did not work to get a sense of whether the client can think of solutions. On the other hand, the toolbox activity can be used to shift the focus from the problem and to create a sense of accomplishment and hope.

References

Asay, T. P., & Lambert, M. J. (1999). The empirical case for the common factors in therapy: Quantitative findings. In M. A. Hubble, B. L. Duncan, & S. C. Miller (Eds.), *The heart and soul of change: What works in therapy* (pp. 23–55). Washington, DC: American Psychological Association.

de Shazer, S., & Molnar, A. (1984). Four useful interventions in brief family therapy. *Journal of Marital and Family Therapy 10*(3), 297–304.

Freedman, J., & Combs, G. (1996). *Narrative therapy: The social construction of preferred realities.* New York: W. W. Norton.

Freeman, E. M., & Couchonnal, G. (2006). Narrative and culturally based approaches in practice with families. *Families in Society, 87*(2), 198–208.

Freeman, J., Epston, D., & Lobovits, D. (1997). *Playful approaches to serious problems: Narrative therapy with children and their families.* New York: W. W. Norton.

Kerr, M. E., & Bowen, M. (1988). *Family evaluation: An approach based on Bowen theory.* New York: W. W. Norton.

Korb, M. P., Gorrell, J., & Van De Riet, V. (1989). *Gestalt therapy: Practice and theory* (2nd ed.). Boston: Allyn and Bacon.

Minuchin, S. (1974). *Families & family therapy.* Cambridge, MA: Harvard University Press.

Payne, M. (2006). *Narrative therapy: An introduction for counselors* (2nd ed.). Thousand Oaks, CA: Sage.

Sharry, J., Madden, B., & Darmody, M. (2001). *Becoming a solution detective: Identifying your clients' strengths in practical brief therapy.* New York: Haworth.

Walter, J. L., & Peller, J. E. (1992). *Becoming solution-focused in brief therapy.* Philadelphia, PA: Brunner/Mazel.

Readings and Resources for the Professional

Beaudoin, M.-N. (2005). Agency and choice in the face of trauma: A narrative therapy map. *Journal of Systemic Therapies, 24*(4), 32–50.

de Shazer, S., & Molnar, A. (1984). Four useful interventions in brief family therapy. *Journal of Marital and Family Therapy 10*(3), 297–304.

Gill, E. (1991). *The healing power of play: Working with abused children.* New York: Guilford.

Gill, E. (1994). *Play in family therapy.* New York: Guilford.

Guha, M. (2006). Narrative therapies with children and their families: A practitioner's guide to concepts and approaches. *Journal of Mental Health, 15*(3), 371.

Kempler, W. (1974). *Principles of Gestalt family therapy: A Gestalt-experiential handbook.* Salt Lake City, UT: Deseret Press.

Korb, M. P., Gorrell, J., & De Riet, V. V. (1989). *Gestalt therapy: Practice and theory* (2nd ed.). Boston: Allyn and Bacon.

Ozeki, T. (2002). "Problems" as resources: A practical guide to addressing clients' description of their problems in solution-focused therapy. *Journal of Systemic Therapy 21*(4), 35–37.

Payne, M. (2006). *Narrative therapy: An introduction for counselors* (2nd ed.). Thousand Oaks, CA: Sage.

Sherman, R., & Fredman, N. (1986). *Handbook of structured techniques in marriage and family therapy.* Bristol, PA: Brunner/Mazel.

Walter, J. L., & Peller, J. E. (1992). *Becoming solution-focused in brief therapy.* Philadelphia, PA: Brunner/Mazel.

Bibliotherapy Sources for the Client

Bang, M. (2004). *When Sophie gets angry—really, really angry.* New York: Scholastic.

Burns, D. D. (1999). *Feeling good: The new mood therapy revised and updated.* New York: HarperCollins.

Satir, V. (1976). *Making contact.* Millbrae, CA: Celestial Arts.

Satir, V. (1988). *The new peoplemaking.* Mountain View, CA: Science and Behavior Books.

Handout 21.1: The Toolbox

– 22 –

Trust Circle and Cradle

Body-Centered Approaches to Help Men Access and Heal Emotions in Groups

William F. Martin

Type of Contribution: Activities

Objectives

The objectives of the trust circle and cradle activities are to help men identify, access, and resolve emotions in a structured group setting. These activities can be utilized either collectively or individually. The activities in this chapter can be used with men in psychotherapy groups or psychodrama groups; with clients who are survivors of trauma or in addictions recovery; or with other structured, ongoing groups led by professional therapists. These activities quickly help men focus on feelings, rather than on thoughts or ideas. The therapist is able to help the client focus on what he is sensing and feeling in his body, rather than what he may be thinking.

The physical intensity of these activities also has the potential to help the client gain greater access to stored emotional memories than traditional talk psychotherapy. As the therapist facilitates greater awareness of internal sensations and feelings, the client has the potential to address and resolve longstanding emotional memories related to unresolved grief and/or trauma. These activities require the context of trust, safety, and support offered by a structured group. They can easily be included in more intense, body-centered therapy methods, such as psychodrama, movement, and dance therapy.

Rationale for Use

The expanding clinical research related to helping clients impacted by trauma has encouraged the integration of more innovative, action-oriented, and body-centered approaches with traditional talk therapy (Rothschild, 2000; Sapolsky, 1994; Sykes Wylie, 2004; van der Kolk, Hopper, & Osterman, 2001). Traditional talk therapy remains very important, but the use of body-centered therapy methods, such as eye movement desensitization response (EMDR), psychodrama, guided imagery, art, dance, and movement therapy, has proven very helpful in the treatment of survivors of trauma (Rothschild).

Researchers studying the neurobiology of post-traumatic stress using clinical interviews, brain imaging technology, and other sophisticated laboratory research methods have made several findings that serve to reinforce the integration of more body-centered therapy methods with traditional talk therapy (Rothschild, 2000; Sapolsky, 1994; van der Kolk et al., 2001). These findings include the following:

1. Traumatic experiences are processed differently than ordinary life experiences. These experiences are associated with sensations and feeling states, rather than words or language (van der Kolk et al., 2001).
2. Memories from traumatic experiences can surface as emotional and sensory states, rather than a description of life events organized in a personal story or narrative. This is to say that some

trauma survivors re-experience the intense feelings associated with the trauma, but may not have access to words to actually describe what happened to them. This is most common with trauma survivors who have delayed recall of trauma (Bremner, Southwick, & Charney, 1999; van der Kolk et al., 2001).

3. Delayed recall of trauma, often called suppressed or repressed memory syndrome, has a biological basis. The brain initiates a process of "active forgetting" until traumatic memories cannot be easily recalled. Also, prolonged stress can impair memory functions and create lasting damage to the physical structure of the brain, especially to the hippocampus, which is directly involved with learning and memory (Bremner, 2001).
4. If traumatic emotional memory remains stored separately from ordinary memories and has not been integrated into a personal narrative, the trauma survivor may often experience intense emotional states, "emotional hijacking" (Goleman, 1995), intrusive memories, behavioral re-enactments, central nervous system hyperarousal, and other trauma symptoms (Rothschild, 2000; Scaer, 2001).

Action-oriented, body-centered therapy methods create more intense internal emotional states and therefore allow the client to consciously choose to open the door to stored emotional memory. Standing up, moving around in the clinical setting as described in these activities, being in a circle of other men being gently moved around the circle, and later held in a cradle can all build emotional intensity and allow for the access of stored emotional memories. The therapist assists by helping the participant track these feelings and build associations to present and previous life events.

Integrating body-centered group activities with traditional talk therapy can help men deal with the complicated emotions associated with traumatic life events. These activities can also be fun and rewarding for therapist, client, and other group members. They can reinforce a sense of connection, cohesion, and, ultimately, trust as each group member works as a whole to offer support and healing to himself and others in the group.

For the purposes of this chapter, the term "therapist" means the facilitator of the group, "participant" means the man in the center of the circle, and "group members" refers to the men in the outer circle.

Evaluating when to do and what types of groups should do these activities. It is extremely important that therapists carefully determine both the timing and the appropriateness of these activities for a particular group. The following list offers readers guidance in determining when and with whom to use these activities:

1. These activities are ideal for psychotherapy, psychodrama, or personal growth groups where each member can reasonably expect to be involved in such things as guided imagery, art, dance or movement therapy, and other experiential methods where physical touch may be involved.
2. They should be utilized only after the therapist has done a comprehensive psychosocial evaluation, including any history of trauma among group members. This enables the therapist to anticipate and be prepared to deal with various trauma issues among the group membership.
3. The participants should also be participating in individual therapy or have access to the group therapist in order to help them process their experience in these activities.
4. The group must be beyond the initial stages of group formation and be able to address the level of emotional and physical intimacy and problem solving that these activities require.
5. The group should be an ongoing or long-term group (3–6 months) so that there is time for the therapist to process any issues, feelings, or memories clients access during these activities.

6. The therapist should be knowledgeable in the research related to trauma, have training in therapy for trauma survivors, and be ready and able to support a participant who may access powerful emotional memories.

Evaluating when these activities should not be utilized. See the "Contraindications for Use" section at the end of this chapter to determine when these activities are not appropriate.

Creating psychological safety. It is essential that therapists establish safety and trust in the group before undertaking the activities in this chapter. Following is a list of suggestions to decrease anxiety and increase psychological safety among participants:

1. The therapist should describe these activities in as much detail as possible and present them as opportunities for self-awareness. It is important to discuss the risk of personal discomfort, anxiety, or even flooding of emotions, so that participants can make a thoughtful choice about their participation.
2. Participation is completely voluntary. No one should feel forced or pressured to participate.
3. Participants should be encouraged to go slowly, that "moving the mountain, one scoopful at a time" is the best approach.
4. Explain that one participant will be in the middle of the circle at a time and will have sufficient time to do any work he chooses. That person will be in charge of what happens. The therapist and other group members will help facilitate, but the participant is in charge.
5. Also clarify that these are group activities, so everyone will have time to explore and process any thoughts or feelings he has about the experience.
6. Anyone can withdraw at any time.
7. Participants must support each other and abstain from the use of ridicule or excessive joking. For example, men should frequently make supportive statements like, "You can trust us" and "We won't let you fall." There is a slight temptation to joke and pretend to drop the participant in the middle of the circle. If there are any problems such as these, the therapist should gently help the group refocus to the task at hand and encourage more positive statements during the exercise.
8. A signal should be identified, such as a raised hand to indicate "Stop!" or "I need more safety," so that each participant is able to stop his participation at any time.
9. The therapist should stress the value of repeating these activities. Like the notion that "practice makes perfect," completing this exercise multiple times can be very effective in resolving intense emotional memories. Each time the activity is experienced, it can become easier for the client.
10. Depending on the therapist's relationship to the group, he may or may not directly participate in the trust circle activity. Some groups encourage the therapist to participate and this can be a good opportunity for connection and modeling of the trust circle activity. The therapist who participates should be clear that his participation is for the group process and not to do any therapeutic work for himself. Any self-disclosure should be minimal and be directed at building group cohesion and trust. The therapist should not be a participant in the cradle activity.

Creating physical safety. These suggestions are important in order to promote physical safety among participants:

1. The space where the activity occurs must be free of any obstructions, furniture, loose carpeting, or anything that may reduce the safety of the activity.
2. Participants' glasses, watches, jewelry, pens in pockets, or other objects should be evaluated and possibly removed to decrease the risk of harm.

3. Participants should be asked if they have any physical illnesses, disabilities, or injuries that may make it difficult to participate in this activity.
4. Participants should be asked to identify anything else that they need to create a safe and supportive environment for the activity.

Problems to avoid during the activity. The therapist should educate participants about the following problems that could occur during these activities. The specific problems to anticipate include:

> Rescuing. This occurs when the therapist and/or men in the group interrupt the process by asking too many questions, giving advice, or in some way distracting the participant from his deeper emotional process. A common example of this is that, when a participant may start to cry, other members may begin to talk or in some way prevent the participant (and perhaps the therapist and other group members) from accessing deeper feelings of grief.
>
> Derailing. This occurs when either the therapist or men in the group try to take control of the man's emotional process. Rather than follow him where he needs to go, they may try to lead him in another direction. An example of this is when a participant may say he is feeling angry and someone else tells him he is probably afraid and he should explore those feelings, rather than the anger he has identified.
>
> Chaos. This occurs when too many men are trying to lead the man's process, and the therapist and other participants are not working collaboratively. When two or more people are trying to lead the participant's process, the result is often too much noise and distraction. If this occurs the participant has more difficulty accessing emotional memory. The end result is that the participant may not benefit from the activity.
>
> Retraumatization. This occurs when a person is flooded with the intense sensations and feelings related to his trauma and re-experiences those feelings in a maladaptive and harmful way. Rather than being able to differentiate between "then and now," the person may feel as powerless and abused as he did during the original trauma experience. If this happens, it is advisable for the therapist to engage the person directly, encourage him to take deep breaths, let him know he is not alone, slowly bring him back to the present moment, and encourage him to ask for what he needs at that moment from the therapist and/or group participants.

If any of these problems surfaces, the therapist must intervene, set limits, and encourage group members to behave more supportively and responsibly during the activity. It is a good idea to "predict" that the feelings experienced during the activity can be intense and that participants might be tempted to use laughter and joking to diminish the intensity of the experience. Participants should be encouraged to be aware of any feelings they experience and to find ways to verbalize these feelings within the context of the activity. On the other hand, humor can be healing, and as long as the group can redirect itself, some humor can add to the overall experience of the activity.

Instructions

The instructions for these activities are described next. Stage I is creating the trust circle, and stage II is creating the cradle. Also included are process questions to be used following each activity.

Stage I. Creating the Trust Circle

1. Invite the men to stand up and form a circle.
2. Instruct the men to stand with shoulders almost touching, in a stance with one foot forward in front of the other, arms bent at the elbow, hands outstretched.
3. Ask for a volunteer from the group and instruct him to stand in the center about 12–15 inches from the outstretched hands of the men in the outer circle.

4. The group members fill in the space created in the outer circle.
5. The therapist instructs the participant to "keep your body rigid and straight as an oak board, and imagine that your shoes are glued to the floor. Cross your arms in front of your chest and place the palms of your hands on opposite shoulders. This will make it easy for the men in the outer circle to catch you and support you as you move around the circle."
6. When the participant is ready, the therapist should say, "Okay, now begin to allow yourself to fall gently forward, backward or sideways into the outstretched hands of the men in the outer circle. As you do this, be aware of any sensations, feelings, or memories that you might experience. Notice how you experience the feelings of trust and mistrust. If and when you choose, let us know what you are experiencing."
7. To the group members in the outer circle, the therapist should say, "Be gentle and encourage [the participant] in the center to trust us that we will not let him fall."
8. The therapist may model this by saying, "You [the participant] can trust us, and we won't let you fall."
9. This may be the time the therapist might have to help the group remain serious and focused, and intervene if the group begins to use laughter and joking too much. The therapist may need to say, "Okay, let's focus now, be gentle and supportive, and help [the participant] be aware of his own experience."
10. As the participant in the center begins to feel more trust in himself and the outer group, he can allow himself to rock gently back and forth into the outstretched hands of the men in the outer circle. The participant in the circle can keep his eyes open or closed. Those forming the circle gently guide the man back and forth and around the circle.
11. During the process, the man can express any random thoughts, feelings, memories or other sensations he is experiencing. It is crucial for the men in the outer circle to remain stable, reliable, and to support the man in the middle if he is to build trust. Joking, sudden movements, or being unable to support the participant in the middle can all create problems at this time during the exercise.
12. After a few minutes, it is time to end the movement of the man around the circle. He stops moving and remains motionless in the center of the circle. The men in the outer circle place one or both of their hands on the shoulders, back or arms of the participant. Participant and group members remain motionless and hold that position for several minutes.
13. Increased intensity can be created by the physical connection of the men in the circle at this time, raising the possibility of the participant accessing deeper feelings and sensations. This is where the state-dependent learning (Rothschild, 2000) concept is useful. The intensity of the participant's experience may be similar to the intensity of emotional experiences in his life. The emotional pathways to previous life experiences or possibly traumatic life experiences may open, so emotional memories previously inaccessible may now be available.
14. The therapist can help build intensity for the man in the center of the circle by asking questions designed to help him access more feelings and images. Helpful questions include:
    - What are you feeling right now?
    - Where do you experience these feelings in your body?
    - When have you felt similar feelings before?
    - What images or memories do you have related to these feelings?
    - If these feelings had a sound, what would they sound like?
    - If these feelings had words, what would they say?
    - If you were to "sculpt" your own body into a posture symbolizing your feelings, what would it look like?
    - If these feelings wanted to take action, what would it look like?
    - If you were to do some more work related to exploring these feelings, what would it look like?

Deciding to do more work can involve many exercises, including more emotional focusing exercises and/or doing more intense body-centered work utilizing the group process, including psychodrama. Participants may say or ask for many different things at this time in the activity. Some examples include:

- "I felt trapped when I was a child when my father was abusing me. I had nowhere to go and no one to help me. So, now I would like everyone to use their hands to press down on my shoulders to re-create that feeling of being trapped."
- "I remember being helpless when my brother was being abused. It was like I couldn't speak and my legs couldn't move. So, now I would like to ask the group to continue to support me while I try to move my legs and say something."
- "I know I really needed to be able to assert myself and do something to protect myself better, but I was so young. So, now I would like someone to stand in and play the role of my parents while I say what I needed to say to them back then, but was unable to express."

These moments can be very moving and powerful for the participant, group, and therapist. It is important to note that due to the intensity of the experience in the group, other group members may also begin to open pathways to emotional memory. This may offer them a chance to identify work that they may do later in the group. While the focus remains on the participant, the therapist should remember to attend to the impact of the experience for others in the group.

For the participant, it can be like he is back in time when the traumatic life events occurred. However, this time he is not alone. He has the support of a group of men that he trusts and is encouraged by the group process to allow his feelings to be expressed. He may be able to re-enact an aspect of a significant life event, but remain engaged in the experience, cope more effectively, and experience himself as a person with more power.

To help the participant transition back to the "here and now" of the group process, the therapist may say or ask the following:

- Slowly return to this room, be aware of the sounds and light, and take some deep breaths.
- When you are ready, open your eyes, look around the circle, see the other men in the group, and let us know what this experience was like for you.
- What are you experiencing or feeling now?
- What new information have you learned about yourself?
- How does this new information fit with your thoughts about yourself?
- What will you take away from this experience?
- When you look around at the eyes of the men in the circle, what do you experience?
- What else do you need right now?
- What else would you like to see happen?
- We could create a cradle experience for you. Would you like us to do that?

At this time, the trust circle activity could either end or evolve into a cradle exercise for the participant. This is a decision for the therapist and participant. As the group becomes more adept at using these activities, a natural flow occurs, and not much needs to be said. Initially, the therapist might transition to the next activity by saying something like, "Would you like us to do a cradle for you?" This can be enough for the participant and group to organize themselves to create the cradle activity. The following is a more elaborate discussion of the cradle exercises.

Stage II. Creating the Cradle

To summarize, the participant remains in the middle of the circle. Rather than transitioning back to the outer circle and ending his participation, he is willing to continue his personal work and potentially deepen his experience. The therapist and group have the option to offer a cradle experience for the participant. A cradle is an exercise where the participant is more fully supported physically by the group. There are several types of cradles, including the standing, support, sitting, and lifting cradles:

> Standing cradle. Perhaps the safest way to create a cradle is for the man to lean back into the arms of several group members, so that he is able to feel them supporting him. He is not completely off his feet, but standing at an angle with his feet on the floor. This is a safe and easy method as it does not involve lifting the man off the floor, where muscles could be strained or injured. There is also no risk of any men falling to the floor.
>
> Support cradle. In this type of cradle the participant stands upright and faces two group members. The participant steps forward, reaches out and holds the two group members around their waist. The two group members reach out and place one arm across the participant's chest and the other around his back. The intensity of this physical connection can quickly enable the participant to access emotional memory. This type of cradle can be utilized effectively when using psychodrama.
>
> Sitting cradle. Another safe method is to have the man drop to the floor where he can sit back into the supportive arms of other group members. The floor provides support and there is no risk of the participant falling or other men being injured. It is helpful during this method to have other group members provide back support to the men who are creating the cradle on the floor. This provides strong support to the men on the floor and enables them to hold this position as long as necessary.
>
> Lifting cradle. The final method is where the participant is actually lifted off the ground and held by other group members. Imagine a cradle holding a baby that easily rocks back and forth. This is the same idea. The group members form two lines and interlock their arms. The participant gently falls back into the arms of the men who lift and hold the participant off the floor. The group then gently rocks the participant. This cradle method offers the most challenges and is not recommended for use unless there are sufficient men to lift and hold the participant, and all the men have had some experience with this specific exercise.

Any type of cradle intensifies the physical contact and connection between the participant and group. As a result, the participant may be able to access other feelings and sensations that provide more information for him to explore. To facilitate the creation of a cradle, the therapist might say or ask:

- You have done a lot of work already, would you like us to create a cradle for you right now?
- The other version of this already mentioned is: "Why don't we create a cradle for you right now?"
- If the participant says no, proceed to transition and end the activity.
- If yes, it is recommended the therapist suggest that the participant select a few men to help support him on the floor.
- Invite the men selected to sit down and create a space for the participant to sit down and rest his back against the supportive cradle of the group members on the floor.
- Other group members should be invited to sit with their backs to the men forming the cradle, so that they can hold this position for a longer period of time without fatigue.

As the participant begins to rest into the cradle, the therapist encourages him to become aware of any thoughts, feelings, or sensations. The therapist might ask:

- How are you feeling?
- What is it like to feel the connection of the men supporting you?
- If your feelings had words, what would they say?
- What images or thoughts are you experiencing?

It is not uncommon for this to be a very emotional experience for men. The close physical connection creates an intensity that again opens emotional pathways. Men participating in a cradle quite often cry and grieve openly. They will say such things as, "I never felt this support before in my life" or "I needed this before, but didn't get it."

The cradle's potential to help men access and express grief makes it an excellent activity to do with survivors of abuse and neglect. Men who did not experience a sense of safety, structure, predictability, love, and nurturance in their family relationships can benefit from this type of intense connection provided by the group during this activity. Participants experience what it feels like to be "cradled" and develop more compassion for their own emotional losses. As they learn to release the grief in their hearts, they create space for love and more positive feelings.

To help reinforce the healing potential of the cradle exercise, the therapist can say:

- Take a few deep breaths and breathe this in.
- Look around at the men who are holding you and feel the strength of their support.
- Notice what you are feeling right now.

There are two other options at this time in this activity. First, it is helpful to have a full-length, lightweight mirror on hand. The therapist can direct group members to lift the mirror and hold it in front or above the participant, who can then be encouraged to look in the mirror and see himself being supported. This serves to provide the participant with images of himself being supported, rather than images of abuse or neglect. He is building other, more positive emotional memories to help him heal and cope more effectively in the world. The second option is to use evocative music to help enhance the participant's and other group members' overall experience.

To end this part of the activity, the therapist might say and do:

- What else do you need right now?
- Is this a good time to end this experience?
- If yes, then the therapist would direct available group members to help the participant up off the floor or down from a cradle in which he is being held.
- At times, it is useful to allow the participant time to just lie on the floor on his back, to reorganize himself and begin to integrate this experience.

The participant then rejoins the other group members. As the man rejoins the group, the therapist should take some time to explore what the other group members may have experienced during the participant's work. The therapist might say to the participant and group:

- How was this experience for you (participant)?
- Do you (participant) or anyone want to talk about your experience and/or feelings being a part of this work?
- Has anyone ever had similar feelings?
- How is your life experience different from what you witnessed?

The therapist should allow the participant and any interested group members to discuss and explore their experience. Then, it is time to move on to another participant, if there is adequate time. If there is not adequate time, it is best to process the experience in the group until time to end the session.

Brief Clinical Vignette I: Support Cradle

David, who was 54 years old, was participating in a psychodrama workshop and was an ongoing member of a men's group. Several of his fellow group members were also participating in the workshop this day. David had participated in psychodrama and other body-centered activities before. During the opening trust circle exercise, David became frozen in the middle of the circle. He was unable to trust the process enough to be gently guided around the circle. He was unable to identify what was happening or why.

The therapist gently suggested that the group create a "standing cradle," to which David agreed. Two volunteers stepped forward and began to hold David, their shoulders touching, and arms wrapped around David. David remained in this position of being held for several minutes. The therapist gently encouraged David to verbalize what he was experiencing. When David was unable to do so, the therapist encouraged him to gently push himself forward into the arms and shoulders of the men holding him. David began to push forward.

Feeling the gentle resistance of the men holding him, David became more intense and emotional. When the therapist asked again what he was experiencing, David was able to explain that he was feeling anger and rage related to childhood abuse by his parents. At this point, David had a better understanding of his own feelings and agreed to participate in a psychodrama where he had the opportunity to access and resolve these feelings more directly.

Brief Clinical Vignette II: Trust Circle and Standing Cradle

During the staff development process for a psychodrama weekend, Tom, a 47-year-old staff person, volunteered to participate in a trust circle activity. He had done this activity before, so he was familiar with the activity. Tom's father was a chronic alcoholic and his parents were divorced when he was 14 years old. His family experience was characterized by chaos and frequent domestic violence. When intoxicated, his father became rueful and threatened his mother and younger sister. Tom described a sense of powerlessness during these episodes and expressed guilt and shame that he was not able to do anything to help himself, his mother, and sister.

The therapist invited the group to form a circle, and Tom moved into the center. The group members were advised to stand in the power stance, with one foot in front of the other and the palms of their hands held forward. Tom was encouraged to stand "rigid as an oak board," keep his feet "glued" firmly to the floor, and cross his arms in front of his chest with his hands placed on opposite shoulders. Having experienced this exercise many times, Tom accomplished this easily. The therapist then invited him to fall into the outstretched hands of the group when he was ready. Tom took a deep breath and began to fall backward into the outstretched hands of the men in the outer circle. He was gently moved in a random motion in the circle. He kept his eyes shut.

When the therapist asked him what he was feeling, Tom replied that he was feeling some anxiety and fear, which he experienced mostly in his legs. Without prompting, he talked about seeing himself as a little boy in a corner of his living room, behind a chair, terrified by his father's rage. The group slowed the movement down until Tom was standing in the middle of the circle. The men kept their hands on his shoulders, back, and arms. Time seemed to stand still. The therapist gently encouraged Tom by saying, "If you want, let us know what you are experiencing." Tom replied that it was like he was back in his childhood, experiencing those events all over again. He described the fear and powerlessness he had felt so long ago.

As Tom continued to verbalize his experience, he talked about beginning to feel sad and tearful. He was able to cry and verbalized that he had a right to be sad and express it. He was able to say, "I was just a little boy ... there was nothing I could do ... someone else should have helped us ..." Tom began to sob and his shoulders and upper body began to move with the waves of grief that reverberated throughout his body.

In a gentle voice the therapist said, "Like you are saying, you were just a little boy ... there was nothing you could do ... you didn't have a place to express these feelings then, but now you do ..." Tom continued to grieve and then talked about beginning to feel anger. He talked about feeling the anger swelling up in his chest. The therapist asked, "What do you need right now?" Tom replied that he wanted to lean forward and have the group put pressure with their hands on his back and provide some resistance for him.

Tom had learned in previous activities that placing his body in a vulnerable, leaning, forward position and feeling restrained by the pressure of the men's hands on his back enabled him to access his own anger and rage. He talked about how feeling the hands of the men on his back and around him created a "sense of being contained," allowing him to access the depth of his own anger and rage, express it, and not disconnect from those feelings. As he pushed up and met the resistance of the men's hands, he intensified his pushing, and then allowed anguished cries of grief and anger to be expressed. After about 3–5 minutes, Tom began to relax. The men loosened their pressure and Tom stood up.

As Tom stood up, the therapist gently suggested that the group could create a standing cradle for him. He agreed and gently fell back into the arms of the men who formed a cradle behind him. He stood motionless as the men in the outer circle supported him in a cradle. Tom reported later that the cradle created by the men in the outer circle helped him feel support, safety, and containment. Rather than anger or sadness, Tom reported feeling safe, warm, nurtured, and supported.

Within the context of the group, Tom was able to go through a range of intense emotional experiences. It helped that he was familiar with the activities and was not intimidated by the prospect of re-experiencing such powerful emotional memories. However, Tom's experience was very moving for the other group members and helped them better understand how they could also benefit from this activity.

Both the therapist and the men in the group were able to offer empathy and support, and serve as witnesses to these memories. Afterward, Tom reported feeling stronger, and more aware and compassionate of his life experiences. This work moved him farther along the path of self-acceptance. Tom was successfully integrating what had happened to him in the past with who he was in the present.

Brief Clinical Vignette III: "Lifting Cradle"

Michael was a 43-year-old man participating in a psychodrama weekend. He had previously completed treatment for substance abuse and had been in recovery for several years. He chose to participate in the workshop to help resolve long-standing conflicts related to his childhood sexual abuse. Michael disclosed that he was HIV positive and suggested that his substance use helped him medicate the pain of being sexually abused, but had also made him vulnerable to being infected with HIV.

Although Michael had completed several treatment programs and actively participated in both individual and group therapy, he was initially reluctant to engage in any intense, action-oriented psychodrama. He expressed fear about becoming flooded and overwhelmed if the experience became too intense. However, Michael agreed to participate in a psychodrama to allow him to verbally explore various aspects of himself, including living with HIV and other issues that he did not ordinarily discuss.

Towards the end of this psychodrama, Michael was offered the opportunity to continue to work on the issue of trust by falling backward into the arms of the men in a "lifting cradle." He agreed and allowed himself to fall safely into the arms of the other group members behind him. The group members gently lifted him off the floor and held him supportively. The therapist played evocative music, while Michael was held and gently rocked by the group. Supportive messages, such as "Michael, you deserve to be held in this way" and "This is the way, with love and support, you should have been held when you were a child," were given by the group members.

The therapist placed a full-length mirror above Michael and encouraged him to observe himself being held and supported by men who cared about him. Michael later verbalized that he felt warmth, connection, and a feeling of being cared for that he had never experienced before. At a follow-up meeting about a year and a half later, Michael reported feeling "goose bumps" and a surge of positive feelings when he remembered being held in the "lifting cradle" by the other men. He further stated that this body-centered work was a turning point in his life, and had helped him in ways that traditional therapy had not.

Brief Clinical Vignette IV: Support Cradle

Robert was a 52-year-old participant at a psychodrama weekend. His stated purpose in attending was to work on issues related to his marriage, conflicts with his adult children, and his history of failed relationships. Robert disclosed that when he was 5 years old, his father had been killed in a car accident coming home from work. He further stated that although no one sat with him to explain what had happened and that he did not attend any wake or funeral for his father, he did not believe his father's death played any active role in his current problems. However, when selecting the main characters for Robert's psychodrama exercise, the therapist encouraged Robert to select someone from the group who could play the role of his father who had been killed, just in case there was some way he would be involved in Robert's work. Robert agreed and selected someone who he said reminded him of his father.

Robert chose to work on the conflict with his oldest son, from whom he was estranged. The therapist helped Robert "set the stage" for the psychodrama, and then placed Robert in a "support cradle." Robert began to push forward into the cradle. The men who formed the cradle were encouraging him to move toward his son, express his feelings about the estrangement, and explore ways of reconnecting with his son.

About 10 minutes into this work, Robert stopped moving, his eyes shifted up and to the right. The therapist, who was one of the men holding Robert in the cradle, noticed this and encouraged Robert to express himself. The therapist said, "It's okay, you can tell us what you are seeing right now." Robert took a few moments and then said, "I am seeing a funeral." The therapist said, "It's safe here to express your thoughts and feelings, whatever they might be. We can bring your father into the psychodrama now and you can see what happens." Robert agreed and within a few moments was engaged in a powerful grieving exercise where he accessed and expressed feelings about his father's death that had been repressed for decades. The support cradle was instrumental in helping Robert feel safe and supported, and it provided enough intensity to begin the grieving process related to his father's death.

Suggestions for Follow-Up

Helping men get in touch with deep feelings, particularly feelings related to trauma, requires time, support, and dedication. Men involved in this work should have an individual therapist to help them process this difficult emotional material. Having the structure and support of an ongoing group is also extremely beneficial. The group provides a larger container for the man to begin to identify, understand, and resolve feelings related to difficult or traumatic life events. The men in the group serve as mirrors to reflect back to the man the importance of his emotional life. The members of the group are witnesses to the power of those life experiences and are a part of the healing process. They offer acceptance, support, and a second chance to address a time in all of their lives when they were powerless, in a way that is both empowering and life changing.

Contraindications for Use

These activities should not be utilized if:

1. The therapist has no training or experience in trauma or action-oriented, body-centered therapy methods.
2. Participants have active substance abuse, mental or physical health concerns, or are using medication that may make it difficult for them to participate.

3. There is no adequate external support system available to participants, including individual therapy relationships to help clients process this experience.
4. There are questions or reservations about these activities that need to be resolved prior to initiating them.

References

Bremner, J. D. (2001). A biological model for delayed recall of childhood abuse. In J. Freyd & A. DePrince (Eds.), *Trauma and cognitive science: A meeting of minds, science, and human experience* (pp. 165–183). New York: Haworth.

Bremner, J. D., Southwick, S., & Charney, D. (1999). Neurobiology of posttraumatic stress disorder: An integration of animal and human research. In P. Saigh (Ed.), *Posttraumatic stress disorder: A comprehensive text.* Boston: Allyn and Bacon

Goleman, D. (1995). *Emotional intelligence: Why it can matter more than IQ.* New York: Bantam Books.

Rothschild, B. (2000). *The body remembers: The psychophysiology of trauma and trauma treatment.* New York: W. W. Norton.

Sapolsky, R. (1994). *Why zebras don't get ulcers: A guide to stress, stress-related diseases.* New York: W. H. Freeman.

Scaer, R. (2001). *The body bears the burden: Trauma, dissociation and disease.* New York: Haworth Medical Press.

Sykes Wylie, M. (2004). The limits of talk: Bessel van der Kolk wants to transform the treatment of trauma. *Psychotherapy Networker, 28*(1), 30–41.

van der Kolk, B., Hopper, J. W., & Osterman, J. E. (2001). Exploring the nature of traumatic memory: Combining clinical knowledge with laboratory methods. In J. Freyd & A. DePrince (Eds.), *Trauma and cognitive science: A meeting of minds, science, and human experience* (pp. 9–31). New York: Haworth Press.

Professional Readings and Resources

Anderson, M. C., Ochsner, K. N., Kuhl, B., Cooper, J., Robertson, E., Gabrieli, S. W., et al. (2004). Neural systems underlying the suppression of unwanted memories. *Science, 303,* 232–235.

Hopper, J. (1995). *Recovered memories of sexual abuse: Scientific research and scholarly resources.* Retrieved May 18, 2006, from Website: http://www.jimhopper.com.

Osofsky, J. (1997). *Children in a violent society.* New York: Guilford.

van der Kolk, B. (2006). Publications available for download by Bessel van der Kolk and his colleagues at the Trauma Center. Retrieved May 31, 2006, from Website: http://www.traumacenter.org/webarticles.html.

Yalom, I. (1995). *The theory and practice of group psychotherapy.* New York: Basic Books.

Bibliotherapy Sources for the Client

Mark, R., & Portugal, B. (1996). *Victories of the heart: The inside story of a pioneer men's group: How men help each other change their lives.* Melbourne, Australia: Element Books.

McKay, M., & Fanning, P. (2000). *Self-esteem: A proven program of cognitive techniques for assessing, improving, and maintaining your self-esteem.* Oakland, CA: New Harbinger.

Pennebaker, J. (1997). *Opening up: The healing power of expressing emotions.* New York: Guilford.

Rossman, M. (1987). *Healing yourself: A step-by-step program for better health through imagery.* Bethesda, MD: The Institute for the Advancement of Health.

Samuels, M., & Samuels, N. (1975). *Seeing with the mind's eye: The history, techniques and uses of visualization.* New York: Random House.

Schiraldi, G. (2000). *Post-traumatic stress disorder sourcebook.* New York: McGraw-Hill.

Schiraldi, G., McKay, M., & Fanning, P. (2001). *The self-esteem workbook.* Oakland, CA: New Harbinger.

O'Neil, M., & Newbold, C. (1994). *Boundary power: How I treat you, how I let you treat me, how I treat myself.* Fort Smith, AR: Sonlight.

Whitfield, C. (1989). *Healing the child within: Discovery and recovery for adult children of dysfunctional families.* Deerfield Beach, FL: Health Communications.

Whitfield, C. (1993). *Boundaries and relationships: Knowing, protecting and enjoying yourself.* Deerfield Beach, FL: Health Communications.

Williams, M.B., & Poijula, S. (2002). *The PTSD workbook: Simple, effective techniques for overcoming traumatic stress symptoms.* Oakland, CA: New Harbinger.

– 23 –

Attachment Injuries
Healing Activity for Survivors of Intimate Partner Abuse

Gunnur Karakurt and Diane E. Jeffries

Type of Contribution: Activity, Handouts

Objective

The objective of this activity is to help adult survivors of intimate partner abuse heal from past attachment injuries that are preventing them from moving forward in life. With this exercise, participants identify an event that is hurtful and traumatic for them. Participants provide supportive thoughts and comfort to themselves during this difficult time. Participants work to identify their own needs in abusive situations and enhance their awareness of these needs. Participants also identify their comforting and supportive skills toward themselves and in turn toward others. This activity can be used in both individual therapy sessions and in a group therapy format.

Rationale for Use

In contemporary society, intimate partner abuse is one of the most worrisome social issues, especially considering the current statistics on the issue. For example, according to the National Violence Against Women Survey, almost two million women were physically assaulted in the year prior to the survey (Tjaden & Thoennes, 1998). Past research also indicated that 12% of all spouses acted violently by pushing, grabbing, shoving, or slapping their intimate partner at least once, while 1–3% of all spouses conducted more extreme measures of violence toward their intimate partner by hitting, kicking, beating up, or threatening with a knife or gun (Dutton, 1992).

Factors that contribute to intimate partner abuse include social pressures that create stressors, cultural values that condone violence, personality pathologies (such as poor impulse control), and drug and alcohol addiction. Moreover, as compared to children who have not witnessed violence between their parents, children who have witnessed violence are more likely to assault their siblings and their parents, commit violent crimes outside the family, and assault their own intimate partners (O'Leary, 1988; Straus & Gelles, 1990).

Cost of intimate partner violence to society is massive. There are not only more salient social costs of intimate partner abuse, such as criminal justice, legal interventions, shelter and advocacy services, and medical care for injured parties, but also more concealed effects of such cost in regard to emotional, relationship, and family functioning of victims (Murphy & Eckhardt, 2005). Violence within the family can also have significant consequences for other family members who are not directly victims. Intimate partner abuse has been associated with long lasting, intense, and negative emotional and behavioral influences on children who witness domestic violence (Jaffe & Sudderman, 1995). Furthermore, intimate partner abuse contributes substantially to family instability, divorce, and homelessness. It also significantly relates to depression, substance abuse, and traumatic stress reactions for both the survivor and the abuser. Moreover, the "inner child" becomes incomplete, empty, hurt, and rejected from abuse, criticism, abandonment, and deceit; thus self worth is decreased over time (Schiraldi, 2001).

This activity has been adapted from Schiraldi's work (2001) for use with domestic violence survivors who suffer from low self-esteem. Schiraldi developed this activity as a self-help exercise to improve self-esteem for individuals. The current authors adapted this exercise to use in group settings for helping the survivors of domestic violence with emphasis on healing attachment injuries caused by physical and psychological abuse.

When intimate partner violence occurs, there is a betrayal of trust by the perpetrator, who is often someone to whom the survivor is emotionally attached. Since the main attachment figure during adulthood is one's romantic partner (Hazan & Shaver, 1987), intimate partner violence often causes problematic attachment relationships. Particularly when one needs to depend on his or her intimate partner for security and support, the fact that this attachment figure is also the cause of pain and hurt may lead to attachment injury (Holzworth-Munroe, Stuart, & Hutchinson, 1997).

Past research indicates that domestic violence survivors are more likely to lack secure attachment styles (Holzworth-Munroe et al., 1997). When someone has a secure attachment style, he or she is comfortable trusting and interacting with others. Attachment theory also elucidates unhealthy relationships as follows: insecurely attached individuals (1) mourn lost attachments (e.g., someone who decides to separate from his or her partner due to the occurrence of violence in the relationship feels loss and sorrow for leaving), (2) engage in inconsistent attachment behaviors (e.g., pursuer and withdrawer patterns), and (3) may suffer from attachment panic (e.g., hold physical and emotional control over a partner) (Millikin, 2000). All of these factors lead to the experience of continuing attachment injury.

Many women experience trauma and ongoing attachment injury due to domestic violence. More severe and frequent exposure to physical violence, including the threat against life, use of weapons, sexual intimate partner violence, and psychological abuse, has been shown to be related to the development of post-traumatic stress disorder (PTSD) (Astin, Lawrence, & Foy, 1993; Dutton et al., 2006). PTSD also often leaves a person feeling isolated and misunderstood. Those who are able to turn to others for support cope well with their trauma (Johnson, 2002). However, for some, talking about it can be extremely hard and shameful. For others, long-term controlling and isolative behavior from their abusive partner eliminates people to whom victims of domestic violence can disclose. Others feel like they are alone in the world and feel no one experiences the same devastating pain and suffering. For many women, getting the support they need at the time of emotional crisis due to physical violence is limited (Millikin, 2000). Therefore, it can be helpful to be in a group with other people who have the same kinds of emotional reactions to domestic violence experience.

This activity helps physical abuse survivors explore their attachment injuries in several ways. First of all, they can identify the attachment injury that is keeping them from moving forward by thinking about past events with which they are struggling. For these experiences, victims of domestic violence can own the injury by acknowledging and admitting that it still hurts and expressing a desire to move toward healing, as well as the need for assistance to do this. In this activity, we work with two parts of self: the "mature self" and the "younger self." The mature self is the present self who has the ability to nurture and offer love. The younger self, on the other hand, is the one who experienced the difficult time and is still suffering due to the abusive events. During this activity, we establish a line of communication between our mature self and younger self. During this process, the mature self, who is more experienced, wiser, and more nurturing, can state the willingness to help and offer ideas about what is needed in order to move on from past traumatizing experiences toward consistently living a healthier and more fulfilling life.

The mature self can also assist in providing supportive and comforting thoughts, personal truth, knowledge, and healing power to the person who is experiencing the past trauma. Furthermore, the mature self can claim the past events, adopt a forward focus, and construct a new dynamic for the current self (i.e., the younger self) about what can be done to help heal future injury that the self may encounter throughout life. Although this exercise is limited to physical abuse victims, it could easily be adapted to be used for other traumatic experiences if the therapist so desires.

Instructions

Participants are instructed to imagine a quiet, comfortable place where they are able to hear the following statements and respond to each thought-provoking image (Bradshaw, 1988). The therapist may dim the lights to set the stage. Clinicians may introduce the activity to individual clients or a group as follows:

> Please keep in mind that this activity is optional since some individuals are willing and ready to neutralize the pain of past events, some others are not willing or ready to revisit their past, or some others might feel more comfortable to revisit their past with the help of a mental health professional in individual therapy. The aim of this exercise is to help you, not to hurt you. Therefore, please be aware that you are in charge of how fast and how intense you want this exercise to be. If you want to stop because this exercise gets too intense or is moving too fast, you can simply stop. Start this activity by preparing to relax. If you prefer, you can loosen your clothing, take off your shoes, and sit comfortably in a chair. You can begin by taking a few deep breaths.
>
> Some relationships we have in life can be stressful and unfortunately some of them can be abusive at times. When we experience physical abuse or violence, it is traumatic. Sometimes we might have emotional injuries from that experience, which we repeatedly remember. Sometimes, these exposures to traumatic memories keep us from moving forward. In other words, we might carry reactions from this past experience that prevent us from forming new and healthy relationships in the future. In our lives, we experience many events. Some life experiences make us stronger. We know our lives and our needs better than anyone. It might be helpful to know how we can support ourselves by providing comfort and positive thoughts about such experiences. In this activity your mature self, who is who you are right now, is going to pay a visit to your younger self that experienced a painful experience. Hearing from your mature self can help you during both negative and positive encounters in life. In order to gain mastery over this exercise, you can start with a smaller event before moving on to larger, more traumatic events. Try to stay with one event and try not to be flooded with other emotional events. If you feel like you are moving to different events or becoming emotionally flooded, you can stop and take a break and can return when you feel ready.
>
> Please close your eyes and think about your past. Think about the abusive events you have gone through that have caused emotional injuries. Remember an event in your life that is still painful for you. Such moments might include people who have hurt you, made fun of you, or criticized you when you felt alone, abandoned, neglected, or empty. Remember how you were feeling at the time and call the person that experienced this painful experience your "younger self." Please remember that your mature self, which is who you are right now, has much insight and wisdom about who you are, and about your life. This mature self has gone through events, survived encounters, and become more powerful. Imagine the mature self traveling back in time to this traumatic event in your life and meeting your younger self. Your younger self trusts you completely. Your younger self is willing to listen to you. Your younger self needs you. Your mature self is talking to the younger self that is experiencing the pain, the hurt, and the sadness. Your mature self asks your younger self, "What is troubling you?" The younger self explains the painful event that is problematic and unresolved. Your mature self is helping you, comforting you, and bringing hope to your life by showing you a positive way out. Your mature self tells your younger self that you are returning to the present and that your love will remain with the younger self always. Notice what that feels like. Allow the feeling of love and reassurance to surround you. You can imagine that your mature self is saying goodbye, and giving a warm hug to your younger self. Let your attention move forward to the present time.... You are awakening back into your real life. You can take a few deep breaths. [Therapist can turn up the lights.]

Brief Clinical Vignette

This activity was used with a support group for adult female survivors of domestic violence. This was an open support group. Participation ranged from one session to several years, and some participants worked on recovery for much longer. Since this was a community support group and not a therapy group in the strict sense, the length of group membership and life experiences varied. Some group members were living functional lives, while others were in more immediate crises and were living at the domestic violence shelter for protection and safety. Group members primarily benefited from this group for community support and continued educational and emotional growth. Both during and outside group sessions, there was a strong sense of community and support.

Group members took turns sharing their experiences with this exercise during the session. One client, Lucy, remembered that when she was a child, her older brother was very critical of her. One day, when the client was about 10 years old, her brother was making fun of her physical appearance, telling her that she had twisted legs. Then, in front of his friends, he told her very angrily, "If we weren't genetically related, I would think that you are stupid" and laughed at her. As an adult, the client remembered how hurt and humiliated she felt and she selected this event to work with during this activity. In imagery, the mature self coached the younger self to ask her brother, "Why are you humiliating me in front of your friends? I am just a child, I am not stupid, and I am beautiful." The mature self protected the younger self from further criticism and saw the sadness in her brother's eyes. Once the younger self was adequately comforted, then the mature self told the younger self that she was going back to the future and that her love would remain with the younger self. She gave her a small smooth stone to keep with herself as a reminder that this love and support could be accessed at any time.

Another client, Melinda, reported an event that happened when she was 18 years old. During that time, she was physically assaulted by her boyfriend. She told her mother about this particular incident. She needed and was naturally expecting a supporting, understanding, and nurturing person to listen to her. She was disappointed with her mother's unresponsiveness and lack of care. After she experienced this negative response, she shut down about the incident and did not talk about it to anyone else, but the thoughts of the incident continued to linger. She started having nightmares and flashbacks of the event. She was terrified much of the time.

In imagery, the mature self trained the younger self to ask her mother, "Why do you not care about me when I need your support and understanding? I need someone to tell me that everything will be OK, I should not worry, and you will be there for me. I am hurt and sad." The mature self protected the younger self from the mother's unresponsiveness and observed the sadness and love in her mother's eyes. The mature self told her, "Don't worry, everything will be all right and I will be there for you." The mature self then gave her a hug and the client wept in the mature self's arms. When it was time, the mature self told the younger self that she is going back to the future, but her love will remain with the younger self. The mature self said that she will always love her, no matter what.

After the exercise, Melinda reported that, with this exercise, she emotionally felt that there was someone there for her. She said that she could not explain it well with words, but, emotionally, she felt like she got the hug, reassurance, and love that she so desperately needed. Another participant who listened intently about this woman's experience compassionately told her that she would be OK and comforted her as the woman processed her life event. The woman reported that the feelings of security, love, and compassion felt great after this exercise.

In general, group members believed that the exercise was beneficial. The women, who largely did not seem to have strong support networks at the time of their emotional injury, were able to bring their mature selves to meet with their younger selves and receive the needed reassurance, love, and comfort. Consequently, they began exploring ways to strengthen themselves during crisis situations whether they were experiencing current crisis or not. Similarly, they began reporting things that were hindering their personal growth. The participants discovered that they were proud of their mature selves and were able to connect to paths of healing from a challenging situation to a more secure point in their lives. Moreover, some women who had difficulty accepting advice from others were able to process their own individual situations, which was a powerful experience for them. They reported that they felt the necessary reassurance and comfort by utilizing the exercise and they felt like this was an exercise that they could use in the future by reflecting on the tools used in this exercise to focus on acceptance and healing from past traumatic experiences.

Many women who experienced emotional injury reported that they were able to bring their mature selves to meet their younger selves and receive the needed reassurance, love, support, and comfort. After this activity, women who had been a victim of physical assault or domestic violence were thinking about the messages that were given by their mature selves. Some of these messages included "Stop hurting me!" "I was lonely, but not anymore," "You made my sister and me cry," "Stop violence!" "It was not my fault," and "I am finally free." Some women reported that they gave up their education because of their abuser and they wanted it back. They also reported that one step that they could take to change their future was to get their GED.

Suggestions for Follow-Up

In order to strengthen the effectiveness of this exercise, clinicians may ask all participants to write down their responses to the questions in Handout 23.1. Writing the exercise puts the past in perspective, which also helps to sharpen and strengthen the solutions to attachment injuries. The therapist can focus on any writing that can illustrate positive changes during the exercises and discuss the use of such positive dialogue to foster a healthy emotional well-being (see Handout 23.2). One can visualize this process by performing a simple exercise that can be utilized with individuals or group participants. Later, it can be discussed. In the context of a support group, it should be made clear that if participants feel uncomfortable, they are not obligated to self-disclose. Sharing their experiences is voluntary.

Contraindications for Use

To conduct this activity, the group should be a safe place. In case of intragroup conflict, it is essential to resolve the conflict as effectively and comprehensively as possible. It is found that, through reducing intragroup conflict and increasing safety, participants can feel more encouraged to self-disclose and feel at ease. Moreover, in order to diversify the experience, group facilitators need to set the tone for valuing sharing with each individual in the group.

This activity should be used carefully, given the nature and intensity of the trauma. The exercises may not work well with women who are just beginning their personal healing process and are still overwhelmed with intense emotions, flashbacks, or crises (Bass & Davis, 1990). This activity can be powerful and may not be appropriate for women who are just embarking on their healing journey or who have more intrinsic needs to cope with.

Some will need extra help with long-term trauma recovery. If fearfulness, nightmares, and depression continue, these may be signs of ongoing PTSD, which would require individual professional help. It might be more appropriate to handle these situations in individual therapy rather than in a group therapy setting.

References

Astin, M. C., Lawrence, K. J., & Foy, D. W. (1993). Posttraumatic stress disorder among battered women: Risk and resiliency factors. *Violence and Victims, 8*(1), 17–28.

Bass, E., & Davis, L. (1990). *The courage to heal: A guide for women survivors of sexual abuse.* New York: Perennial Library, Harper & Row.

Bradshaw, J. (1988). *Healing the shame that binds you.* Deerfield Beach, FL.: Health Communications.

Dutton, D. G. (1992). Theoretical and empirical perspectives on the etiology and prevention of wife assault. In R. D. Peters, R. J. McCahon, & V. L. Quinsey (Eds.), *Aggression and violence throughout the lifespan* (pp. 192–221). Newbury Park, CA: Sage.

Dutton, M. A., Green, B. L., Kaltman, S. I., Roesch, D. M., Zeffiro, T. A., & Krause, E. D. (2006). Intimate partner violence, PTSD, and adverse health outcomes. *Journal of Interpersonal Violence, 21,* 955–968.

Hazan, C., & Shaver, P. R. (1987). Romantic love conceptualized as an attachment process. *Journal of Personality and Social Psychology, 52,* 511–534.

Holzworth-Munroe, A., Stuart, G. L., & Hutchinson, G. (1997). Violent versus nonviolent husbands: Differences in attachment patterns, dependency, and jealousy. *Journal of Family Psychology, 11,* 314–331.

Jaffe, J. H., & Sudderman, M. (1995). Child witnesses of woman abuse: Research and community responses. In S. Stith & M. Straus (Eds.), *Understanding partner violence: Prevalence, causes, consequences and solutions* (pp. 213–222). Minneapolis, MN: National Council on Family Relations.

Johnson, S. (2002). *Emotionally focused couple therapy with trauma survivors: Strengthening attachment bonds.* New York: Guilford.

Millikin, J. W. (2000). *Resolving attachment injuries in couples using emotionally focused therapy: A process study.* Unpublished doctoral dissertation. Virginia Polytechnic Institute and State University.

Murphy, C. M., & Eckhardt, C. I. (2005). *Treating the abusive partner.* New York: Guilford.

O'Leary, K. D. (1988). Physical aggression between spouses: A social learning theory perspective. In V. B. Van Hasselt & R. L. Morrison (Eds.), *Handbook of family violence* (pp. 31–55). New York: Plenum Press.

Schiraldi, G. R. (2001). *The self-esteem workbook.* Oakland, CA: New Harbinger.

Straus, M. A., & Gelles, R. J. (1990). *Physical violence in American families: Risk factors and adaptations to violence in 8,145 families.* New Brunswick, NJ: Transaction.

Tjaden, P., & Thoennes, N. (1998). Battering in America: Findings from the National Violence Against Women Survey. *Research in Brief* (pp. 60–66). Washington, DC: National Institute of Justice, U.S. Department of Justice.

Professional Readings and Resources

Cameron, C. (2000). *Resolving childhood trauma: A long-term study of abuse survivors.* Thousand Oaks, CA: Sage.

Holzworth-Munroe, A., Stuart, G. L., & Hutchinson, G. (1997). Violent versus nonviolent husbands: Differences in attachment patterns, dependency, and jealousy. *Journal of Family Psychology, 11,* 314–331.

Jacobson, N., & Gottman, J. (1998). *When men batter women: New insights into ending abusive relationships.* New York: Simon & Schuster.

Johnson, M. P. (1995). Patriarchal terrorism and common couple violence: Two forms of violence against women. *Journal of Marriage and the Family, 57,* 283–294.

Johnson, S., & Talitman, E. (1997). Predictors of success in emotionally focused marital therapy. *Journal of Marital and Family Therapy, 23*(2), 135–152.

Stith, S. M., Rosen, K. H., & McCollum, E. E. (2002). Domestic violence. In D. Sprenkle (Ed.), *Effectiveness research in marriage and family therapy* (pp. 223–254). Alexandria, VA: AAMFT.

Bibliotherapy Sources for the Client

Bass, E., & Davis, L. (1990). *The courage to heal: A guide for women survivors of sexual abuse.* New York: Perennial Library, Harper & Row.

Rich, P. (1999). *The healing journey through grief: Your journal for reflection and recovery.* New York: John Wiley & Sons.

Schiraldi, G. R. (2001). *The self-esteem workbook.* Oakland, CA; New Harbinger.

Taylor, C. L. (1991). *The inner child workbook: What to do with your past when it just won't go away.* New York: Jeremy Tarcher.

Handout 23.1: Process Questions to Be Used Following the Visualization Activity

Questions that can be used to facilitate discussion might include the following:

How did it feel to talk to your younger self as your mature self?

Were you surprised by any of the things that you heard?

Did you feel supported? How so?

Were there things that made you feel supported as you completed this exercise?

Did you feel unsupported? How?

Were there things that your mature self talked about that made you feel unsupported?

Is there anything you would like to change about your past? If so, what?

Did you feel comforted? How?

Did this activity show new ways to deal with your trauma? If so, what are these new ways?

What are the messages that you want to give to your younger self?

If there is something that you want to change about your past, what is one step you could take to work toward that change?

Handout 23.2: Suggestions for Supporting Yourself

You ask your younger self, "What would make this situation better for you?" You offer solutions to the problem by fulfilling a need by offering:

1. A genuine understanding of the situation. Examples include phrases such as "I know how hard it is for you," "You must be very sad that this is happening to you," "You have the right to be angry," and "It is not your fault."
2. Instruction to equip the younger self with effective skills that you can teach the younger self to learn about the event.
3. Unconditional support by offering statements such as "You can do this," "Life will get better," and "I am here for you."
4. Protection by offering statements such as "That is not right…children should not be treated that way" and "I will protect you."
5. Advice to enable the mature and younger selves to think together to come up with successful solutions. Work together to focus on the positives of your life. Praise the younger self for working with you to discover solutions and making good choices. Remind the younger self of such things as praises for making good choices, that mistakes do happen, how we can learn from mistakes, how feelings are very real and genuine and need to be expressed, and that making amends with the past can create peace from within,
6. Communicate love effectively by offering a hug; a reassuring look; a soft, soothing touch; and, most importantly, loving words such as "I love you" and "You mean so much to me."

Index

Made in the USA
Coppell, TX
09 November 2020

41032158R00136